# HOUSING A METROPOLIS—
# CHICAGO

# Housing

# A Metropolis—

# Chicago

*By* Beverly Duncan

*and* Philip M. Hauser

*The Free Press of Glencoe, Illinois*

# Contents

*v*

*vi*

# List of Illustrations

# List of Tables

*xii*

# Preface

THE ANALYSES reported here were undertaken with two purposes in mind. First, we have sought to describe current housing conditions in Chicago from several perspectives. The composition of the housing inventory and recent changes therein are explored and compared with characteristics of the inventory in other major metropolitan areas. Within the City of Chicago, the housing conditions of families with lower incomes are contrasted with those of higher-income families. The housing of nonwhite households is compared with the housing of white households. Differences between "young" and "older" families with respect to housing are examined. Second, on the assumption that readers may wish to analyze or re-analyze the basic data for specific purposes, we have given explicit attention to methodology. The nature of the available data and pitfalls in their interpretation are discussed at some length, and a variety of techniques for manipulating the data are illustrated.

This monograph is another product of the co-operative research program between the Chicago Community Inventory of the University of Chicago and governmental agencies of the City of Chicago. The Chicago Community Inventory performs general statistical, research, and service functions for the Department of City Planning and is, also, available for special studies like this one. This co-operative arrangement is designed, on the one hand, to stimulate research on important local problems and, on the other, to provide city agencies with a sound factual basis for policy formulation and administration. The program of co-operative research has resulted in a monograph concerning the Negro population in Chicago (Duncan and Duncan, 1957), the "Population Estimates and Projections" series of bulletins, and research reports dealing with such topics as housing conditions in the Chicago area, living arrangements of older persons in Chicago, and the types of local housing statistics available in the decennial Censuses. (A complete listing of publications is available in "Population Research and Training Center and the Chicago Community Inventory, University of Chicago: Statement of Program and Summary Report, 1947–58.")

By and large, this study is based on the unique body of data which became available through the National Housing Inventory survey and the Chicago Supplement thereto which were conducted by the Bureau of the Census at the close of 1956. The Chicago supplementation to the National Housing Inventory took three forms: (1) the sample of dwellings drawn in the City of Chicago was expanded substantially; (2) special items

*xviii*

were added to the schedule used in the National Housing Inventory; and (3) a special tabulation program was arranged. Provision was made for the basic data obtained through the Chicago Supplement to the National Housing Inventory to be analyzed and published through the Chicago Community Inventory, University of Chicago. The costs involved in procuring, analyzing, and publishing these data were underwritten by five local agencies—the Chicago Housing Authority, the Chicago Land Clearance Commission, the Office of the Housing and Redevelopment Coordinator, the Chicago Plan Commission, and the Community Conservation Board.

The basic data obtained through the Chicago Supplement to the National Housing Inventory were made available for general use in a series of "CSNHI Bulletins," which were submitted to the Chicago Housing Authority by the Chicago Community Inventory. The nine Bulletins, each of which included a summary of major findings along with the basic statistical tables, were published during the summer of 1958. The analysis of these data is a central part of this monograph. However, the analyses reported here also draw on statistics published by the Bureau of the Census in their National Housing Inventory reports and on other sources of data.

Although we accept full responsibility for the accuracy of the factual materials in this monograph and the general conclusions drawn from them, we would be remiss if we failed to acknowledge the "joint" nature of this undertaking. The Advisory Committee on the Chicago Supplementation of the National Housing Inventory, under the chairmanship of D. E. Mackelmann, at present Commissioner, Community Conservation Board, City of Chicago, provided valuable suggestions at the several stages of the project. The over-all design of the study and preparation of tabulation specifications for the Chicago supplementation were handled skillfully by our colleagues,

Donald J. Bogue and Evelyn M. Kitagawa, in collaboration with George Akahoshi, then with the Chicago Housing Authority, and the staff of the Housing Division, United States Bureau of the Census. Dr. Kitagawa assumed major responsibility for Bulletins 1, 2, and 6 of the CSNHI. Dr. Ethel Shanas of the National Opinion Research Center, University of Chicago, took primary responsibility for CSNHI Bulletins 3, 7, 8, and 9 and also undertook an analysis of the housing conditions of older persons on which Chapter 7 draws heavily. The tedious compilation of data presented in the Bulletins was carried out by Rose Stamler and Hal H. Winsborough, Research Assistants at the Chicago Community Inventory. Some 90 tables which form the bulk of the CSNHI Bulletins were patiently typed by Johnnie Williams.

Our work in preparing the monograph was lightened by the able assistance of Alma Ficks who checked the computations and proofed the manuscript, by Mary Thomas who typed the manuscript, and by Karel Kansky who executed the graphics. We are indebted also to our colleague, Otis Dudley Duncan, for a critical reading of the entire manuscript and to Beulah Washabaugh, Housing Division of the Bureau of the Census, for her comments on Chapter 2 as well as her prompt replies to our many queries. Finally, we should like to thank Hana Okamoto, our Administrative Assistant, for maintaining a working atmosphere in which we could prepare this monograph.

The interpretation of substantive findings is, of course, the responsibility of the authors. The conclusions reached do not necessarily represent the point of view of any of the agencies which have contracted for or contributed to the study.

BEVERLY DUNCAN
PHILIP M. HAUSER

# Chicago Supplement to 1956 National Housing Inventory

*Co-operating City Agencies*

    Chicago Housing Authority
Chicago Land Clearance Commission
Chicago Plan Commission
Community Conservation Board
Office of the Housing and Redevelopment Coordinator

*Advisory Committee Members*

    D. E. Mackelmann, Department of City Planning, CHAIRMAN
Yuan Liang, Department of City Planning, SECRETARY

Anthony Allison, Chicago Real Estate Board
J. R. Brady, Chicago Daily News
George Cloos, Federal Reserve Bank of Chicago
John Downs, Chicago Metropolitan Home Builders
Phil A. Doyle, Chicago Land Clearance Commission
William Findeisen, Pacific Mutual Life Insurance Company
Paul Freedman, Cook County Housing Authority
Raymond Goodpasture, Illinois Bell Telephone Company
Kenneth Green, Chicago Urban League
Don Hanson, Community Conservation Board
George Hartman, Housing and Home Finance Agency
Philip Hauser, University of Chicago
Paul Hedden, Chicago Real Estate Board
Don Klein, Chicago Tribune
Francis McPeek, Commission on Human Relations
George A. Morgan, People's Gas Light & Coke Company
Joseph A. Nowicki, Society of Residential Appraisers
Paul Oppermann, Northeastern Illinois Planning Commission
Lillian G. Peterson, Chicago Housing Authority
Warren B. Pursell, Pursell Public Relations
George Ramsey, Department of Buildings
Dorothy Rubel, Metropolitan Housing & Planning Council
Arnold Schumacher, Chicago Title & Trust Company
Robert Seidner, Chicago American
DeVer Sholes, Chicago Association of Commerce & Industry
Jack Silverman, Chicago Housing Authority
Dean Swartzel, Metropolitan Center for Neighborhood Renewal
Martin Tarpey, Chicago Sun-Times
H. Hoyt Thompson, Chicago Mortgage Bankers Association
Lawrence Trimble, Commonwealth Edison Company
Theodore Veenstra, Public Housing Administration
Barbara Wallace, Welfare Council of Metropolitan Chicago
W. K. Wittausch, First Federal Savings & Loan Association
Paul N. Zimmerer, Department of City Planning

# HOUSING A METROPOLIS— CHICAGO

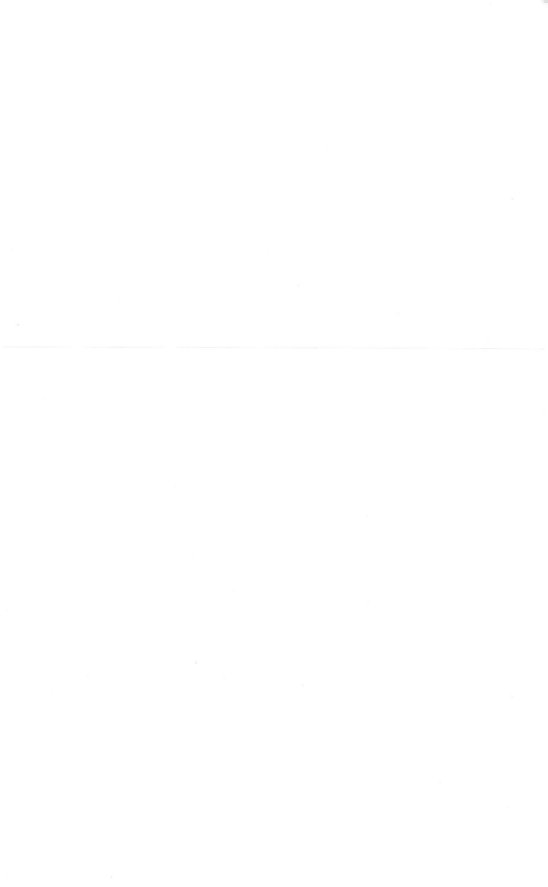

# 1

# Overview

CONSCIOUSNESS of housing as a metropolitan social problem rose sharply in the 1930's. An interplay of factors accounted for growing public recognition of the problematic aspects of housing. The trend toward population concentration in metropolitan centers had become evident. The spread or "decentralization" of the metropolitan community, spurred by the great expansion in use of the automobile and truck, pointed to a changing residential structure. A growing number of social surveys in metropolitan centers detailed the pervasiveness of deterioration and obsolescence. The onset of the depression and concomitant curtailment of private residential construction touched

*1*

off the movement for housing reform. One manifestation of this movement is the growth of dwelling units supervised by the Public Housing Administration—from 800 in 1936, to 8,000 in 1937 to 61,000 in 1940.

The curtailment of residential construction during the depression years was marked. The value (in constant dollars) of new private residential construction fell from 11.5 billion in 1925 to 2.5 billion in 1935, and the value of public residential construction, initiated in the 1930's, amounted to only 22 million in 1935. During the war years, the cities experienced a sizeable influx of population. Wartime restrictions, however, prevented a concomitant expansion of the housing inventory. In 1945, the value of residential construction amounted to only 1.6 billion in the private sector and 115 million in the public sector. By the end of the war, deterioration, obsolescence, and congestion were widespread in the metropolitan residential areas.

A concerted effort at urban renewal has characterized the postwar period. Coping with deterioration, obsolescence, and congestion in a period of accelerating population growth and a war-induced housing shortage in metropolitan areas has been no easy task. Although the value of private residential construction in the post-war period has averaged nearly 10 billion per year, and that in the public sector 350 million per year, much of the increment to the metropolitan housing inventory was required to house a growing population rather than to replace obsolescent dwellings.

A continuing population "explosion" in the United States is in prospect. No abatement of the trend toward metropolitan concentration is in sight. New dimensions and exigencies in the metropolitan housing problem have emerged since housing reforms were activated in the 1930's. A renewed effort on the part of social scientists to understand metropolitan housing on the macroscopic level is in order.

The increasing need and demand for information about the housing inventory and its utilization are mirrored in the expanding housing program of the Bureau of the Census. Prior to 1940, the only housing items collected in the decennial Censuses of the United States were counts of occupied dwellings by tenure, color of occupants, and residence, and data on homes which were mortgaged. The first fairly comprehensive and standardized body of statistics on housing became available in the 1930's when Real Property Inventories or Surveys were carried out in some 400 cities. These surveys, initiated by federal agencies, stimulated interest in the inclusion of housing items in the 1940 Census. The first Census of Housing, a comprehensive survey of the quality, characteristics, and utilization of the nation's dwellings, was taken in 1940. By the mid-1940's, special reports on housing were appearing: for example, Housing—Special Reports (H-46) presented characteristics of occupied dwellings for the nation; Current Population Reports—Housing (P-70, P-71, and P-72) made available occupancy status and selected other characteristics for regions, 34 metropolitan districts, and some 187 localities. In the 1950's, the series of Housing and Construction Reports was initiated by the Bureau of the Census: Alterations and Repairs (H-101); Housing Vacancies (H-111); and Housing Characteristics (H-121), for example. The National Housing Inventory conducted by the Bureau of the Census at the close of 1956 represented a major "break-through" in the housing statistics program. For the first time, statistics on the components of change in the size and composition of the housing inventory were obtained.

With the NHI (National Housing Inventory), we can measure not only the net change in number of dwelling units between

*3*

1950 and the close of 1956, but also gross change in the inventory. Estimates of the numbers of dwellings demolished, merged, converted, constructed, or otherwise lost from or added to the housing inventory are available. For certain key characteristics of the inventory, such as occupancy status or quality of housing, it is possible to decompose the 1950–56 change in composition into that part attributable to dwellings lost from or added to the inventory and that part attributable to changes in the characteristics of dwellings which remained in the inventory. From the NHI, then, information can be obtained about increments to the housing inventory in the post-1950 period and about the quality, characteristics, and utilization of the housing inventory at the end of 1956. Of primary importance is the information available on the processes by which change in the size and composition of the inventory come about.

The 1960 Census probably will cover all aspects of housing which were touched on by the NHI as well as certain other items. However, all the results of the forthcoming Census are unlikely to be available until 1962. The NHI results are, in a sense, a preview of the 1960 Census results. The NHI has recorded the changes in housing which occurred in the initial seven years of the decade 1950 to 1960. Unless the patterns of change reverse during the terminal three years of the decade, results of the 1960 Census are to a considerable extent anticipated by the NHI results.

Perhaps because mass survey or census data on housing have been collected for a relatively short time, methods for analyzing housing statistics are relatively undeveloped. The 1940 and 1950 Censuses of Housing were not strictly comparable in the definition of such items as vacant units, type of structure, or condition and water supply. Household and family concepts were revised in the 1940's. The components-of-change concept first appears in the 1956 NHI. The family-life-cycle

*4*

concept is beginning to appear in housing studies. Changes in concept and measurement are essential in the development of an appropriate methodology. However, each innovation poses special problems in analysis and interpretation. Analysis of the NHI data points to certain pitfalls and windfalls which are likely to obtain in the data of the 1960 Census of Housing.

The NHI and the Chicago Supplement to the NHI were designed to provide data for the intercensal period which were necessary for the formulation and execution of housing programs. Summaries or analyses of portions of the NHI and CSNHI (Chicago Supplement to the NHI) data have appeared, focusing for the most part on problematic aspects of housing. This monograph attempts to meet a somewhat different need— that for an overview of the housing situation in relation to which planners, administrators, and interested citizens can evaluate particular problems in the area of housing. We also have attempted to detail certain analytical and interpretive issues which arise in using the housing statistics. It is just as important to recognize the limitations of these data as to exploit their unusual potentialities. Failure to recognize these limitations, which are not immediately apparent, may lead to erroneous conclusions about the housing situation.

On the substantive side, the major topics treated in the monograph are patterns of change in the size and composition of metropolitan housing inventories during the 1950's, the relationship of income to housing, differentials in the housing of whites and nonwhites, and the housing of families at different stages of the family life cycle. Several critical housing problems confronting the metropolis are illuminated by these analyses. For example, there is concern that the demolition entailed in urban renewal will exacerbate the depression and war-induced housing shortage in metropolitan areas. It is relevant that although about 4 per cent of the 1950 housing inventory had been demolished or otherwise lost in the post-1950 period, the number of available vacancies increased between 1950 and 1956 in each of the nation's six largest metropolitan centers. Housing the growing nonwhite population of metropolitan centers is another problem faced by the metropolis. It is shown that, at least in the case of Chicago, discrimination in the housing market as well as residential segregation aggravates the problem. There is the perennial problem of providing adequate shelter for the lower-income groups—white as well as nonwhite. Although in comparison with levels of housing elsewhere in the world, it can scarcely be held that the lower economic third of the people in the nation, or in Chicago, are "ill-housed," it is apparent from the data presented that lower-income groups have a difficult time providing their families with adequate shelter and amenities. Finally, there is the emergent problem of housing our rapidly increasing aged population. Growing concern with this problem is evident throughout the nation. The data, at least for Chicago, show that some of the opinions held on the inferior housing conditions of the aged are unfounded; and they provide a factual basis for the consideration and solution of such problems as there are.

On the methodological side, we emphasize problems in the analysis of "turnover" data, in particular the statistics on quality shifts among the same dwellings. Given the unreliability in the classification by quality, the reported numbers of units shifting from the standard to the substandard group and vice versa greatly overstate the "actual" numbers of units which change in quality status. A formal analysis of rent-income relationships demonstrates that the "rules of thumb" in current usage are poor descriptions of the existing patterns. Techniques of direct and indirect standardization and the analysis of components of differences among rates are exploited rather more fully than in conventional studies of housing characteristics.

*6*

Part I of the monograph is a comparative study of post-1950 changes in the size and composition of the housing inventory in the nation's six largest SMA's (Standard Metropolitan Areas) and the Cities of Chicago and Philadelphia. Special attention is given the components-of-change data obtained through the NHI. The mode of analysis illustrates one way of handling the sorts of "change" statistics which are likely to appear in the 1960 Census. Part II of the monograph is based on the special tabulations of housing statistics by tenure, color of occupant, and quality of dwelling for the City of Chicago obtained through the CSNHI. Such data are not available for areas other than the City of Chicago, and are unlikely to appear in equal detail in the regular tabulations of the 1960 Census. The detail of the tabulations permits more revealing study of a number of relationships, particularly white-nonwhite differentials in housing, than has been possible heretofore. The data by stage in the family life cycle, presence of minor children in the family, presence of older persons in the household, and migration status also are unusual. The analyses may be useful in developing special tabulation plans for the forthcoming Census, which would make possible comparative study of housing utilization in metropolitan centers.

Before presenting the detailed analyses which constitute Parts I and II of the monograph, we set forth succinctly what we regard as major findings of the study. This overview both highlights results of general import and provides a preview of the study's substance.

This study although based primarily on materials for Chicago and thus necessarily affected by the unique aspects of the Chicago situation, nevertheless has a number of generic implications. Comparative analysis of patterns of change in the housing inventory of the six largest SMA's and two cities brings out striking inter-area similarities. Insofar as differences are observed, they typically hinge on the differential rates of new construction.

In general, the housing situation in these metropolitan areas improved between 1950 and the close of 1956 both quantitatively and qualitatively. The available vacancy rate more than doubled in the Boston, Chicago, Detroit, and Philadelphia SMA's and increased by a fifth in the New York SMA. In the Los Angeles SMA, the available vacancy rate fell by a sixth; but in both years it was above the metropolitan average. The proportion of the housing inventory classified substandard dropped by a third to a half in each SMA except New York, where a decrease of a twelfth was observed. Loosening of the housing market and upgrading of the housing supply also are evident in the cities. The available vacancy rate doubled in Chicago and tripled in Philadelphia. The proportion substandard fell by a third in each city.

At the outset, a few comments about the areas for which statistics are available seem in order. The SMA's differ greatly in date of settlement, residential maturity, population density, and other factors which are likely to be associated with the composition of the housing inventory and changes therein. The number of areas for which data are available is too small, however, to "control" for such differences. Statistics also are available for the central cities of two of these SMA's—Chicago and Philadelphia. The central city typically has been settled at an earlier date, is more mature residentially, and is more densely populated than the outlying or suburban part of an SMA. The sample design does not permit us to compare central and suburban parts of the Chicago and Philadelphia SMA's although such comparisons would be invaluable.

We may tend to overemphasize similarities and minimize differences among the areas. The concepts of change employed in the NHI are new, and measures of the components of change are subject to relatively large sampling errors. Many differences which are of doubtful statistical significance may be important substantively. Such differences will be revealed by analysis of the 1960 Census results, based on a larger sample and available for a wider range of areas.

Growth of the housing inventory and area growth differentials are accounted for primarily by the volume of new construction. In both the SMA's and the cities, about 92 per cent of the dwellings which existed in 1950 remained intact in the 1956 housing inventory. Some 2 per cent of the 1950 dwellings had been demolished in the seven-year period. Four per cent of the 1950 dwellings were involved in merger or conversion. However, losses through merger were offset by additions through conversion, and jointly merger and conversion processes had a negligible effect on the size of the housing inventory. Losses by "other means" generally were offset by additions from "other sources." Thus, the rate at which an area's housing inventory grew depended almost wholly on the local rate of residential construction. Los Angeles, with a 40 per cent increase in housing between 1950 and 1956, was the most rapidly growing of the six SMA's. Boston grew most slowly, with an increase of 10 per cent. Growth rates in the other SMA's ranged from 17 to 26 per cent. In the Cities of Chicago and Philadelphia, both relatively old and densely settled compared with their suburban rings, the housing supply increased more slowly, on the order of 5 per cent.

Standard housing increased by nearly half in the Los Angeles SMA, roughly a third in Chicago, Detroit, and Philadelphia, and at least a sixth in the Boston and New York SMA's. Increases in standard dwellings of nearly a sixth are reported in the cities. In each area, new construction was the chief source of increase in standard housing. Upgrading of dwellings which existed in 1950 contributed a smaller, but nonetheless note-

*9*

worthy, number of units to the supply of standard housing in each area except the New York SMA, where a net downgrading of the 1950 inventory apparently occurred.

Substandard housing was reduced by a third or more in the Chicago, Detroit, Los Angeles, and Philadelphia SMA's and by over a fourth in Boston. In the New York SMA, however, the supply of substandard housing may have increased slightly. In both the cities of Chicago and Philadelphia, substandard dwellings decreased by almost a third. Substandard dwellings merged, demolished, or otherwise lost to the inventory were somewhat more numerous than substandard dwellings added through conversion or new construction. In the Boston, Detroit, and Philadelphia SMA's, on the order of a third of the total decrease in substandard housing is attributable to these change processes and two thirds is accounted for by net upgrading of existing dwellings. A fifth of the decrease in the Chicago, and a sixth of the decrease in the Los Angeles, SMA can be attributed to the change processes. In the New York SMA, net downgrading of the existing inventory more than offset the net loss of substandard dwellings which resulted in a small increase in substandard housing. A third of the decrease in the City of Chicago and half the decrease in the City of Philadelphia is accounted for by net losses of substandard dwellings through the change processes.

The change processes—in particular, new construction—accounted for most of the increase in standard housing. In the case of substandard housing, the change processes jointly resulted in moderate decreases in each area. The upgrading, or in the case of New York downgrading, of the existing housing supply was of primary importance in changing the supply of substandard housing.

Home ownership became more prevalent in each area between 1950 and 1956. Accounting for this increase were primarily new construction and to a lesser extent tenure-occupancy shifts within the existing housing supply. Rental housing decreased both as a proportion of the total inventory and in volume in the Boston, Chicago, Detroit, and Philadelphia SMA's. In the Los Angeles and New York SMA's, the proportion of renters decreased, although the supply of rental housing increased. In each city, both the number and proportion of renters decreased. New construction added some rental units to the housing supply in each area; but these additions were in large part offset by demolition and other losses of rental housing. Among existing dwellings, a net shift away from the rental sector is observed in each area except Los Angeles.

In general, the 1950's were a period of growing home ownership and lessening importance of rental housing. The patterns of change in the Los Angeles SMA, however, should not be overlooked. As in the other areas, home ownership became more prevalent; but conditions were conducive to substantial new construction in the rental sector and to a net shift to rental housing within the unchanged 1950 inventory.

Examination of the effects of demolition and new construction on the composition of the housing inventory reveals a fairly consistent pattern over the areas. With respect to many characteristics, demolition and construction reinforce one another in producing compositional changes in the inventory. They tend to raise the proportion of home ownership and reduce the proportion of renters; to increase the proportion standard and reduce the proportion substandard; to lower the median age of the inventory; to raise the proportion of single-family dwellings and lower the proportion of units in multi-unit structures; and to reduce the proportions of small and large units and increase the proportion of units with three to six rooms.

Before-and-after views of converted and merged units suggest that their effects on the composition of the inventory are

*11*

largely offsetting. For example, conversion tended to reduce home ownership, merger to increase it. Conversion typically increased the proportion of substandard housing, whereas merger improved housing quality. Conversion appears to be undertaken as a solution for the "too-large" dwelling, but results in "too-small" dwellings. The converse, of course, applies for mergers.

The available statistics on residential mobility indicate that over four-fifths of the moves which terminate in these metropolitan areas involve a change of dwelling within the same SMA rather than in-movement to the SMA from other areas. Vacancies occurring in the city appear most likely to be filled by city residents, whereas vacancies occurring in the ring are more likely to be filled by residents of the suburban ring. This suggests the existence of a "city housing market" and a "ring housing market" within the metropolitan market.

The NHI provides less adequate information about differentials in the housing of various segments of the population, such as lower-income families, nonwhite families, or "older" families, than about changes in the housing inventory. However, data of the CSNHI permit fairly intensive study of such differentials. We suspect that, in general, the differences by income, color, or stage of the family cycle observed in Chicago obtain in other major cities although the details probably are unique to Chicago.

First, some housing and family characteristics which vary with income may be noted. As family income increases, increases are observed in: prevalence of home ownership; the proportion of normal families, those which comprise married couples and their relatives; the size of the average family. As family income increases, decreases are observed in: prevalence of substandard housing; the proportion of nonwhite families; the proportion of families headed by persons 65 and over.

For convenience, families in the lowest fifth of the income

*12*

distribution are designated "lower-income." Only a fifth of the lower-income families were home owners. These families who owned their home were likely to consist of an older family head with one or two adult relatives; and the family was unlikely to be living in substandard housing. The inferior housing conditions of lower-income families who rent is apparent from the fact that a third were living in substandard dwellings. Half these renter families were nonwhite, as compared with a fourth of all renter families or a seventh of all lower-income home owners. A majority of the lower-income renter families included at least one minor child, and a sixth were "broken" families with a child.

Some 15,000 standard dwellings available in public-housing projects mitigate the housing situation of lower-income families. Although such units comprise only 1 per cent of the city's housing supply, 10 per cent of all standard dwellings rented by lower income families lie within the projects. Families in the projects, as compared with other lower-income renters, are likely to be nonwhite, to be large, to include minor children, and to consist of an atypical family group.

A loose relationship between rent and income on a household basis is indicated by the finding that only a sixth of the variation among households in rent is accounted for by differences among them in income. Households paying the same rent vary substantially in their income, and households with the same income pay a wide range of rents. There is, nonetheless, a strong average tendency for rent to increase as income increases and, conversely, for income to increase as rent increases. These relationships, along with the nature of the data, lead to an average tendency for the rent/income ratio to decrease as income increases and to increase as rent increases.

The ratio of gross rent to current income for lower-income families is high as compared with rent/income ratios for families with greater current incomes. Very possibly gross rent also accounts for a higher proportion of the total expenditures of lower-income families or of their permanent income, although these ratios presumably vary less with income than does the rent/income ratio. Lower-income families occupying standard dwellings pay higher rentals and consequently have higher ratios of rent to current income than do those families in substandard housing. This suggests that disproportionate numbers of the families in substandard dwellings are families with low permanent incomes to which their housing expenditures are geared.

During the past two decades, Chicago's nonwhite population has grown rapidly while the white population has decreased somewhat. During the 1940's, the rapid in-migration of nonwhites coupled with a housing shortage encouraged doubling up of nonwhite families and other somewhat irregular living arrangements. In the improved economic climate of the post-1950 period, the nonwhite population appears to have "caught up" in terms of household formation. There also is some evidence that although substantial differences remain, white and nonwhite households are becoming more alike in terms of their distributions by size and type. White households include relatively high proportions of small normal families and persons living alone. Nonwhite households include relatively high proportions of large normal families, atypical family groups, and persons sharing their dwelling with nonrelatives. An over-all decrease in room crowding is evident for both white and nonwhite households in the post-1950 period. Their differential in crowding may have lessened somewhat although the proportion crowded for nonwhites remains at least four times as great as that for whites.

Nonwhites in Chicago pay rentals more or less equivalent to

those paid by whites and can do so only by allocating larger proportions of their income to housing. Although in the 1950's, the housing of nonwhite renters improved more than that of white renters, the proportion of nonwhites in substandard housing still is at least double that for whites. This white-nonwhite differential is accounted for not by differences in the rents paid by white and nonwhite families but by the fact that nonwhite families receive less "quality" per dollar spent on housing than do white families. When white and nonwhite families paying the same rent are compared, the nonwhite families consistently have a higher proportion in substandard dwellings. There is no evidence that the nonwhites "sacrifice" quality for space. They get less desirable housing but apparently no more housing space for a given rental than do white families. Differences in the economic status and composition of white and nonwhite families also fail to account for their differential in housing quality.

Residential discrimination against nonwhites can be inferred from the finding that nonwhites pay significantly more than whites for housing of roughly equivalent quality and spaciousness. Such discrimination is evident among families living in the Chicago area for at least two years as well as among recent in-migrants. Given the high degree of nonwhite residential segregation in Chicago, white and nonwhite households may be competing in separate housing markets. If so, the heavy demand in the nonwhite housing market engendered by nonwhite population increase may produce residential discrimination as well as "piling up" or congestion in nonwhite residential areas.

By and large, nonwhites gained additional housing by taking up occupancy in dwellings formerly occupied by whites rather than by occupying new dwellings. Although large numbers of dwellings were "turning over" from white to nonwhite occupancy, very few dwellings reverted from nonwhite to white occupancy. This also suggests separate white and nonwhite housing markets.

Although new construction was concentrated in the outlying sections of the city, increases in vacant dwellings and improvement in housing quality occurred in all parts of the city during the 1950's. At the end of 1956, however, housing conditions still were less favorable in the central than in the peripheral areas. In the outlying parts, housing tended to be newer and in better condition and to provide more adequate facilities. "Family living" also appears more prevalent in the outlying areas, for the rate of home ownership is high and households are likely to be large and to consist of normal families.

Both white and nonwhite residential areas are found in the central, more deteriorated section of the city. Housing conditions generally appear more desirable in the white areas. For example, substandard housing is only half as prevalent as in the nonwhite central area where, despite improvements between 1950 and 1956, over half of all housing was substandard. "Family living" seems more widespread in the white residential areas also.

The "middle" section of the city has sizeable numbers of both white and nonwhite residents. The transition from white to nonwhite occupancy during the 1950's occurred largely within this area. Insofar as we can tell, the housing conditions and patterns of family living for nonwhites in this area are about the same as those of the white residents, and the housing situation is considerably better than that in either the white or nonwhite central residential area. The outlying part of the city, in which housing conditions are superior and "family living" is more prevalent, is an almost exclusively white residential area.

Families typically undergo a series of stages, termed the "family life cycle," the major elements of which may be de-

*16*

scribed as formation, expansion, contraction, and dissolution. Substandard housing is widespread among young couples, becomes less prevalent as the family passes through its expanding phase, and then rises slightly among older couples whose children have left the parental home. On the other hand, home ownership, occupancy of single-family homes, and occupancy of newly built units become more frequent as the family expands and then become slightly less frequent as the family contracts. On the economic side, the pattern of change is more complicated. The situation perhaps is most acute for younger couples with pre-school children. Their need for spacious housing of relatively good quality must be met from a relatively limited income.

Typically older persons in Chicago share a dwelling with their relatives. Of the households which included at least one person aged 65 or over, half consisted of an older family head sharing his dwelling with relatives. Younger family heads sharing their dwellings with elderly relatives accounted for a fourth. Older persons living alone made up a sixth. A tenth consisted of elderly persons sharing a dwelling with nonrelatives.

Households which include an older person are no more likely to live in substandard housing than are other households. It is true that a third of the older persons living alone and a fourth of those living with nonrelatives live in substandard dwellings, but the proportions substandard are equally high among the dwellings of younger persons living alone or with nonrelatives. The current income of older families and older persons living alone is lower than that of the younger, and the ratios of rent to current income among the old are relatively high. However, current income may be a poor indicator of the financial status of older households and tend to overstate their economic disadvantage. No information is available on the financial status of elderly persons who share the dwelling of younger relatives, but it should be noted that the families which include elderly relatives have current incomes well above those of other families.

*Part I*

# THE HOUSING INVENTORY:
# CHICAGO AND OTHER AREAS

# Introduction to Part I

DURING DECEMBER, 1956 and January, 1957, the Bureau of the Census conducted a survey of housing in the United States. This National Housing Inventory was the outgrowth of several years' experimentation with techniques for obtaining information about the housing market on a sample basis in a non-census year. The 1956 NHI (National Housing Inventory) was designed to provide measures of change in the housing supply which had occurred since the 1950 Census of Housing and to describe the 1956 housing inventory.

Chapters 2 and 3 are concerned with measures of change in the housing supply. From the 1956 NHI, we can determine not only how much or how rapidly an area's housing inventory grew between 1950 and 1956 but also the components of this growth, such as the loss through demolition, the additions from residential construction activity, or changes resulting from conversion and merger. In addition, we can learn something about the ways in which the composition of the housing inventory changed between 1950 and 1956—for example, the role of demolition in reducing substandard housing or the relationship of residential construction activity and home ownership. Because the 1956 NHI is the first large-scale survey to collect information on components of change, the concepts are somewhat unfamiliar and there are no conventional methods of analysis to rely on.

The reader may feel that we give undue attention to the concepts, nature of the data, and methods of analysis and underemphasize the implications of the observed changes. However, any special skills which we can bring to bear on the NHI data are analytical; a major function of this monograph is to point out pitfalls in the treatment and interpretation of the statistics.

Our approach is to examine the components of change in the housing inventory of each of the six largest Standard Metropolitan Areas. Such a comparative framework provides some indication of the variety of change patterns characteristic of the nation's major metropolitan centers and a broader perspective on the changes taking place within Chicago. A variety of analytical techniques are introduced to suggest alternative ways of handling the data, for we are confident that many readers will wish to examine somewhat special aspects of change which we have been unable to cover.

The composition of the 1956 housing inventory in the several areas is examined in Chapter 4. For the most part, the inventory is described in terms of conventional summary statistics, such as the proportion of home owners, the proportion of substandard dwellings, or median rental; consequently less attention is given to methodological issues.

Part I, then, comprises a series of exploratory analyses of data derived from the 1956 NHI. It does not purport to be comprehensive or to exhaust the possibilities for analysis; however, we do touch upon many of the more significant changes in the size and composition of the housing inventory.

# 2

# Patterns of Change
# in the Housing Inventory

MEASURES OF net change in an area's housing inventory, or in the total number of dwelling units in the area, frequently are cited. For example, the housing inventory in the City of Chicago increased by 116,600 dwelling units, or 12 per cent, during the decade 1940 to 1950. Although we know the net change in the City's housing inventory between 1940 and 1950, we know very little about the components of this change. Results of the 1950 Census of Housing indicate that 51,200 dwelling units were added to the City's housing inventory by new construction during the decade 1940 to 1950. Thus, a net increase of 65,400 dwelling units (116,600 minus 51,200) occurred between 1940 and 1950 which is not accounted for by new construction. But we do not know how many dwellings were gained through conversion of existing units or how many dwellings were gained by converting nonresidential structures into living quarters; nor do we know how many dwelling units which existed in 1940 were lost to the inventory between 1940 and 1950 by demolition, fire, or other means.

The 1956 NHI conducted by the Bureau of the Census is the first large-scale survey from which statistics on gross change in the housing inventory over a period of several years are available. Using data for the City of Chicago again, we will examine gross change in the City's housing inventory between April, 1950 and December, 1956 as it is revealed by the NHI. The City's 1950 housing inventory consisted of 1,106,000 dwelling units. About 86,000 of these dwelling units were lost to the inventory between 1950 and 1956—13,000 by conversion, 31,000 by merger, 26,000 by demolition, and 16,000 by other means. The remaining 1,020,000 units in the 1950 housing inventory (1,106,000 minus 86,000) were unchanged during the period 1950 to 1956. Additions to the City's housing inventory between 1950 and 1956 numbered 145,000 dwelling units—28,000 added by conversion, 14,000 by merger, 84,000 by new construction, and 19,000 by other sources. The City's 1956 housing inventory consisted of 1,165,000 dwelling units —the 1,106,000 units of the 1950 housing inventory minus the 86,000 units of the 1950 inventory lost between 1950 and 1956 plus the 145,000 units added to the inventory between 1950 and 1956. The net increase in dwelling units in the City of Chicago between 1950 and 1956 was 59,000 units (1,165,000 minus 1,106,000). Gross change in the City's housing inventory during the period consisted of a loss of 86,000 units and a gain of 145,000 units.

To obtain data on components of change in the housing inventory, some new concepts and techniques of measurement were introduced in the NHI. We can define the universe of dwelling units covered by the NHI as all units existing in 1950 and all units existing in 1956. Each unit in the universe is classified by its status in 1950 and its status in 1956. Let us look first at the kinds of units which would be classified as "unchanged 1950 to 1956." The 1956 NHI enumerator records a dwelling unit, i.e., room(s) intended for occupancy as separate living quarters for person(s); the enumerator, then, compares the dwelling unit with the returns of the 1950 Census of Housing. If, on the basis of this check, it appears that the living quarters enumerated as one dwelling unit in 1956 existed as one dwelling unit in 1950, the enumerator records the status of the dwelling unit as "unchanged 1950 to 1956."

The enumerator may find that the living quarters enumerated as one dwelling unit in 1956 did not exist as one dwelling unit in 1950; the unit then falls in the category "additions to the inventory, 1950–56." The 1956 unit may be in a structure built between 1950 and 1956; if so, the source of the additional unit is new construction. If the 1956 unit was created by dividing a dwelling unit which existed in 1950 into two or more units through structural alteration or change in use, the source of the additional unit is conversion of a 1950 unit. If the 1956 unit was created by combining two or more dwelling units which existed in 1950 into one dwelling unit through structural alteration or change in use, the source of the additional unit is merger of 1950 units. Or the 1956 unit may have been added through other sources. Examples would be units created from living quarters classified as nondwelling-unit quarters in 1950 such as a sleeping room in a rooming house, units created from nonresidential space such as a garage, and units moved to the site between 1950 and 1956 such as a trailer.

The third broad component of change in the inventory is "losses to the inventory, 1950–56." It includes dwelling units which existed in 1950 but did not exist in 1956. The enumerator secured information on losses through conversion and losses through merger in the part of the survey already described. However, to gain information on the number of units lost to the inventory by virtue of an entire structure being demolished or otherwise lost to the inventory, an alternative survey technique had to be introduced. The 1956 NHI enumerator was supplied with a list of addresses drawn from the returns of the 1950 Census of Housing; the enumerator, then, located the address and reported whether the structure still contained living quarters or whether it had been demolished, burned, abandoned, changed to nonresidential use, or otherwise lost to the inventory since 1950.

It is difficult to assess the accuracy with which the various components of change in the housing inventory between 1950 and 1956 have been measured. The errors associated with sampling presumably can be specified with some confidence although the estimation procedures in the NHI were complicated. Errors in field work and in the compilation of statistics are present, of course, in any survey or census. We also know on the basis of past investigations that respondents sometimes are unable or unwilling to provide accurate information. We suspect that this last problem is particularly serious in measuring the components of change.

Let us look at the data for the City of Chicago. Some 1,020,000 dwelling units in the City were classified as "unchanged 1950 to 1956." Of the units recorded in 1956, some 945,000 could be matched with units enumerated in the 1950 Census of Housing; but 75,000 or 7 per cent, apparently could not be matched and we infer that they were classified as unchanged on the basis of information provided by the house-holder or neighbors. Inasmuch as three-fourths of the house-holds in Chicago at the time of the NHI had moved into their present dwelling since the 1950 Census (1956 NHI, Vol. III, Table 2), we question whether a majority of householders could provide adequate information about the 1950 status of their present dwelling. The same problem arises in connection with the measurement of other components of change; for example, the Bureau of the Census states (1956 NHI, Vol. I, pp. 3–4): "Because of the difficulty of ascertaining the actual cause of the disappearance of a unit, due to the time period involved and the difficulty of locating a reliable respondent, it is possible that some units recorded as destroyed by fire, flood, or other cause had actually been demolished, and vice versa." We do not know just how often the NHI enumerator had to assign a dwelling to a change category on the basis of information provided by a respondent, nor do we know how reliable the respondent's in-formation was. However, users of the NHI data should be aware of this potential source of error.

Because the categories of change are unfamiliar and com-parable data are not available for other time periods, we often find ourselves at a loss in deciding whether, say, a rate of con-version should be regarded as "high" or "low." To help over-come this difficulty, statistics from the 1956 NHI are presented for six SMA's (Standard Metropolitan Areas) including Chi-cago and Philadelphia and for the Cities of Chicago and Phila-delphia. Three of the SMA's are in the eastern part of the country—Boston, New York-Northeastern New Jersey, and Philadelphia; two are located in the north central area—Chi-cago and Detroit; and Los Angeles is in the "Far West." In 1950, these six SMA's were the largest in the nation in terms of population size. Each had a 1950 housing inventory in excess of a half million dwelling units. (With respect to size of 1950 housing inventory, the San Francisco-Oakland SMA ranked sixth and the Boston SMA seventh.) In terms of population the Cities of Chicago and Philadelphia ranked second and third respectively among the nation's cities in 1950; they ranked second and fourth respectively in terms of size of 1950 housing inventory.

## THE TOTAL INVENTORY

The 1950 and 1956 housing inventories of the six SMA's are as follows:

| SMA | MILLIONS OF UNITS | |
|-----|-----|-----|
| | 1950 | 1956 |
| New York | 4.0 | 4.6 |
| **Chicago** | 1.6 | 1.9 |
| Los Angeles | 1.5 | 2.1 |
| Philadelphia | 1.1 | 1.3 |
| Detroit | 0.9 | 1.1 |
| Boston | 0.7 | 0.7 |

With respect to size of the inventory, only one change in rank occurred among the six SMA's between 1950 and 1956. The Chicago SMA ranked second in 1950 with an inventory of 1.6 million units; its 1956 inventory of 1.9 million units ranked third. The Los Angeles SMA ranked third in 1950 with an inventory of 1.5 million units; its 1956 inventory of 2.1 million units ranked second.

Expansion of the housing inventory, both in numerical and relative terms, was most rapid in the Los Angeles SMA and least rapid in the Boston SMA. Net changes in the several

SMA's are shown below in schematic form, and the inter-area variation in growth rates also can be observed in Figure 2–1.

| NUMERICAL INCREASE, 1950–1956 (IN THOUSANDS) | PERCENTAGE INCREASE, 1950–1956 | | |
|---|---|---|---|
| | 10–17 | 22–26 | 40 |
| 610 to 677 | New York | . . . | Los Angeles |
| 225 to 285 | **Chicago** | Philadelphia Detroit | . . . |
| 69 | Boston | . . . | . . . |

Information on change in housing inventory is available for only two cities—Chicago and Philadelphia. Dwellings in the City of Chicago increased from 1,106,000 to 1,165,000 in the period; this represents a net gain of 59,000 units or a relative increase of 5 per cent. Dwellings in the City of Philadelphia increased by 41,000 units, from 600,000 in 1950 to 641,000 in 1956; this represents a 7 per cent increase in the Philadelphia housing inventory.

Components of the net change in dwelling units are shown in Table 2–1 for the six SMA's and two cities. By and large, the number of units in a change category varies directly with size of the total inventory. Therefore, to facilitate inter-area comparisons, we introduce the summary measures in Table 2–2 which take account of differences in size of inventory among the SMA's. Our first question is what became of the 1950 housing inventory during the period 1950 to 1956? As Figure 2–1 shows, the vast majority of the dwelling units included in the 1950 inventory remained unchanged in the 1956 inventory. The proportion of the 1950 housing inventory which remained unchanged ranged from 94 per cent in the Boston and New York SMA's to 91 per cent in the Detroit SMA. Units lost to the housing inventory between 1950 and 1956 are classified according to the means by which they were lost: namely, conversion; merger; demolition; other means. The four categories

## Table 2-1
## Disposition of the 1950 Housing Inventory and Source of the 1956 Housing Inventory: Selected Standard Metropolitan Areas and Cities

| HOUSING INVENTORY AND COMPONENTS OF CHANGE | STANDARD METROPOLITAN AREA | | | | | | CITY | |
|---|---|---|---|---|---|---|---|---|
| | Boston | Chicago | Detroit | Los Angeles | New York | Phila-delphia | Chicago | Phila-delphia |
| | thousands of units | | | | | | | |
| Total dwelling units, 1950 | 668 | 1,646 | 858 | 1,522 | 3,954 | 1,052 | 1,106 | 600 |
| 1950 units lost 1950–56 | 41 | 115 | 77 | 109 | 248 | 74 | 86 | 47 |
| By conversion | 13 | 23 | 17 | 8 | 51 | 19 | 13 | 12 |
| By merger | 13 | 40 | 27 | 14 | 71 | 32 | 31 | 22 |
| By demolition | 5 | 31 | 22 | 29 | 72 | 8 | 26 | 4 |
| By other means | 10 | 21 | 11 | 58 | 54 | 15 | 16 | 9 |
| 1950 units remaining unchanged in 1956 inventory | 627 | 1,531 | 781 | 1,413 | 3,706 | 978 | 1,020 | 553 |
| Units added 1950–56 | 110 | 400 | 302 | 719 | 925 | 300 | 145 | 88 |
| By conversion of 1950 units | 28 | 49 | 33 | 19 | 109 | 42 | 28 | 27 |
| By merger of 1950 units | 6 | 19 | 14 | 7 | 35 | 16 | 14 | 11 |
| By new construction | 69 | 307 | 247 | 630 | 737 | 235 | 84 | 45 |
| By other sources | 7 | 25 | 8 | 63 | 44 | 7 | 19 | 5 |
| Total dwelling units, 1956 | 737 | 1,931 | 1,083 | 2,132 | 4,631 | 1,278 | 1,165 | 641 |

Source: 1956 NHI, Vol. I, Tables A and B.

## Table 2-2
## Summary Measures of Change in Housing Inventory, 1950–56: Selected Standard Metropolitan Areas and Cities

| SUMMARY MEASURE | STANDARD METROPOLITAN AREA | | | | | | CITY | |
|---|---|---|---|---|---|---|---|---|
| | Boston | Chicago | Detroit | Los Angeles | New York | Phila-delphia | Chicago | Phila-delphia |
| Net change in inventory, 1950–56 (in thousands) | 69 | 285 | 225 | 610 | 677 | 226 | 59 | 41 |
| Percentage change in inventory, 1950–56 | 10 | 17 | 26 | 40 | 17 | 22 | 5 | 7 |
| Disposition of 1950 inventory (percentage distribution): | | | | | | | | |
| Total dwelling units, 1950 | 100 | 100 | 100 | 100 | 100 | 100 | 100 | 100 |
| Converted | 2 | 1 | 2 | ... | 1 | 2 | 1 | 2 |
| Merged | 2 | 2 | 3 | 1 | 2 | 3 | 3 | 4 |
| Demolished | 1 | 2 | 3 | 2 | 2 | 1 | 2 | 1 |
| Lost by other means | 2 | 1 | 1 | 4 | 1 | 1 | 1 | 2 |
| Remained unchanged | 94 | 93 | 91 | 93 | 94 | 93 | 92 | 92 |
| Source of 1956 inventory (percentage distribution): | | | | | | | | |
| Total dwelling units, 1956 | 100 | 100 | 100 | 100 | 100 | 100 | 100 | 100 |
| Conversion of 1950 units | 4 | 2 | 3 | 1 | 2 | 3 | 2 | 4 |
| Merger of 1950 units | 1 | 1 | 1 | ... | 1 | 1 | 1 | 2 |
| New construction | 9 | 16 | 23 | 30 | 16 | 18 | 7 | 7 |
| Other sources | 1 | 1 | 1 | 3 | 1 | ... | 2 | 1 |
| Unchanged 1950 units | 85 | 79 | 72 | 66 | 80 | 76 | 88 | 86 |

. . . 0.5 per cent or less.

Source: Table 2–1.

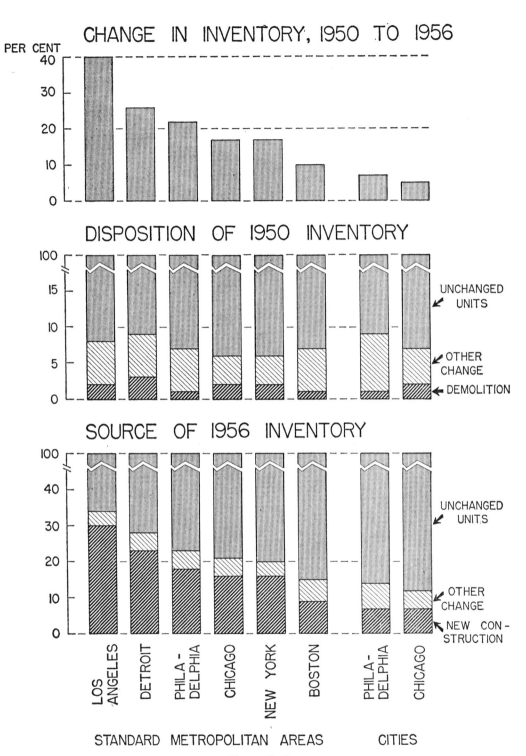

**Figure 2–1**

*Change in Housing Inventory, 1950 to 1956: Selected Standard Metropolitan Areas and Cities. (Source: Table 2–2)*

account for roughly equal proportions of the 1950 units lost to the inventory between 1950 and 1956. On the order of 2 per cent of the units existing in 1950 were converted between 1950 and 1956, 2 per cent were merged, 2 per cent were demolished, and 2 per cent were lost by other means.

Given the size of the sampling errors attached to the components of change, we are reluctant to regard the observed interarea differences in disposition of the 1950 inventory as significant. The similarities among areas rather than the differences among areas in disposition of the 1950 housing inventory are the striking feature brought out by the analysis.

We suspect that the casual observer would overestimate the relative importance of demolition as a means by which units are lost. The fact that sizeable clusters of structures frequently are demolished at the same time and often with a formidable array of wrecking equipment calls attention to it. Conversion, merger, abandonment, or other means of loss of more or less isolated structures may go unnoticed. The data indicate, however, that only about 2 per cent of all units or about a fourth of all units lost to the inventory between 1950 and 1956 were demolished on the initiative of a public agency or as a result of action on the part of the owner.

A second question now is posed: where did the 1956 housing inventory come from? In the Boston SMA, about 85 per cent of the 1956 housing inventory consisted of dwellings which existed in 1950 and remained in the inventory unchanged between 1950 and 1956. Unchanged dwellings accounted for about 80 per cent of the 1956 housing inventory in the New York, Chicago, and Philadelphia SMA's, and on the order of 70 per cent of the 1956 inventory in the Detroit and Los Angeles SMA's. New construction accounted for about 10 per cent of the 1956 inventory in the Boston SMA, about 15 per cent of the 1956 inventory in the

New York, Chicago, and Philadelphia SMA's, and about 25 per cent of the 1956 inventory in the Detroit and Los Angeles SMA's. Roughly 2 per cent of the 1956 housing inventory in each SMA was created by the conversion of units existing in 1950, about 1 per cent was created by the merger of units existing in 1950, and about 1 per cent was added from other sources. In the main, the inter-SMA differences in the relative importance of conversion, merger, and other sources are too small to be meaningful.

Unchanged 1950 units accounted for 86 to 88 per cent of the 1956 inventory in the Cities of Chicago and Philadelphia; 7 per cent of the 1956 inventory had been constructed since 1950. Unchanged units were a somewhat more important source of the 1956 inventory and new construction was a somewhat less important source in the Cities than in the SMA's.

The key factor in our observed differences among areas in sources of their 1956 housing inventories is new construction. (See Figure 2–1.) We already have seen that the 1950 inventories in the several areas were disposed of in the same way. About 92 per cent of the dwellings were retained unchanged and 8 per cent were lost between 1950 and 1956. Thus the inter-area differences in sources of the 1956 housing inventory result from variation among the areas in rate of new construction during the period 1950 to 1956. Any explanation of the differences among areas in new construction would call for a careful analysis of the determinants of population growth and household formation in the several areas. Such an analysis falls outside the scope of this monograph.

One other aspect of the components of change merits special attention: the effect of conversion and merger on the housing inventory. The data summarized in Table 2–3 indicate that the two types of change are more or less offsetting—the net gain in units through the conversion process is roughly equal to the net

## Table 2–3
### Change in Housing Inventory through Conversion and Merger, 1950–56: Selected Standard Metropolitan Areas and Cities

| COMPONENT OF CHANGE | STANDARD METROPOLITAN AREA | | | | | | CITY | |
| --- | --- | --- | --- | --- | --- | --- | --- | --- |
| | Boston | Chicago | Detroit | Los Angeles | New York | Phila-delphia | Chicago | Phila-delphia |
| | thousands of units | | | | | | | |
| 1950 units lost by conversion | 13 | 23 | 17 | 8 | 51 | 19 | 13 | 12 |
| 1956 units added by conversion | 28 | 49 | 33 | 19 | 109 | 42 | 28 | 27 |
| Net change by conversion, 1950–56 | 15 | 26 | 16 | 11 | 58 | 23 | 15 | 15 |
| 1950 units lost by merger | 13 | 40 | 27 | 14 | 71 | 32 | 31 | 22 |
| 1956 units added by merger | 6 | 19 | 14 | 7 | 35 | 16 | 14 | 11 |
| Net change by merger, 1950–56 | —7 | —21 | —13 | —7 | —36 | —16 | —17 | —11 |
| Net change by conversion and merger, 1950–56 | 8 | 5 | 3 | 4 | 22 | 7 | —2 | 4 |

Source: Table 2-1.

loss in units through merger during the period 1950 to 1956. Conversion typically involves the creation of two units from one existing unit, and merger typically involves the creation of one unit from two existing units. It will be recalled that conversion and merger as defined in the NHI can take place without any alteration of the structure itself. Conversion calls for nothing more than locking a door and merger for nothing more than unlocking a door. We do not know how often the conversion or merger results from structural alteration as compared with a simple change in use. Although we have no information on the point, it may be that "matching" with 1950 Census records was particularly difficult for units in these change categories.

We have found that the disposition of the 1950 inventory was much the same in each area. Between 1950 and 1956, about 8 per cent of the 1950 inventory underwent change—conversion, merger, demolition, and other losses each removed about 2 per cent of the dwellings; about 92 per cent of the 1950 inventory remained intact in the 1956 inventory. We do not dismiss the possibility that the rates of conversion, merger, demolition, and other loss varied from area to area; but the area-to-area consistency in disposition of the 1950 inventory is noteworthy. The analyses also make it clear that the housing inventory expanded more rapidly in some areas than in others. Apparently this differential growth reflects differences among the areas in residential construction activity rather than in disposition of the existing housing supply.

It is an open question whether a similar pattern would be observed in a different time period. There is reason to suppose that the disposition of the inventory was different in the war years when materials for residential construction were scarce, normal family life was disrupted, and population mobility was high. Likewise we are reluctant to project the 1950–56 pattern into the future.

*37*

## OCCUPANCY STATUS

This section focuses on change in the inventories of owner-occupied, rental, and vacant dwellings which occurred in the six SMA's and two cities between 1950 and 1956. Components of change in the inventories by occupancy status are shown in Table 2–4. The change categories are the same as those presented in Table 2–1 which pertains to the total inventory. Aside from certain minor discrepancies which stem from rounding procedures, the sum of owner, renter, and vacant dwellings in a given category (Table 2–4) equals the total dwellings in that category (Table 2–1).

One feature of the statistics on change for dwellings of a given status, e.g., owner, rental, or vacant, calls for comment. The inventory of dwellings of a given status changes in two ways: first, dwellings of the given status are removed from the housing inventory by demolition and other processes and are added to the housing inventory through new construction and from other sources; second, dwellings which remain in the housing inventory throughout the period can shift their status, e.g., a rental unit becomes vacant, a vacant unit is occupied by its owner. The first type of change we will refer to as change in inventory attributable to specific components of change; the second type will be referred to as change in inventory attributable to status shifts among identical, or unchanged, dwellings.

Here we can only summarize certain patterns of change which appear in the several areas. Although the reader may wish to examine the data in Table 2–4 in detail, our comments are based on the summary measures in Table 2–5 for the most part. The number of home owners increased substantially in each area between 1950 and 1956. The net increase in owner-occupied dwellings was 400 to 500 thousand in the Los Angeles and New York SMA's, 200 to 300 thousand in the Chicago, Detroit, and

Philadelphia SMA's, and about 60,000 in the Boston SMA. These numerical increases in the metropolitan owner inventories represent increases of 55 per cent in Los Angeles, on the order of 40 per cent in Chicago, Detroit, New York, and Philadelphia, and 20 per cent in Boston. Owner-occupied dwellings increased by about 50,000, or 15 per cent, in the Cities of Chicago and Philadelphia.

In each area, the growth of home ownership is attributable primarily to construction activity in the owner sector. Additions from new construction and other sources resulted in increases in the 1950 owner inventory ranging from 58 per cent in the Los Angeles SMA to 18 per cent in the Boston SMA and 17 and 10 per cent in the Cities of Chicago and Philadelphia respectively. The other change processes, in combination, had a negligible influence on the owner inventory; and tenure-occupancy shifts among identical dwellings resulted in increases of only 1 to 7 per cent in the 1950 owner inventory.

The rental inventory expanded by about 175,000 dwellings in the Los Angeles and New York SMA's. In each other SMA, the number of rental units decreased; reductions in rental housing ranged from 5,000 units in Chicago to 41,000 units in Philadelphia. Growth of the rental inventory amounted to 26 per cent in the Los Angeles SMA and 7 per cent in the New York SMA. Rental units decreased by less than 4 per cent in the Boston, Detroit, and Chicago SMA's and by 11 per cent in the Philadelphia SMA. In the City of Chicago, rental housing decreased by 9,000 units or 1 per cent. The decrease in Philadelphia was 31,000 units or 12 per cent.

The pattern of change in the Los Angeles rental inventory differs from that observed in the other areas. In Los Angeles, an increase of 30 per cent is accounted for by new construction and other sources and a decrease of 8 per cent is accounted for by demolition and other means. In combination the change

*39*

## Table 2-4
### Components of Change in the Inventories of Owner-Occupied, Renter-Occupied, and Vacant Dwelling Units, 1950–56: Selected Standard Metropolitan Areas and Cities

| HOUSING INVENTORY AND COMPONENTS OF CHANGE | STANDARD METROPOLITAN AREA | | | | | | CITY | |
| --- | --- | --- | --- | --- | --- | --- | --- | --- |
| | Boston | Chicago | Detroit | Los Angeles | New York | Phila-delphia | Chicago | Phila-delphia |
| | thousands of units | | | | | | | |
| **Owner-occupied:** | | | | | | | | |
| Total owner-occupied units, 1950 | 288 | 671 | 513 | 779 | 1,198 | 630 | 330 | 328 |
| 1950 units lost 1950–56 | | | | | | | | |
| By conversion | 6 | 13 | 7 | 6 | 24 | 11 | 7 | 7 |
| By merger | 4 | 9 | 7 | 3 | 24 | 8 | 6 | 5 |
| By demolition | ... | 5 | 2 | 9 | 2 | 2 | 3 | ... |
| By other means | 2 | 4 | 4 | 22 | 7 | 5 | 2 | 2 |
| 1950 status of unchanged units | 276 | 640 | 493 | 739 | 1,141 | 604 | 312 | 314 |
| 1956 status of unchanged units | 281 | 657 | 498 | 744 | 1,221 | 645 | 314 | 328 |
| Units added 1950–56 | | | | | | | | |
| By conversion of 1950 units | 8 | 18 | 4 | 7 | 23 | 13 | 8 | 8 |
| By merger of 1950 units | 4 | 10 | 4 | 3 | 24 | 8 | 7 | 4 |
| By new construction | 52 | 252 | 216 | 438 | 398 | 188 | 53 | 33 |
| By other sources | ... | 5 | 2 | 17 | 5 | 1 | 2 | 1 |
| Total owner-occupied units, 1956 | 345 | 943 | 724 | 1,209 | 1,670 | 856 | 384 | 375 |
| **Renter-occupied:** | | | | | | | | |
| Total renter-occupied units, 1950 | 358 | 936 | 316 | 661 | 2,576 | 388 | 757 | 257 |
| 1950 units lost 1950–56 | | | | | | | | |
| By conversion | 7 | 10 | 10 | 2 | 24 | 7 | 6 | 5 |
| By merger | 8 | 31 | 19 | 10 | 39 | 22 | 25 | 16 |
| By demolition | 4 | 24 | 18 | 18 | 52 | 6 | 20 | 4 |
| By other means | 7 | 15 | 6 | 33 | 45 | 7 | 13 | 5 |

| | | | | | | | | |
|---|---|---|---|---|---|---|---|---|
| 1950 status of unchanged units | 332 | 856 | 263 | 598 | 2,416 | 346 | 693 | 227 |
| 1956 status of unchanged units | 311 | 840 | 248 | 618 | 2,351 | 280 | 682 | 191 |
| Units added 1950–56 | | | | | | | | |
| By conversion of 1950 units | 18 | 28 | 24 | 11 | 78 | 24 | 20 | 16 |
| By merger of 1950 units | 1 | 8 | 8 | 3 | 10 | 6 | 7 | 5 |
| By new construction | 14 | 37 | 19 | 156 | 283 | 32 | 23 | 10 |
| By other sources | 6 | 18 | 5 | 43 | 36 | 5 | 17 | 4 |
| Total renter-occupied units, 1956 | 350 | 932 | 303 | 832 | 2,758 | 347 | 748 | 226 |
| Vacant: | | | | | | | | |
| Total vacant units, 1950 | 21 | 43 | 29 | 81 | 180 | 35 | 19 | 15 |
| 1950 units lost 1950–56 | | | | | | | | |
| By conversion | ... | ... | ... | ... | 3 | 1 | ... | ... |
| By merger | ... | 1 | 1 | 2 | 9 | 2 | 1 | 1 |
| By demolition | ... | 2 | 2 | 2 | 18 | ... | 2 | ... |
| By other means | 1 | 2 | 1 | 3 | 2 | 2 | 1 | 1 |
| 1950 status of unchanged units | 20 | 38 | 25 | 74 | 148 | 30 | 15 | 13 |
| 1956 status of unchanged units | 34 | 34 | 36 | 50 | 135 | 53 | 24 | 33 |
| Units added 1950–56 | | | | | | | | |
| By conversion of 1950 units | 2 | 3 | 4 | 1 | 8 | 5 | ... | 3 |
| By merger of 1950 units | ... | ... | 2 | ... | 1 | 2 | ... | 1 |
| By new construction | 3 | 18 | 13 | 35 | 57 | 15 | 8 | 2 |
| By other sources | 1 | 1 | 1 | 3 | 3 | ... | ... | ... |
| Total vacant units, 1956 | 41 | 56 | 56 | 90 | 203 | 75 | 32 | 40 |

... Less than 500.

Source: 1956 NHI, Vol. I, Tables 1, 2, and 3, and Vol. III, Table 1.

## Table 2-5
### Summary Measures of Change in the Inventories of Owner-Occupied and Renter-Occupied Dwelling Units, 1950–56: Selected Standard Metropolitan Areas and Cities

| SUMMARY MEASURE | STANDARD METROPOLITAN AREA | | | | | | CITY | |
| --- | --- | --- | --- | --- | --- | --- | --- | --- |
| | Boston | Chicago | Detroit | Los Angeles | New York | Phila-delphia | Chicago | Phila-delphia |
| **Owner-occupied:** | | | | | | | | |
| Net change in units, 1950–56 (in thousands) | 58 | 272 | 212 | 430 | 472 | 226 | 55 | 47 |
| Percentage change in units, 1950–56 | 20 | 40 | 41 | 55 | 39 | 36 | 17 | 14 |
| Percentage change resulting from: | | | | | | | | |
| Conversion and merger | 1 | 1 | –1 | ... | ... | ... | 1 | ... |
| Demolition and other means | –1 | –1 | –1 | –4 | –1 | –1 | –2 | –1 |
| New construction and other sources | 18 | 38 | 42 | 58 | 34 | 30 | 17 | 10 |
| Tenure-occupancy shifts in unchanged units | 2 | 3 | 1 | 1 | 7 | 7 | 1 | 4 |
| **Renter-occupied:** | | | | | | | | |
| Net change in units, 1950–56 (in thousands) | –8 | –4 | –13 | 170 | 182 | –41 | –9 | –31 |
| Percentage change in units, 1950–56 | –2 | ... | –4 | 26 | 7 | –11 | –1 | –12 |
| Percentage change resulting from: | | | | | | | | |
| Conversion and merger | 1 | –1 | 1 | ... | 1 | ... | –1 | ... |
| Demolition and other means | –3 | –4 | –8 | –8 | –4 | –3 | –4 | –4 |
| New construction and other sources | 6 | 6 | 8 | 30 | 12 | 10 | 5 | 5 |
| Tenure-occupancy shifts in unchanged units | –6 | –2 | –5 | 3 | –3 | –17 | –1 | –14 |

... 0.5 per cent or less.
Source: Table 2–4.

processes resulted in an increase of 22 per cent in rental housing. A net tenure-occupancy shift toward the rental sector resulted in a 3 per cent growth of rental housing. In the other areas, the change processes jointly resulted in small increases in rental housing which ranged from 1 to 9 per cent. Net tenure-occupancy shifts resulted in decreases ranging from 2 to 17 per cent.

Vacancies were more numerous in 1956 than in 1950 in each of the six SMA's and two cities. Components of change are available only for total vacancies (Table 2–4) although available vacancies, i.e., vacant units on the market for rent or sale which are suitable for year-round occupancy and are not dilapidated, generally are regarded as a more meaningful category. Table 2–6 shows the net change in total and available vacant dwellings, but no attempt is made to analyze the components of change in total vacancies. Both available and total vacancies increased in each area. Numerical increases in available vacancies ranged from 9,000 in the Los Angeles SMA to 29,000 in the Philadelphia SMA. These changes represent a tripling of available vacancies in Philadelphia, more than a doubling in Boston, Detroit, and Chicago, and increases of 40 and 20 per cent in New York and Los Angeles respectively. The increase of 11,000 available vacancies in the City of Chicago represented a doubling, and the increase of 17,000 in Philadelphia represented a tripling.

To recapitulate, home ownership increased substantially in each area. The increases were attributable in the main to the specific change components—in particular, new construction, although net tenure-occupancy shifts among identical dwellings also added to the owner inventory. Rental housing evidenced substantial expansion only in Los Angeles, where conditions were conducive both to substantial residential construction in

## Table 2–6
## Change in the Inventory of Vacant Dwelling Units between 1950 and 1956: Selected Standard Metropolitan Areas and Cities

| SIZE OF INVENTORY AND MEASURES OF CHANGE | STANDARD METROPOLITAN AREA | | | | | | CITY | |
|---|---|---|---|---|---|---|---|---|
| | Boston | Chicago | Detroit | Los Angeles | New York | Phila-delphia | Chicago | Phila-delphia |
| **Vacant:** | | | | | | | | |
| 1950 inventory (in thousands) | 21 | 43 | 29 | 81 | 180 | 35 | 19 | 15 |
| 1956 inventory (in thousands) | 41 | 56 | 56 | 90 | 203 | 75 | 32 | 40 |
| Net change in units, 1950–56 (in thousands) | 20 | 13 | 27 | 9 | 23 | 40 | 13 | 25 |
| Percentage change in units, 1950–56 | 92 | 30 | 92 | 11 | 13 | 115 | 70 | 171 |
| **Available vacant:** | | | | | | | | |
| 1950 inventory (in thousands) | 7 | 15 | 11 | 45 | 50 | 13 | 9 | 8 |
| 1956 inventory (in thousands) | 18 | 36 | 30 | 54 | 69 | 42 | 20 | 25 |
| Net change in units, 1950–56 (in thousands) | 11 | 22 | 20 | 9 | 20 | 29 | 11 | 17 |
| Percentage change in units, 1950–56 | 161 | 146 | 185 | 20 | 39 | 224 | 122 | 222 |

Source: 1956 NHI, Vol. III, Table 1.

the rental sector and a net shift to the rental sector among identical dwellings. In each other area, the components of change together increased rental housing somewhat. However, small to moderate net shifts away from the rental sector occurred among identical dwellings. On balance, the two types of change resulted in relatively rapid growth of rental housing in Los Angeles, moderate growth of rental housing in New York, and a small to moderate reduction in rental housing in each other area. The supply of vacant dwellings and available vacancies was greater in 1956 than in 1950 in each of the six SMA's and two cities although the rate of increase varied considerably by area.

To complete our overview, we examine the distributions of the 1950 and 1956 inventories by occupancy status. Figure 2–2, which is based on the data in Table 2–7, shows that the proportion of home owners increased and the proportion of renters decreased between 1950 and 1956 in each of the six SMA's and two cities. The rank of the several areas with respect to proportion renters is, by and large, the reverse of the ranking with respect to home ownership. In both years, Detroit and Philadelphia stand out as areas of high home ownership. Two-thirds of the 1956 inventory in these areas were owner-occupied. Home ownership is least frequent in the New York SMA, where only a third of the 1956 inventory was owner-occupied. The data in Table 2–7 also indicate that disproportionate numbers of owner-occupied dwellings were added to the housing inventory between 1950 and 1956, whereas disproportionate numbers of rental units were demolished or otherwise removed from the inventory.

The remainder of this section concerns changes in available vacancy rates. In the Los Angeles SMA the 1950 available vacancy rate was 3.0 per cent and the 1956 available vacancy rate was 2.5 per cent. In the Boston, Chicago, Detroit, and Philadelphia SMA's, and in the Cities of Chicago and Philadelphia,

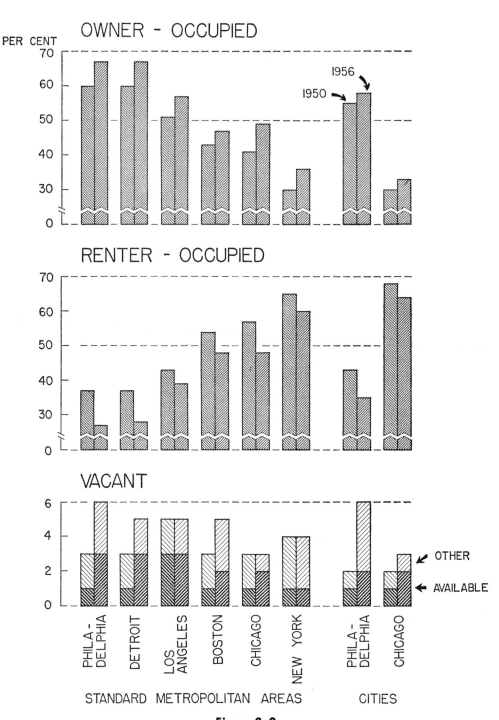

**Figure 2–2**

*Occupancy Status of the 1950 and 1956 Housing Inventories: Selected Standard Metropolitan Areas and Cities. (Source: Table 2–7)*

## Table 2-7
### Percentage Distribution by Occupancy Status of the 1950 and 1956 Housing Inventories and of Dwellings in Selected Change Categories: Selected Standard Metropolitan Areas and Cities

| OCCUPANCY STATUS | STANDARD METROPOLITAN AREA | | | | | | CITY | |
|---|---|---|---|---|---|---|---|---|
| | Boston | Chicago | Detroit | Los Angeles | New York | Phila-delphia | Chicago | Phila-delphia |
| **1950 inventory:** | 100 | 100 | 100 | 100 | 100 | 100 | 100 | 100 |
| Owner-occupied | 43 | 41 | 60 | 51 | 30 | 60 | 30 | 55 |
| Renter-occupied | 54 | 57 | 37 | 44 | 65 | 37 | 68 | 43 |
| Vacant | 3 | 3 | 3 | 5 | 4 | 3 | 2 | 2 |
| Available vacant | 1 | 1 | 1 | 3 | 1 | 1 | 1 | 1 |
| Other vacant | 2 | 2 | 2 | 2 | 3 | 2 | 1 | 1 |
| **Losses to 1950 inventory:** | 100 | 100 | 100 | 100 | 100 | 100 | 100 | 100 |
| Owner-occupied | 30 | 28 | 26 | 36 | 23 | 36 | 21 | 30 |
| Renter-occupied | 66 | 69 | 69 | 57 | 65 | 57 | 74 | 64 |
| Vacant | 4 | 4 | 5 | 6 | 13 | 7 | 5 | 6 |
| **Additions to 1950 inventory:** | 100 | 100 | 100 | 100 | 100 | 100 | 100 | 100 |
| Owner-occupied | 58 | 72 | 75 | 65 | 49 | 70 | 48 | 52 |
| Renter-occupied | 35 | 23 | 18 | 30 | 44 | 22 | 46 | 40 |
| Vacant | 6 | 6 | 7 | 6 | 7 | 7 | 6 | 8 |
| Available vacant | 3 | 4 | 5 | 4 | 3 | 4 | 3 | 5 |
| Other vacant | 3 | 2 | 1 | 2 | 4 | 3 | 2 | 3 |
| **1956 inventory:** | 100 | 100 | 100 | 100 | 100 | 100 | 100 | 100 |
| Owner-occupied | 47 | 49 | 67 | 57 | 36 | 67 | 33 | 58 |
| Renter-occupied | 48 | 48 | 28 | 39 | 60 | 27 | 64 | 35 |
| Vacant | 6 | 3 | 5 | 4 | 4 | 6 | 3 | 6 |
| Available vacant | 2 | 2 | 3 | 2 | 2 | 3 | 2 | 4 |
| Other vacant | 3 | 1 | 2 | 2 | 3 | 3 | 1 | 2 |

Source: 1956, NHI, Vol. I, Tables 1 and 2, and Vol. III, Table 1.

1950 available vacancy rates ranged from 0.8 to 1.3 per cent and 1956 available vacancy rates, which ranged from 1.7 to 3.8 per cent, were double or triple the 1950 rates. The available vacancy rate in the New York SMA was 1.3 per cent in 1950 and 1.5 per cent in 1956. The foregoing figures, drawn from Table 2–8, suggest a three-fold classification of areas: Los Angeles, with a relatively high 1950 available vacancy rate and a relatively high 1956 available vacancy rate; New York, with a relatively low 1950 available vacancy rate and a relatively low 1956 available vacancy rate; the remaining four SMA's and two cities, with relatively low 1950 available vacancy rates and relatively high 1956 available vacancy rates. A thorough analysis of area differentials in available vacancy rates falls outside the scope of this monograph. However, we will call attention to some aspects of the available vacancy rates which may be helpful in interpreting our observations.

In the first place, on the basis of data for the metropolitan United States as a whole, we question whether the available vacancy rates in the New York and Los Angeles SMA's actually were more or less constant over the period 1950 to 1956 and whether the available vacancy rates in the other areas actually were increasing throughout the period 1950 to 1956. In the metropolitan United States, the available vacancy rate in April 1950 was 1.6 per cent; rates of 2.2 per cent for the fourth quarter of 1956 and 2.0 per cent for the first quarter of 1957— the approximate date of the NHI—are reported. However, the available vacancy rate had been on the order of 2.4 to 2.5 per cent in the year preceding the NHI. (The figures are taken from Bureau of the Census, Housing and Construction Reports, Series H–111.) This at least suggests that if an annual series of available vacancy rates were available for the several areas, we might classify them differently with respect to level of and change in available vacancies.

## Table 2-8
### Available Vacancy Rates, 1950 and 1956, and Percentages of the 1950 and 1956 Housing Inventories Accounted for by New Construction: Selected Standard Metropolitan Areas and Cities

| AREA | AVAILABLE VACANCY RATE 1956 (1) | AVAILABLE VACANCY RATE 1950 (2) | PER CENT OF 1956 INVENTORY BUILT 1950–56 (3) | PER CENT OF 1950 INVENTORY BUILT 1945–50 (4) | (1) DIVIDED BY (2) (5) | (3) DIVIDED BY (4) (6) |
|---|---|---|---|---|---|---|
| SMA: | | | | | | |
| Boston | 2.5 | 1.0 | 9.4 | 5.2 | 2.5 | 1.8 |
| **Chicago** | 1.9 | 0.9 | 16.0 | 7.3 | 2.1 | 2.2 |
| Detroit | 2.8 | 1.2 | 23.0 | 13.4 | 2.3 | 1.7 |
| Los Angeles | 2.5 | 3.0 | 29.7 | 21.7 | 0.8 | 1.4 |
| New York | 1.5 | 1.3 | 15.9 | 8.1 | 1.2 | 2.0 |
| Philadelphia | 3.3 | 1.2 | 18.5 | 7.5 | 2.8 | 2.5 |
| City: | | | | | | |
| **Chicago** | 1.7 | 0.8 | 7.2 | 2.8 | 2.1 | 2.6 |
| Philadelphia | 3.8 | 1.3 | 7.1 | 3.9 | 2.9 | 1.8 |

Source: 1956 NHI, Vol. III, Table 1.

It also is worth noting that at least in 1950 the available vacancy rate was closely associated with the rates of population growth and new construction on an area-by-area basis. The following correlation analysis based on 52 SMA's with 1950 housing inventories of 100,000 or more is suggestive. Let $X_1 =$ the 1950 available vacancy rate, $X_2 =$ percentage change in population, 1940 to 1950, and $X_3 =$ percentage of the 1950 housing inventory accounted for by new construction, 1945 to 1950. The results are:

$$r_{12} = .78 \qquad r_{12.3} = .16$$
$$r_{13} = .87 \qquad r_{13.2} = .61$$
$$r_{23} = .86$$

The available vacancy rate is, on the average, higher in areas of rapid population growth than in areas of slow population growth and in areas with substantial new construction than in areas with negligible new construction. Of course, areas of rapid population growth tend to have substantial new construction and areas of slow population growth tend to have negligible new construction. When we hold constant (in a statistical sense) the relative volume of new construction, we find little association between the available vacancy rate and the rate of population growth. However, when we hold constant the rate of population growth, we find an average tendency for the available vacancy rate to increase as the relative volume of new construction increases. This exploratory analysis should not be over-interpreted; but it does suggest a positive association between the available vacancy rate and expansion of the housing inventory which is independent of population growth.

Factors which "explain" a substantial proportion of the variation among areas in the available vacancy rate at a given point in time may fail to "explain" differential change among these areas through time (Duncan and Cuzzort, 1958). And with data available for only six SMA's and two cities, we are unable to test our hypothesis that level of and change in the available vacancy rate are dependent on residential construction activity. However, we note that with regard to the six SMA's, both the relative increase in new construction and the relative increase in the available vacancy rate were highest in the Philadelphia SMA and lowest in the Los Angeles SMA.

On the basis of these results, it seems quite possible that available vacancy rates tend to increase as the rate of new construction increases more or less independently of the demand for housing. Some newly constructed dwellings will be awaiting occupancy; others will be recently occupied and the former dwellings of their occupants will be awaiting occupancy. We offer this only as a possible explanation of our observed differences among areas with respect to vacancy rates and changes therein. The discussion does serve, however, to point up the complexity of the determinants of the available vacancy rate.

## STANDARD AND SUBSTANDARD DWELLINGS

Analysis of components of change in the inventories of standard and substandard dwellings is more difficult than the analysis of components of change in the total housing inventory. In both cases we are working with estimates based on a sample survey and hence subject to sampling error; and our comments about possible misclassification of dwellings by change status apply both to the total inventory and to the quality-specific inventories. However, two features of the data on the inventory by quality and change status present special problems in tracing changes in substandard and standard housing between 1950 and 1956.

First, quality is not reported for all dwellings; second, the classification of dwellings as standard and substandard is not wholly reliable.

As a preliminary to the change analysis, each dwelling in the 1950 and 1956 total housing inventories must be assigned to a quality category. Perhaps the most common way to allocate nonreporting dwellings to quality groups, i.e., standard or substandard, is to assume that their distribution by quality is proportional to the quality distribution of reported units. If we follow this procedure of allocation, we obtain the "B" estimates of the 1950 and 1956 inventories by quality in Table 2–9. However, to examine the change fully, we need to know not only the net change in standard and substandard housing but the components of this change, i.e., change resulting from conversion, change resulting from merger, and so forth. Our several components of change should add algebraically to our net change. If within each component-of-change category we allocate nonreporting units proportionally to the quality distribution of reporting units, our components will not add to these net change totals because the proportion of units reporting varies from one change category to another change category. The discrepancy in totals obtained by the two allocation procedures arises from the inter-category variation in proportion reporting. This can be shown algebraically.

Let us define: $T$, total dwellings; $S$, total standard dwellings; $t$, reporting dwellings; and $s$, reporting standard dwellings. Nonreporting dwellings can be expressed as $T - t$ and nonreporting standard dwellings can be expressed as $S - s$. Then, $S = T(s/t)$, if $s/t = (S - s)/(T - t)$. Suppose the dwellings are classified into two groups, say "changed" and "unchanged"; identify the groups by the subscripts $i$ and $j$ respectively. Now, $S_i = T_i(s_i/t_i)$, if $s_i/t_i = (S_i - s_i)/(T_i - t_i)$; and $S_j = T_j(s_j/t_j)$, if $s_j/t_j = (S_j - s_j)/(T_j - t_j)$. However, $S = S_i + S_j$ only if $t_i/T_i = t_j/T_j$.

The complications involved in trying to allocate the non-reporting units proportionally within each component-of-change category become apparent when we recall that there are some eleven change categories. Operationally, the independent rounding, usually to nearest thousand, of each quality-change category in the basic tables also is troublesome; note that in Table 2–9 the estimates of standard and substandard dwellings do not always sum to reported totals. (In the Chicago Supplement to the NHI, Table 1–2, estimates of standard and substandard units were obtained by allocating nonreporting units proportionally to reporting units within occupancy status-color groups; the estimates differ slightly from those shown in Table 2–9 because the proportion reporting varies by occupancy status-color group.)

Even more important than these technical difficulties is the fact that the quality distribution of nonreporting units probably is not identical with the quality distribution of reporting units; this, of course, is contrary to the assumption underlying proportional allocation. To simplify the allocation procedure and to remind the user of uncertainty about the "true" magnitudes of change, we show the range of possible changes, estimates A and C in Table 2–9, as well as the proportional allocation estimate B.

The second problem—unreliability—is discussed only briefly at this point. Two enumerators viewing the same structure frequently will disagree with respect to its quality. A standard dwelling has adequate plumbing facilities, i.e., both a flush toilet and a bathtub or shower inside the structure for the exclusive use of its occupants and hot running water on a year-round basis; in addition, it is not dilapidated. A substandard unit lacks adequate plumbing facilities and/or is dilapidated. Occasionally enumerators will disagree with respect to the presence of adequate plumbing facilities; more

## Table 2–9
### 1950 and 1956 Inventories of Standard and Substandard Dwelling Units: Selected Standard Metropolitan Areas and Cities

| AREA AND ESTIMATE OF INVENTORY | 1956 INVENTORY | | | 1950 INVENTORY | | | NET CHANGE, 1950–56 | | |
|---|---|---|---|---|---|---|---|---|---|
| | Total | Standard | Sub-standard | Total | Standard | Sub-standard | Total | Standard | Sub-standard |
| | | | | | thousands of units | | | | |
| SMA: | | | | | | | | | |
| Boston | | | | | | | | | |
| A | 737 | 680 | 56 | 667 | 573 | 94 | 70 | 107 | —38 |
| B | 737 | 678 | 59 | 667 | 586 | 81 | 70 | 92 | —22 |
| C | 737 | 648 | 89 | 667 | 588 | 80 | 70 | 60 | 9 |
| **Chicago** | | | | | | | | | |
| A | 1,931 | 1,691 | 240 | 1,650 | 1,248 | 402 | 281 | 443 | —162 |
| B | 1,931 | 1,690 | 241 | 1,650 | 1,291 | 359 | 281 | 399 | —118 |
| C | 1,931 | 1,681 | 250 | 1,650 | 1,303 | 348 | 281 | 378 | —98 |
| Detroit | | | | | | | | | |
| A | 1,083 | 1,017 | 67 | 858 | 724 | 134 | 225 | 293 | —67 |
| B | 1,083 | 1,015 | 68 | 858 | 745 | 113 | 225 | 270 | —45 |
| C | 1,083 | 991 | 93 | 858 | 748 | 110 | 225 | 243 | —17 |
| Los Angeles | | | | | | | | | |
| A | 2,132 | 2,046 | 85 | 1,522 | 1,357 | 165 | 610 | 689 | —80 |
| B | 2,132 | 2,045 | 87 | 1,522 | 1,385 | 137 | 610 | 660 | —50 |
| C | 2,132 | 1,999 | 132 | 1,522 | 1,388 | 134 | 610 | 611 | —2 |

| | | | | | | | | | |
|---|---|---|---|---|---|---|---|---|---|
| **New York** | | | | | | | | | |
| A | 4,631 | 4,146 | 484 | 3,954 | 3,342 | 612 | 677 | 804 | −128 |
| B | 4,631 | 4,133 | 498 | 3,954 | 3,471 | 483 | 677 | 662 | 15 |
| C | 4,631 | 4,012 | 618 | 3,954 | 3,489 | 465 | 677 | 523 | 153 |
| **Philadelphia** | | | | | | | | | |
| A | 1,278 | 1,184 | 94 | 1,053 | 872 | 180 | 225 | 312 | −86 |
| B | 1,278 | 1,182 | 96 | 1,053 | 901 | 151 | 225 | 281 | −55 |
| C | 1,278 | 1,157 | 120 | 1,053 | 906 | 147 | 225 | 251 | −27 |
| **City:** | | | | | | | | | |
| **Chicago** | | | | | | | | | |
| A | 1,165 | 989 | 177 | 1,106 | 822 | 284 | 59 | 167 | −107 |
| B | 1,165 | 988 | 177 | 1,106 | 852 | 254 | 59 | 136 | −77 |
| C | 1,165 | 983 | 183 | 1,106 | 860 | 246 | 59 | 123 | −63 |
| **Philadelphia** | | | | | | | | | |
| A | 641 | 585 | 56 | 599 | 501 | 98 | 42 | 84 | −42 |
| B | 641 | 584 | 57 | 599 | 519 | 81 | 42 | 65 | −24 |
| C | 641 | 572 | 68 | 599 | 521 | 78 | 42 | 51 | −10 |

Note: A assumes all units with quality not reported were standard in 1956, substandard in 1950; B assumes quality distribution of nonreporting units proportional to quality distribution of reporting units in each year; C assumes all units with quality not reported were substandard in 1956, standard in 1950.

Source: 1956 NHI, Vol. III, Table 1.

often, they will disagree with respect to the condition of the unit. Does the dwelling evidence "substantial sagging of floors, walls, or roof"? If so, it is dilapidated. Does the unit have "makeshift walls"? If so, it is dilapidated. Although enumerators are provided with detailed oral and written instructions and with visual aids to assist them in classifying dwellings by condition, the element of individual judgment remains. As we shall indicate later, the differences in classification between enumerators tend to cancel out so that different enumerators report about the same number of standard (or substandard) dwellings. Thus, the unreliability problem is not particularly serious when we are concerned with change in number of standard or substandard units over a period of time or with quality differences among areas. However, it does pose a major obstacle in assessing turnover among quality categories for so-called unchanged or identical dwellings.

Turning now to the data, we undertake an overview of changes in standard and substandard housing in each of six SMA's and two cities. Probably the most widely used figures on changes in the standard and substandard inventories between 1950 and 1956 will be the estimates obtained by proportional allocation, here designated estimate B. On the basis of these estimates, it appears that the supply of standard housing increased by some 650,000 to 700,000 units in the Los Angeles and New York SMA's, by about 400,000 in the Chicago SMA, 250,000 to 300,000 in the Detroit and Philadelphia SMA's, and 100,000 in the Boston SMA. Standard dwellings in the City of Chicago increased by roughly 140,000; an increase of some 60,000 units occurred in the City of Philadelphia. The largest numerical decrease in substandard dwellings is observed in the Chicago SMA where a net loss of about 120,000 substandard units took place. Substandard units were reduced by about 50,000 in the Detroit, Los Angeles, and Philadelphia SMA's and by some 20,000 in the Boston SMA. Only in the New York SMA did the supply of substandard housing increase; the net gain amounted to some 15,000 units between 1950 and 1956. Both the City of Chicago and the City of Philadelphia experienced a decrease in substandard housing—a loss of about 75,000 units in Chicago, and about 25,000 units in Philadelphia. In part of course, the inter-area differences in numerical change in standard or substandard housing reflect differences in size of the housing inventory. For additional comparisons among areas, we focus on the percentage changes summarized in Table 2–10 and also shown in Figure 2–3.

Between 1950 and 1956, the supply of standard housing in the Los Angeles SMA increased by nearly 50 per cent if we accept the estimates based on proportional allocation. Increases on the order of 30 to 35 per cent took place in the Chicago, Detroit, and Philadelphia SMA's; in the Boston and New York SMA's standard housing expanded by 15 to 20 per cent. Increases in standard dwellings in the Cities of Chicago and Philadelphia amounted to about 15 per cent. We will show subsequently that by and large these inter-area differences in growth of the standard housing inventory reflect differences in new construction. The pattern of inter-area variation in relative change in substandard housing is quite different from that just described. In each SMA with the exception of New York and in the Cities of Chicago and Philadelphia, substandard housing was reduced 30 to 40 per cent between 1950 and 1956. In the New York SMA, by contrast, the supply of substandard housing apparently increased by some 3 per cent. Before undertaking a final assessment of inter-area differences in quality change, the effects of the several components of change are examined.

Quality changes resulting from conversion, merger, new construction, demolition, and other means and sources are shown in numerical terms in Table 2–11. (We defer consideration of

**Table 2–10**

**Percentage Change in Standard and Substandard Inventories
between 1950 and 1956: Selected Standard Metropolitan
Areas and Cities**

| AREA | PERCENTAGE CHANGE IN STANDARD DWELLINGS | | PERCENTAGE CHANGE IN SUBSTANDARD DWELLINGS | |
|---|---|---|---|---|
| | Estimate B | Possible range | Estimate B | Possible range |
| SMA: | | | | |
| Boston | 16 | 10 to 19 | −27 | 11 to −40 |
| **Chicago** | 31 | 29 to 35 | −33 | −28 to −40 |
| Detroit | 36 | 32 to 40 | −40 | −15 to −50 |
| Los Angeles | 48 | 44 to 51 | −36 | − 1 to −48 |
| New York | 19 | 15 to 24 | 3 | 33 to −21 |
| Philadelphia | 31 | 28 to 36 | −36 | −18 to −48 |
| City: | | | | |
| **Chicago** | 16 | 14 to 20 | −30 | −26 to −38 |
| Philadelphia | 13 | 10 to 17 | −30 | −13 to −43 |

Source: Table 2–9.

quality shifts among identical dwellings, i.e., 1950 units remaining unchanged in the 1956 inventory.) The reader may wish to examine the numbers of units in the several quality-change status categories in particular areas, but only a few general points can be made here.

Conversion resulted in net increases in both standard and substandard housing in each area. In several areas, however, the conversion process operated in the direction of downgrading the quality of the total inventory by adding disproportionate numbers of substandard dwellings to the housing supply. Recall that in the total inventory in each area, there were no more than one or two substandard dwellings for every ten standard dwellings. For every ten standard dwellings gained through the conversion process, five or six substandard dwellings were added in the Detroit SMA. Conversion added six or seven substandard dwellings for every ten standard dwellings in the City

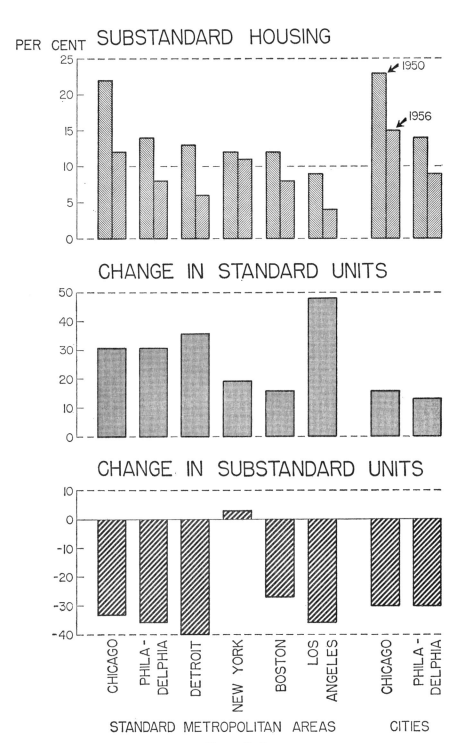

**Figure 2–3**
*Quality of the 1950 and 1956 Housing Inventories: Selected Standard
Metropolitan Areas and Cities. (Source: Tables 2–10 and 2–14)*

of Chicago. It is doubtful that conversion upgraded quality in any of the areas.

Merger, on the other hand, consistently operated in the direction of upgrading quality in the total inventory. For example, in the City of Chicago, at least seven substandard dwellings were removed for each standard dwelling lost through merger. At least five substandard dwellings were removed for each standard dwelling lost through merger in the Detroit SMA. In each area except the New York SMA, substandard units lost through merger were more numerous than standard units lost through merger. In New York, the numbers of standard and substandard units were about equal.

Demolition also removed disproportionate numbers of substandard dwellings and hence upgraded overall quality. However, the substandard/standard ratio for units lost through demolition was considerably lower than the substandard/standard ratio for units lost through merger. On first mention, it may seem surprising that the number of substandard units demolished was actually less than the number of standard units demolished in the Boston, Detroit, Los Angeles, and New York SMA's. Only in Philadelphia and Chicago, SMA and City, did the number of substandard units demolished equal or exceed the number of standard units demolished. However, demolition frequently is undertaken in conjunction with highway programs and the like rather than as a "slum clearance" program. For example, in the City of Chicago, some 3,600 families and unrelated individuals were relocated during the first nine months of 1958; 1,900 of these were relocated in conjunction with highway programs (Department of City Planning, City of Chicago, 1958).

Dwellings added through new construction are, by and large, of standard quality. In each SMA with the possible exception of Boston, a few thousand substandard, recently built

**Table 2-11**

**Change in Standard and Substandard Inventories between 1950 and 1956 Accounted for by Specified Components of Change: Selected Standard Metropolitan Areas and Cities**

| AREA AND QUALITY | COMPONENT OF CHANGE | | | | |
|---|---|---|---|---|---|
| | Conversion | Merger | New construction thousands of units | Demolition | Other means and sources |
| **SMA:** | | | | | |
| Boston | | | | | |
| Standard | 13 to 14 | −1 to −2 | 67 to 69 | −3 | −2 |
| Substandard | 1 to 2 | −4 to −5 | 0 to 2 | −2 | −2 |
| **Chicago** | | | | | |
| Standard | 18 to 20 | −1 to −4 | 299 to 301 | −12 to −15 | 3 to 6 |
| Substandard | 7 to 9 | −18 to −21 | 7 to 9 | −16 to −19 | 0 to −3 |
| Detroit | | | | | |
| Standard | 10 | 0 to −2 | 239 to 244 | −15 to −16 | 0 to 1 |
| Substandard | 5 to 6 | −10 to −13 | 3 to 8 | −7 | −3 to −4 |
| Los Angeles | | | | | |
| Standard | 8 | −1 to −3 | 604 to 619 | −18 to −19 | 11 to 14 |
| Substandard | 3 | −4 to −6 | 12 to 27 | −10 to −11 | −7 to −10 |
| New York | | | | | |
| Standard | 45 to 49 | −15 to −22 | 716 to 728 | −36 to −46 | −18 to −22 |
| Substandard | 9 to 13 | −14 to −21 | 10 to 22 | −27 to −37 | 6 to 10 |
| Philadelphia | | | | | |
| Standard | 20 to 22 | −1 to −3 | 228 to 232 | −2 | −1 to −3 |
| Substandard | 2 to 3 | −13 to −16 | 3 to 7 | −6 | −5 to −7 |
| **City:** | | | | | |
| **Chicago** | | | | | |
| Standard | 9 to 10 | 0 to −2 | 83 to 84 | −8 to −10 | 2 to 4 |
| Substandard | 6 to 7 | −15 to −17 | 0 to 1 | −15 to −17 | 0 to 2 |
| Philadelphia | | | | | |
| Standard | 12 to 13 | 0 to −2 | 44 to 45 | −2 | 0 to −1 |
| Substandard | 2 to 3 | −9 to −11 | 0 to 1 | −2 | −3 to −4 |

Source: 1956 NHI, Vol. I, Tables 1 and 2.

units are reported however. In the Cities of Chicago and Philadelphia, fewer than a thousand substandard dwellings were added by new construction between 1950 and 1956. In each area, of course, new construction upgraded over-all housing quality.

It is difficult to interpret substantively change through "other means and sources." The category includes units added or lost through planned action, such as change from non-dwelling quarters to dwelling quarters as well as units lost through such diverse causes as fire, flood, or hurricane. This heterogeneity probably accounts for the fact that no consistent pattern is observed from area to area.

To get some notion of the impact of these several types of change on the supply of standard and substandard housing respectively, we express the number of dwellings in a given quality-change status category (Table 2–11) as a percentage of the 1950 inventory of dwellings of the given quality (estimate B, Table 2–9). The pattern with regard to standard housing is clear cut. The data in Table 2–12 show that new construction has a far greater impact on expansion of standard housing than does any other of the components of change. Considered alone, new construction would have resulted in a 45 per cent growth of standard housing in the Los Angeles SMA, a 33 per cent increase in the Detroit SMA, a 20 to 25 per cent increase in the Chicago, New York, and Philadelphia SMA's, and a 10 per cent growth of standard housing in the Boston SMA and the Cities of Chicago and Philadelphia. Conversion alone would have produced a 1 or 2 per cent increase in standard dwellings in each of the six SMA's and two cities; merger would have resulted in a decrease of less than 1 per cent in standard housing in each area. Demolition removed about 1 per cent of the standard dwellings in each area; other means and sources generally produced a change of less than 1 per cent in standard housing.

The picture is quite different with regard to substandard dwellings. The five types of change had more nearly equal impacts on the supply of substandard housing. The processes which could increase substandard housing are, of course, conversion and new construction. Conversion alone typically resulted in a 2 or 3 per cent increase in substandard dwellings. In the Cities of Chicago and Philadelphia, substandard housing increased by less than 1 per cent through new construction. In each SMA except Los Angeles, new construction accounted for an increase on the order of 3 per cent; in Los Angeles, the increase in substandard housing resulting from new construction was not less than 9 per cent.

Merger and demolition result in decreases in substandard housing. Merger **reduced substandard** housing by about 4 per cent in the Los Angeles and New York SMA's, on the order of 6 per cent in Boston and Chicago, some 10 per cent in the Detroit and Philadelphia SMA's. Demolition removed 2 to 6 per cent of the substandard dwellings in each SMA. Substandard housing in Philadelphia City was reduced perhaps 12 per cent by merger and 2 per cent by demolition. In the City of Chicago, merger and demolition each accounted for a decrease of 6 per cent. On the average the reduction in substandard housing attributable to merger is as large as the reduction accounted for by demolition. Changes from other means and other sources occasionally increased the supply of substandard units and other times reduced substandard housing; typically, the change amounted to less than 5 per cent.

The supply of standard or substandard housing also can be changed by quality shifts among identical dwellings, i.e., units which appear in both the 1950 and 1956 inventories. Net quality shifts among identical dwellings can be estimated by

**Table 2-12**

**Percentage Change in Standard and Substandard Inventories between 1950 and 1956 Accounted for by Specified Components of Change: Selected Standard Metropolitan Areas and Cities**

| QUALITY AND AREA | COMPONENT OF CHANGE | | | | |
|---|---|---|---|---|---|
| | Conversion | Merger | New construction | Demolition | Other means and sources |
| **Standard:** | | | | | |
| SMA | | | | | |
| Boston | 2 | ... | 11 to 12 | —1 | ... |
| **Chicago** | 1 to 2 | ... | 23 | —1 | ... |
| Detroit | 1 | ... | 32 to 33 | —2 | ... |
| Los Angeles | 1 | ... | 44 to 45 | —1 | 1 |
| New York | 1 | 0 to —1 | 21 | —1 | —1 |
| Philadelphia | 2 | ... | 25 to 26 | ... | ... |
| City | | | | | |
| **Chicago** | 1 | ... | 10 | —1 | ... |
| Philadelphia | 2 to 3 | ... | 8 to 9 | ... | ... |
| **Substandard:** | | | | | |
| SMA | | | | | |
| Boston | 1 to 2 | —5 to —6 | 0 to 2 | —2 | —2 |
| **Chicago** | 2 to 3 | —5 to —6 | 2 to 3 | —4 to —5 | 0 to —1 |
| Detroit | 4 to 5 | —9 to —12 | 3 to 7 | —6 | —3 to —4 |
| Los Angeles | 2 | —3 to —4 | 9 to 20 | —7 to —8 | —5 to —7 |
| New York | 2 to 3 | —3 to —4 | 2 to 5 | —6 to —8 | 1 to 2 |
| Philadelphia | 1 to 2 | —9 to —11 | 2 to 5 | —4 | —3 to —5 |
| City | | | | | |
| **Chicago** | 2 to 3 | —6 to —7 | ... | —6 to —7 | 0 to 1 |
| Philadelphia | 2 to 4 | —11 to —14 | 0 to 1 | —2 | —4 to —5 |

... 0.5 per cent or less.
Source: Tables 2–9 and 2–11.

subtracting from the net change in dwellings of a given quality the change accounted for by the specific change processes, i.e., conversion, merger, new construction, demolition, and other means and sources. Specifically, we subtract losses to the inventory by quality (proportional allocation applied to data in 1956 NHI, Vol. I, Table 2) and add gains to the inventory by quality (proportional allocation applied to data in 1956 NHI, Vol. I, Table 1) from and to the 1950 inventory by quality (estimate B, Table 2–9). The estimates in Table 2–13 are rough, but we regard them as adequate for identifying major inter-area differences in net quality shifts and their impact on standard and substandard housing.

Numerically, the net shift from substandard to standard among identical dwellings is estimated to have been largest in the Chicago SMA—a net upgrading of 93,000 units. Only the New York SMA evidences a net shift from standard to substandard—perhaps on the order of 31,000. The impact of net quality shifts on the inventory of standard housing typically was small, ranging among the SMA's from a 7 per cent increase in Chicago to a 1 per cent decrease in New York. Net upgrading increased standard housing by 6 per cent in the City of Chicago and 2 per cent in the City of Philadelphia. The impact of net quality shifts on the inventory of substandard dwellings, however, was marked. Decreases in substandard housing resulting from net upgrading ranged from 31 per cent in the Los Angeles SMA to 17 per cent in the Boston SMA. The increase in substandard housing resulting from net downgrading amounted to 6 per cent in the New York SMA. The Cities of Chicago and Philadelphia experienced decreases of 20 and 14 per cent respectively in substandard housing as a result of net upgrading.

The growth of standard housing is accounted for primarily by the specific change processes in combination rather than by net quality shifts among identical dwellings. New construction

## Table 2-13
### Change in Standard and Substandard Inventories between 1950 and 1956 Accounted for by Specified Components of Change and by Quality Shifts among Identical Dwellings: Selected Standard Metropolitan Areas and Cities

| QUALITY AND AREA | CHANGE (THOUSANDS OF UNITS) | | | PERCENTAGE CHANGE | | |
|---|---|---|---|---|---|---|
| | Total | Components of change | Quality shifts | Total | Components of change | Quality shifts |
| **Standard:** | | | | | | |
| SMA | | | | | | |
| Boston | 92 | 78 | 14 | 16 | 14 | 2 |
| **Chicago** | 399 | 306 | 93 | 31 | 24 | 7 |
| Detroit | 270 | 239 | 31 | 36 | 32 | 4 |
| Los Angeles | 660 | 618 | 42 | 48 | 45 | 3 |
| New York | 662 | 693 | −31 | 19 | 20 | −1 |
| Philadelphia | 281 | 247 | 34 | 31 | 27 | 4 |
| City | | | | | | |
| **Chicago** | 136 | 84 | 52 | 16 | 10 | 6 |
| Philadelphia | 65 | 54 | 11 | 13 | 11 | 2 |
| **Substandard:** | | | | | | |
| SMA | | | | | | |
| Boston | −22 | −8 | −14 | −27 | −10 | −17 |
| **Chicago** | −118 | −25 | −93 | −33 | −7 | −26 |
| Detroit | −45 | −14 | −31 | −40 | −13 | −27 |
| Los Angeles | −50 | −8 | −42 | −36 | −5 | −31 |
| New York | 15 | −16 | 31 | 3 | −3 | 6 |
| Philadelphia | −55 | −21 | −34 | −36 | −13 | −23 |
| City | | | | | | |
| **Chicago** | −77 | −25 | −52 | −30 | −10 | −20 |
| Philadelphia | −24 | −13 | −11 | −30 | −16 | −14 |

Source: Tables 2–9 and 2–10; 1956 NHI, Vol. I, Tables 1 and 2.

appears as the key factor in expansion of standard housing. However, the impact of net quality shifts on the inventory of substandard units generally was greater than the impact of the several components of change. We are not confident enough about the accuracy of the net quality-shift estimates to attempt more detailed analysis.

To complete our overview of quality changes between 1950 and 1956, the proportions of the total inventory classified substandard in 1950 and in 1956 are shown in Table 2–14. The patterns also can be observed in Figure 2–3 which appeared earlier. The proportion substandard was lower in 1956 than in 1950 in each SMA with the possible exception of New York and in both cities. The rank of the areas with respect to prevalence of substandard housing was much the same in the two years. In 1956, the proportion substandard was relatively high in Chicago and New York as compared with the other SMA's. In the case of Chicago, substandard housing was relatively

**Table 2–14**
**Substandard Dwellings as a Percentage of Total Inventory, 1950 and 1956: Selected Standard Metropolitan Areas and Cities**

| AREA | PERCENTAGE SUBSTANDARD | | | |
| | 1956 | | 1950 | |
| | Estimate B | Possible range | Estimate B | Possible range |
| --- | --- | --- | --- | --- |
| SMA: | | | | |
| Boston | 8 | 8 to 12 | 12 | 12 to 14 |
| **Chicago** | 12 | 12 to 13 | 22 | 21 to 24 |
| Detroit | 6 | 6 to 9 | 13 | 13 to 16 |
| Los Angeles | 4 | 4 to 6 | 9 | 9 to 11 |
| New York | 11 | 10 to 13 | 12 | 12 to 15 |
| Philadelphia | 8 | 7 to 9 | 14 | 14 to 17 |
| City: | | | | |
| **Chicago** | 15 | 15 to 16 | 23 | 22 to 26 |
| Philadelphia | 9 | 9 to 11 | 14 | 13 to 16 |

Source: Table 2–9.

prevalent in 1950; but improvements in housing quality kept pace with those in other areas between 1950 and 1956. In New York, however, the 1950 proportion substandard was about the same as in the other SMA's; but improvements in housing quality were less than in the other areas in the 1950's. The proportion substandard was substantially higher in the City of Chicago than in the City of Philadelphia both in 1950 and in 1956. In each city, the proportion substandard was reduced by a third in the post-1950 period.

The remainder of this section concerns quality shifts among identical dwellings. We alluded earlier to the difficulty in assessing gross quality shifts, or quality turnover, among identical dwellings which stems from the unreliability in quality classification; we also indicated that the implications of unreliability are less serious when we are examining net quality shifts such as those just discussed. (Formally, our problem is much the same as that dealt with in "Pitfalls in the Analysis of Panel Data," Maccoby, 1956.)

Statistics are presented in the 1956 NHI (Vol. I, Table 4) which show the number of identical dwellings which were standard in 1950 and substandard in 1956, not dilapidated in 1950 and dilapidated in 1956, and so forth. In our judgment, the data as reported present a false picture of the quality shifts which actually occurred. Although the reader may find it tedious to follow in detail our exposition of the problem, the issue warrants detailed examination. At the outset, it should be made clear that the data are not without value. From a technical standpoint, the identical dwelling data may be important in sample design; from a substantive standpoint, useful estimates of actual shifts can be derived from the published figures.

A "Post-enumeration Survey," hereafter referred to as PES, was conducted by the Bureau of the Census in conjunction with the 1950 Census of Housing; results indicate that enumerators often disagree with respect to a dwelling's quality—in particular, whether the unit is dilapidated or not. From the Census-PES study, we have a tabulation of urban occupied dwellings by quality reported by a Census enumerator and quality reported by a PES enumerator (Table 2, Results Memorandum No. 22, Post-enumeration Survey, 1950). Throughout the analysis we employ three categories of housing quality: standard; substandard, lacking facilities though not dilapidated, which is identified hereafter as W/o fac., not dilap.; and substandard, dilapidated. The quality classification—standard versus substandard—was not developed by the Bureau of the Census although it is based on their classification of units by condition and plumbing facilities. Shown below is the percentage distribution of dwellings in each Census quality group (quality reported by a Census enumerator) by PES quality (quality reported by a PES enumerator).

| CENSUS QUALITY | | PES QUALITY | | |
| --- | --- | --- | --- | --- |
| | ALL DWELLINGS | STAND-ARD | SUBSTANDARD | |
| | | | W/o fac., not dilap. | Dilapi-dated |
| Standard | 100 | 96 | 3 | 1 |
| Substandard: | | | | |
| W/o fac., not dilap. | 100 | 8 | 80 | 12 |
| Dilapidated | 100 | 25 | 43 | 32 |

Thus, of the dwellings reported standard by a Census enumerator, 96 per cent were reported standard by a PES enumerator, 3 per cent were reported substandard, lacking facilities though not dilapidated, and so forth.

Consider the identical dwellings classified by 1950 and 1956 quality. The 1950 quality classification was made by a Census enumerator; the 1956 quality classification was made by an NHI enumerator. Assume that the differences with respect to classifying dwellings by quality are the same between Census and NHI enumerators as between Census and PES enumerators. Then, if no shifts in quality actually occurred among identical dwellings, we would find 96 per cent of the dwellings classified standard in 1950 classified standard in 1956, 3 per cent of the dwellings classified standard in 1950 classified substandard, lacking facilities though not dilapidated in 1956, and so forth.

First, we take up the unreliability problem alone; later, we will consider the unreliability and nonreporting problems simultaneously. Throughout this section, we will be working with statistics for the City of Chicago. Quality in both 1950 and 1956 is reported for 907,000 identical dwellings (1956 NHI, Vol. I, Table 4). The distribution of these dwellings by 1950 quality and 1956 quality as reported in the NHI volume is shown in the first panel of Table 2–15; it is identified A: reported distribution. On the basis of the reported distribution, 32,000 dwellings shifted from standard to substandard and 73,000 dwellings shifted from substandard to standard between 1950 and 1956. Thus 105,000 of the 907,000 dwellings "turned over" with respect to quality. To get some notion of the effect of unreliability in quality classification, we assume that the distribution of dwellings in each 1950 Census quality group by 1956 NHI quality would be the same as the distribution of dwellings in each 1950 Census quality group by PES quality *if* there actually had been no quality shifts among identical dwellings. The second panel in Table 2–15, identified B: distribution with no actual shift but with unreliability, is based on the foregoing assumption. Operationally, we classify 96 per cent of the 741,000 dwellings which were standard in 1950, or 714,000 dwellings, standard in 1956; we classify 3 per cent of the 1950 standard dwellings, or 18,000 dwellings, substandard, lacking facilities though not dilapidated in 1956, and so forth. In the absence of any actual quality shifts, unreliability of quality classification would result in a reported shift of 27,000 dwellings from stand-

**Table 2–15**

**Distributions of Identical Dwellings with 1950 and 1956 Quality Reported by Quality in 1950 and Quality in 1956 as Reported in NHI and as Estimated Assuming No Actual Quality Shift but Unreliability in Quality Classification: City of Chicago**

| 1950 QUALITY | ALL DWELLINGS | STANDARD | 1956 QUALITY SUBSTANDARD | | |
|---|---|---|---|---|---|
| | | | All | W/o fac., not dilap. | Dilapidated |
| | | | *thousands of units* | | |
| | | | A: *Reported Distribution* | | |
| All dwellings | 907 | 782 | 125 | 93 | 32 |
| Standard | 741 | 709 | 32 | 20 | 12 |
| Substandard | 166 | 73 | 93 | 73 | 20 |
| Without all facilities, not dilapidated | 125 | 51 | 74 | 64 | 10 |
| Dilapidated | 41 | 22 | 19 | 9 | 10 |
| | | | B: *Distribution with No Actual Shift but with Unreliability* | | |
| All dwellings | 907 | 734 | 173 | 135 | 38 |
| Standard | 741 | 714 | 27 | 18 | 9 |
| Substandard | 166 | 20 | 146 | 117 | 29 |
| Without all facilities, not dilapidated | 125 | 10 | 115 | 99 | 16 |
| Dilapidated | 41 | 10 | 31 | 18 | 13 |

Note: See text for explanation and sources.

ard to substandard and 20,000 dwellings from substandard to standard; 47,000 of the 907,000 dwellings would have turned over with respect to quality. Hence, we estimate that the actual quality turnover was about 58,000 (105,000 minus 47,000) rather than the reported 105,000.

The unreliability and nonreporting problems now are dealt with simultaneously. The NHI reports 1,020,000 identical dwellings in the City of Chicago. Quality in 1956 is available for 1,015,000 or virtually all dwellings, whereas reports on 1950 quality are available for only 90 per cent of the dwellings. As the tabulation below brings out, the 1956 quality distribution of dwellings with 1950 quality reported differs considerably from the 1956 quality distribution of dwellings with 1950 quality not reported.

| GROUP OF DWELLINGS | | 1956 QUALITY | | |
| --- | --- | --- | --- | --- |
| | ALL DWELLINGS | STAND-ARD | SUBSTANDARD W/o fac., not dilap. | Dilapi-dated |
| All identical dwellings (thousands) | 1,020 | 864 | 114 | 42 |
| Quality reported, 1950 | 907 | 782 | 93 | 32 |
| Quality not reported, 1950 | 113 | 82 | 21 | 10 |

Because it seems improbable that the 1950 quality distributions of reporting and nonreporting dwellings were the same, the assumption underlying proportional allocation, we have chosen an alternative allocation procedure. The 82,000 dwellings classified standard in 1956 and nonreporting in 1950 have been allocated to 1950 quality groups in proportion to the 1950 quality distribution of the 782,000 dwellings classified standard in 1956 and reporting in 1950 (first panel, Table 2–15). The same procedure has been followed for the other two quality groups (the 21,000 nonreporting distributed proportionally to the 93,000 reporting, the 10,000 nonreporting distributed proportionally to the 32,000 reporting). The estimated 1950 quality distribution of the 113,000 nonreporting dwellings obtained is: 84,000 standard; 22,000 substandard, lacking facilities though not dilapidated; 7,000 substandard, dilapidated. (On the assumption that no actual quality shifts occurred and that PES-Census unreliability factors obtain, the 1950 quality distribution of the 113,000 nonreporting dwellings is: 84,000 standard; 20,000 substandard, lacking facilities though not dilapidated; 9,000 substandard, dilapidated).

The estimated distribution by 1950 and 1956 quality of the 113,000 nonreporting dwellings is combined with the reported distribution of the 907,000 reporting dwellings (first panel,

Table 2–15) to obtain an estimated distribution of all identical dwellings by 1950 and 1956 quality. This distribution is shown in the first panel of Table 2–16 and identified A: estimated reported distribution. In the second panel of Table 2–16, identified B: distribution with no actual shift but with unreliability, is shown the distribution of all identical dwellings by 1950 and 1956 quality which would have resulted from unreliability in classification in the absence of any actual quality shifts among identical dwellings. (The B distribution has been derived from the A distribution in the manner described in connection with Table 2–15.) From the distributions in Table 2–16, we will obtain our estimates of the quality shifts which actually took place among identical dwellings in the City of Chicago between 1950 and 1956.

It should be clear by now that our "actual shift" figures are only estimates of a crude sort. The unreliability factors derived from the Census-PES study are assumed to apply to the Census-NHI data for Chicago. In fact, we do not know whether they overstate or understate the unreliability actually obtaining in the Census-NHI data for Chicago. The procedures followed in allocating nonreporting dwellings to quality groups may be inappropriate. We suspect that unreliability in classification may increase as the proportion nonreporting increases, on the assumption that both are indicative of field-work difficulties. Our estimating procedures have been spelled out in considerable detail so that the reader, if he desires, can evaluate them independently. In our opinion, the "actual shift" estimates provide a more faithful picture of the quality shifts which took place than do the reported figures. In any case, they serve a useful function by showing that the reported shifts must not be accepted without reservation.

In Table 2–17, we compare reported and estimated actual net quality shifts among identical dwellings. We estimate that

**Table 2–16**
**Estimated Distributions of All Identical Dwellings by Quality in 1950 and Quality in 1956 as Reported in NHI and Assuming No Actual Quality Shift but Unreliability in Quality Classification: City of Chicago**

| 1950 QUALITY | 1956 QUALITY | | | | |
|---|---|---|---|---|---|
| | ALL DWELLINGS | STANDARD | SUBSTANDARD | | |
| | | | All | W/o fac., not dilap. | Dilapidated |
| | | | *thousands of units* | | |
| | | | A: *Estimated Reported Distribution* | | |
| All dwellings | 1,020 | 864 | 156 | 114 | 42 |
| Standard | 825 | 784 | 41 | 25 | 16 |
| Substandard | 195 | 80 | 115 | 89 | 26 |
| Without all facilities, not dilapidated | 147 | 56 | 91 | 78 | 13 |
| Dilapidated | 48 | 24 | 24 | 11 | 13 |
| | | | B: *Distribution with No Actual Shift but with Unreliability* | | |
| All dwellings | 1,020 | 819 | 201 | 158 | 43 |
| Standard | 825 | 795 | 30 | 21 | 9 |
| Substandard | 195 | 24 | 171 | 137 | 34 |
| Without all facilities, not dilapidated | 147 | 12 | 135 | 117 | 18 |
| Dilapidated | 48 | 12 | 36 | 20 | 16 |

Note: See text for explanation and sources.

the net shift of dwellings from substandard to standard quality was 45,000 as compared with a reported shift of 39,000. The estimates indicate a 5 per cent increase in standard identical dwellings and a 23 per cent decrease in substandard identical dwellings; the reported figures indicate a 5 per cent increase in standard identical dwellings and a 20 per cent decrease in substandard identical dwellings. (Incidentally, recall that the residual estimate of net upgrading shown in Table 2–13 was 52,000. Given the problems of estimation, the residual estimate compares rather favorably with the more careful estimate cited above. At the same time, their difference is another indicator of the uncertainty which obtains with respect to the "true" magnitudes of change.)

Also shown in Table 2–17 are reported and estimated actual net shifts in substandard dwellings, lacking facilities though not dilapidated and in substandard dwellings, dilapidated. The estimated actual net decrease in substandard dwellings, lacking facilities though not dilapidated is 44,000 as compared with a reported 33,000, or an estimated 30 per cent reduction as compared with a reported 22 per cent reduction. The actual net decrease in substandard dwellings, dilapidated is estimated as 1,000 rather than the reported 6,000, or 2 rather than 12 per cent. These estimated actual changes seem plausible to us, for by and large it should be a simpler matter to install adequate plumbing facilities in a nondilapidated dwelling to upgrade its quality than to undertake the correction of major structural deficiencies and in many cases also install adequate plumbing facilities to upgrade a dilapidated dwelling.

On the basis of the reported figures, 121,000 of the 1,020,000 identical units shifted from standard to substandard or vice versa between 1950 and 1956. The estimated actual turnover, however, is 67,000. Whereas 80,000 dwellings are reported as shifting from substandard to standard, the estimated actual upgrading is 56,000. Whereas 41,000 dwellings are reported as shifting from standard to substandard, the estimated actual downgrading is 11,000. Also shown in Table 2–18 are reported and estimated actual percentage shifts. The proportion of identical dwellings which turned over in terms of quality is reported as 12 per cent; our estimated actual percentage turnover is 7 per cent. We estimate that 29 per cent of the 1950 substandard identical dwellings were upgraded, as compared with a reported 41 per cent. We estimate that 1 per cent of the 1950 standard identical dwellings were downgraded, as compared with a reported 5 per cent.

**Table 2-17**

**Net Quality Shifts Among Identical Dwellings between 1950 and 1956, Reported and Estimated Actual:**
**City of Chicago**

| Quality group | Reported 1950 | Reported 1956 | Reported shift | Shift due to unreliability | Estimated actual shift |
|---|---|---|---|---|---|
| | | | thousands of units | | |
| Standard dwellings | 825 | 864 | 39 | —6 | 45 |
| Substandard dwellings | 195 | 156 | —39 | 6 | —45 |
| Without all facilities, not dilapidated | 147 | 114 | —33 | 11 | —44 |
| Dilapidated | 48 | 42 | —6 | —5 | —1 |

Source: Table 2-16

## Table 2–18

## Gross Quality Shifts among Identical Dwellings between 1950 and 1956, Reported and Estimated Actual: City of Chicago

| QUALITY GROUPS AND TYPE OF SHIFT | REPORTED SHIFT | SHIFT DUE TO UNRELIABILITY | ESTIMATED ACTUAL SHIFT | BASE | PERCENTAGE SHIFT | |
|---|---|---|---|---|---|---|
| | | thousands of units | | | Reported | Estimated actual |
| *Standard—Substandard:* | | | | | | |
| Total turnover | 121 | 54 | 67 | 1,020 | 12 | 7 |
| Upgrading | 80 | 24 | 56 | 195 | 41 | 29 |
| Downgrading | 41 | 30 | 11 | 825 | 5 | 1 |
| *Not Dilapidated—Dilapidated:* | | | | | | |
| Total turnover | 64 | 59 | 5 | 1,020 | 6 | ... |
| Upgrading | 35 | 32 | 3 | 48 | 73 | 6 |
| Downgrading | 29 | 27 | 2 | 972 | 3 | ... |
| *Standard—Without All Facilities, Not Dilapidated—Dilapidated:* | | | | | | |
| Total turnover | 145 | 92 | 53 | | | |
| W/o fac., not dilap. to std. | 56 | 12 | 44 | | | |
| Std. to w/o fac., not dilap. | 25 | 21 | 4 | | | |
| Dilap. to std. | 24 | 12 | 12 | | | |
| Std. to dilap. | 16 | 9 | 7 | | | |
| Dilap. to w/o fac., not dilap. | 11 | 20 | −9 | | | |
| W/o fac., not dilap. to dilap. | 13 | 18 | −5 | | | |

... 0.5 per cent or less
Source: Table 2–16.

About 64,000 dwellings are reported as shifting from not dilapidated to dilapidated or vice versa between 1950 and 1956; however, the estimated actual turnover is 5,000. Whereas 35,000 dwellings are reported as shifting from dilapidated to not dilapidated, the estimated actual upgrading is 3,000. Whereas 29,000 dwellings are reported as shifting from not dilapidated to dilapidated, the estimated actual downgrading is 2,000. The proportion of identical dwellings which turned over in terms of condition is reported as 6 per cent; our estimated actual percentage turnover is less than 1 per cent. We estimate that 6 per cent of the 1950 dilapidated identical dwellings were upgraded, as compared with a reported 73 per cent. We estimate that less than 1 per cent of the 1950 not dilapidated identical dwellings were downgraded, as compared with a reported 3 per cent.

Also shown in Table 2–18 is the estimated turnover among three quality-condition groups, i.e., standard; substandard, lacking facilities though not dilapidated; substandard, dilapidated. Note that the reported shift between some quality-condition categories is less than the shift due to unreliability; consequently, the estimated actual shift is negative in sign. This, of course, has no substantive interpretation and merely indicates that the unreliability factors based on the Census-PES study are not wholly appropriate for use with the Census-NHI data. The estimates are shown primarily to remind the reader that although we are confident that actual turnover was substantially less than reported turnover, we cannot specify the magnitude of the difference with any great precision.

However, the foregoing analyses make it clear that the reported figures on quality turnover and gross upgrading and downgrading can be used only with careful qualification.

# 3

# Differentials among Categories
# of Change

IN THE PRECEDING CHAPTER, the impact of the several change components on the total inventory and its composition by occupancy status and quality was explored. Only incidental attention was given to characteristics of demolished dwellings, newly constructed dwellings, and converted or merged dwellings. Here, we first undertake a comparison of demolished and newly constructed dwellings in terms of their occupancy and physical characteristics. For example, a third to three-fourths of the dwellings demolished in each area were of substandard quality; virtually none of the newly built dwellings were substandard. Then, other things being equal, an increase in the rates of demolition and new construction will tend to accelerate improvement in an area's housing supply. Later our analysis turns to comparing dwellings which underwent conversion with the dwellings which resulted from conversion. On the basis of these "before and after" comparisons, we conclude, for example, that an increase in the rate of conversion tends to downgrade the over-all quality of the housing supply, since the proportion substandard typically is higher among dwellings created through conversion than among dwellings which undergo conversion. "Before and after" comparisons of merged dwellings indicate that an increase in the rate of merger tends to upgrade over-all quality of the housing supply since the proportion substandard consistently is lower among dwellings created through merger than among dwellings which are merged. We cite these examples to provide the reader with a general notion of the sorts of findings to be reported.

## DEMOLITION AND NEW CONSTRUCTION

The numbers of dwellings in the several change categories were reported in Table 2–1. Demolitions per 100 dwellings in the 1950 inventory ranged from one to three in the six SMA's and two cities. Newly constructed dwellings per 100 dwellings in the 1950 inventory ranged from ten to forty in these areas. Thus, the impact of new construction on the existing housing supply was substantially greater than the impact of demolition during the period 1950 to 1956 in each area.

In Tables 3–1 and 3–2, characteristics of demolished and newly constructed dwellings in each area are shown. The data are a sufficient basis for drawing generalizations about differen-

*80*

tials between demolished and newly built dwellings when a more or less consistent pattern is observed in each area. We caution the reader, however, about attempting inter-area comparisons with regard to characteristics of new and, particularly, demolished dwellings. Given the relatively large sampling errors which obtain, rather sizeable differences often are not significant in the statistical sense.

In 1950, the dwellings subsequently demolished were somewhat more likely to be vacant than the housing inventory as a whole. Vacancy rates also appear relatively high among newly constructed units. We suspect that the relatively high total vacancy rate for units subsequently demolished is accounted for, at least in part, by vacancies in structures slated for demolition though still standing. Perhaps the relatively high vacancy rate among newly built units is accounted for, to some extent, by vacant dwellings virtually completed but not yet occupied. Data are not readily available with which to explore these possibilities.

Demolition removed relatively few dwellings from the home-owner sector and new construction added dwellings primarily to the home-owner sector. These processes, separately and jointly, operated in the direction of increasing home ownership. Demolition removed disproportionate numbers of dwellings from the substandard sector, whereas new construction added virtually no dwellings to the substandard sector. These processes, separately and jointly, tended to upgrade over-all housing quality. Disproportionate numbers of the demolished dwellings were occupied by nonwhite households prior to demolition; nonwhite occupancy occurred relatively infrequently among newly built dwellings.

The foregoing observations with respect to tenure, quality, and color-of-occupant characteristics of demolished dwellings are not unrelated. Presumably demolition, in the main, is di-

## Table 3-1
## Occupancy Characteristics and Quality for the 1950 Housing Inventory, Demolitions, and Units Built between 1950 and 1956: Selected Standard Metropolitan Areas and Cities

| CHARACTERISTIC AND GROUP OF DWELLING UNITS | STANDARD METROPOLITAN AREA | | | | | | CITY | |
|---|---|---|---|---|---|---|---|---|
| | Boston | Chicago | Detroit | Los Angeles | New York | Phila-delphia | Chicago | Phila-delphia |
| **Occupancy status:** | | | | | | | | |
| Per cent vacant | | | | | | | | |
| 1950 inventory | 3 | 3 | 3 | 5 | 4 | 3 | 2 | 2 |
| Units demolished, 1950–56 | 4 | 6 | 7 | 7 | 25 | 3 | 8 | 4 |
| Units built, 1950–56 | 4 | 6 | 5 | 6 | 8 | 6 | 10 | 5 |
| **Tenure:** | | | | | | | | |
| Per cent owner-occupied | | | | | | | | |
| 1950 inventory | 43 | 41 | 60 | 51 | 30 | 60 | 30 | 55 |
| Units demolished, 1950–56 | 10 | 17 | 11 | 33 | 4 | 26 | 12 | 7 |
| Units built, 1950–56 | 78 | 87 | 92 | 74 | 58 | 85 | 70 | 76 |
| **Quality:** | | | | | | | | |
| Per cent substandard | | | | | | | | |
| 1950 inventory | 12 | 22 | 13 | 9 | 12 | 14 | 23 | 14 |
| Units demolished, 1950–56 | 46 | 57 | 30 | 36 | 44 | 74 | 62 | 52 |
| Units built, 1950–56 | ... | 2 | 1 | 2 | 1 | 1 | ... | ... |
| **Color of occupant:** | | | | | | | | |
| Per cent nonwhite | | | | | | | | |
| 1950 inventory | 2 | 9 | 9 | 5 | 6 | 12 | 12 | 17 |
| Units demolished, 1950–56 | 22 | 45 | 33 | 19 | 46 | 55 | 52 | 63 |
| Units built, 1950–56 | 2 | 6 | 3 | 2 | 5 | 2 | 12 | 5 |

... 0.5 per cent or less.
Source: 1956 NHI, Vol. I, Tables 1 and 2, and Vol. III, Table 1.

## Table 3–2
## Structural Characteristics for the 1950 Housing Inventory, Demolitions, and Units Built between 1950 and 1956: Selected Standard Metropolitan Areas and Cities

| CHARACTERISTIC AND GROUP OF DWELLING UNITS | STANDARD METROPOLITAN AREA | | | | | | CITY | |
| --- | --- | --- | --- | --- | --- | --- | --- | --- |
| | Boston | Chicago | Detroit | Los Angeles | New York | Phila-delphia | Chicago | Phila-delphia |
| **Year built:** | | | | | | | | |
| Per cent built in 1929 or earlier | | | | | | | | |
| 1950 inventory | 85 | 82 | 60 | 46 | 76 | 80 | 92 | 87 |
| Units demolished, 1950–56 | 82 | 86 | 66 | 55 | 83 | 100 | 95 | 100 |
| Units built, 1950–56 | ... | ... | ... | ... | ... | ... | ... | ... |
| **Size of structure:** | | | | | | | | |
| Per cent 1 dwelling unit | | | | | | | | |
| 1950 inventory* | 34 to 37 | 34 to 35 | 61 to 63 | 67 to 71 | 26 to 30 | 63 to 75 | 18 to 19 | 61 to 69 |
| Units demolished, 1950–56 | 27 | 23 | 30 | 66 | 12 | 49 | 19 | 36 |
| Units built, 1950–56 | 84 | 87 | 93 | 81 | 57 | 91 | 63 | 75 |
| **Number of rooms:** | | | | | | | | |
| Per cent 1 and 2 rooms | | | | | | | | |
| 1950 inventory | 6 | 14 | 6 | 14 | 9 | 8 | 18 | 11 |
| Units demolished, 1950–56 | 2 | 18 | 15 | 21 | 4 | 43 | 21 | 49 |
| Units built, 1950–56 | ... | 2 | 2 | 6 | 7 | 1 | 4 | 2 |
| Per cent 7 rooms or more | | | | | | | | |
| 1950 inventory | 21 | 9 | 14 | 8 | 11 | 24 | 6 | 20 |
| Units demolished, 1950–56 | 4 | 7 | 1 | 7 | ... | 4 | 4 | 7 |
| Units built, 1950–56 | 12 | 5 | 6 | 6 | 12 | 12 | 4 | 3 |

* Excluding and including "1 and 2 dwelling unit, semidetached."

... 0.5 per cent or less.

Source: 1956 NHI, Vol. I, Tables 1 and 2 and Vol. III, Table 1; 1950 Census of Housing, Vol. I, Part I, Tables 22 and 27.

rected toward reducing an area's substandard inventory although, as we noted earlier, it may be undertaken for purposes of land acquisition in conjunction with highway construction or the like. Now, the proportion of home owners typically is lower in the substandard than in the standard sector; hence, insofar as demolition is directed toward the reduction of substandard housing, relatively few owner-occupied dwellings and relatively many rental dwellings will be demolished. To illustrate the point, we note that in the 1950 standard occupied inventory of the City of Chicago, 36 per cent of the dwellings were owner-occupied, 64 per cent were rented. In the 1950 substandard inventory, 11 per cent of the dwellings were owner-occupied, 89 per cent were rented (CSNHI, Table 1–2). Demolition removed 8,000 standard dwellings and 15,000 substandard dwellings which had been occupied in 1950 (1956 NHI, Vol. I, Table 2). We then expect about 4,500 of the dwellings demolished to have been owner-occupied in 1950 (36 per cent of 8,000 plus 11 per cent of 15,000) and 18,500 of the dwellings demolished to have been rented in 1950 (64 per cent of 8,000 plus 89 per cent of 15,000), on the basis of the quality-specific tenure distributions. The tenure distribution of the demolished dwellings is "explained" in large part by their quality distribution and the quality-specific tenure distributions, as the following tabulation shows.

| | 1950 TENURE OF DEMOLITIONS | |
| | Owner | Renter |
| --- | --- | --- |
| Reported in NHI | 3,000 | 20,000 |
| Expected | 4,500 | 18,500 |

Given the quality distribution of demolished dwellings and the quality-specific tenure distributions of all dwellings, the expected distribution of demolished dwellings by 1950 tenure would be 4,500 owner and 18,500 renter. The reported distribution of demolished dwellings by 1950 tenure is 3,000 owner and

20,000 renter. We conclude that the chance of an owner-occupied substandard dwelling being demolished is about the same as the chance that a rental substandard dwelling will be demolished; and the chance of an owner-occupied standard dwelling being demolished is about the same as the chance that a rental standard dwelling will be demolished.

The proportion of nonwhite households typically is lower in the standard than in the substandard sector. Hence, if demolition is directed toward reducing the substandard inventory, the proportion of nonwhite households in units subsequently demolished would be higher than the proportion of nonwhite households in the total housing inventory. For example, in 1950, about 93 per cent of the standard dwellings in Chicago City were occupied by white households, 7 per cent were occupied by nonwhite households; 70 per cent of the substandard dwellings were occupied by white households, 30 per cent were occupied by nonwhite households (CSNHI, Table 1–2). Given the quality distribution of demolished dwellings and the quality-specific distributions of all dwellings by color of occupant, the expected distribution of demolished dwellings by color of occupant in 1950 would be 18,000 white and 5,000 nonwhite. However, the reported distribution of demolished dwellings by color of occupant in 1950 is 12,000 white and 12,000 nonwhite (the discrepancy in total demolitions arises from rounding). Hence, color-of-occupant distribution of demolitions is not accounted for in any substantial degree by the quality distribution of demolitions and the quality-specific distributions of all dwellings by color of occupant. A standard dwelling with nonwhite occupants is somewhat more likely to be demolished than is a standard dwelling occupied by whites. A substandard dwelling occupied by nonwhites is somewhat more likely to be demolished than is a substandard dwelling with white occupants.

The demolition rate is higher for substandard, dilapidated

units than for substandard, lacking facilities though not dilapidated units. And the proportion of dwellings with nonwhite occupants is higher for substandard dilapidated units than for substandard, lacking facilities though not dilapidated units. Thus, although the color-of-occupant distribution of demolitions was not accounted for by the quality distribution of demolitions, it might be accounted for by the quality-condition distribution of demolitions. The distribution of demolitions by quality and condition is 8,000 standard, 6,000 substandard, lacking facilities though not dilapidated, and 9,000 substandard, dilapidated (1956 NHI, Vol. I, Table 2). In 1956, the proportion nonwhite for all substandard dwellings was about 40 per cent in Chicago City; the proportion nonwhite for substandard dwellings, lacking facilities though not dilapidated was about 30 per cent, whereas the proportion nonwhite for substandard dwellings, dilapidated was about 65 per cent (tabulations from the CSNHI). We assume that in 1950, when the proportion nonwhite for all substandard dwellings was 30 per cent, the proportion nonwhite for substandard dwellings, lacking facilities though not dilapidated was 20 per cent and the proportion nonwhite for substandard dwellings, dilapidated was 55 per cent. Given the quality and condition distribution of demolished dwellings and the quality-condition-specific distributions of all dwellings by color of occupant in 1950, the expected distribution of demolished dwellings by color of occupant in 1950 is 16,000 white and 7,000 nonwhite. By comparison, the reported distribution is 12,000 white and 12,000 nonwhite. Part, but by no means all, of the color-of-occupant distribution of demolitions is accounted for by the quality-condition distribution of demolitions and the quality-condition-specific distributions of all dwellings by color of occupant. Thus, the chance that a dwelling of a given quality and condition will be demolished appears to be somewhat less if the occupants are white than if they are nonwhite. Were a

*86*

more detailed classification of dwellings by "quality" available —e.g., one which indicated the types of deficiencies—a more complete "explanation" of the distribution of demolitions by color of occupant prior to demolition might be possible.

With regard to the newly built units, we note that they are concentrated in the home-owner sector, they are virtually all of standard quality, and relatively few are occupied by nonwhite households. The complex of economic, social, and psychological factors conducive to residential construction in the home-owner sector cannot be explored here. The standard quality of the new dwellings calls for no particular comment. The small percentage of nonwhite households occupying new dwellings perhaps can be explained primarily in economic terms. Although no systematic test of this explanation can be undertaken here, some statistics for the City of Chicago may be illuminating.

Twelve per cent of the households in the City in 1950 and 19 per cent of the households in 1956 were nonwhite. In 1956, nonwhites occupied 9,000, or 12 per cent, of the 76,000 newly constructed (built between 1950 and 1956) occupied dwellings in the City of Chicago. About 6,000 of the new units were within projects of the Chicago Housing Authority which are restricted to lower-income families. Of the new CHA dwellings, 92 per cent were occupied by nonwhites (Chicago Housing Authority, 1957). Inasmuch as only 39 per cent of the families with incomes below $4,000 are nonwhite, it appears that the proportion nonwhite in new CHA dwellings is as high or higher than would be expected on the basis of income. Five per cent of the new units outside CHA projects had nonwhite occupants in 1956. Virtually all new owner-occupied units were valued in excess of $15,000, and over three-fourths of the new, private rental units had rents in excess of $100 per month (1956 NHI, Vol. I, Table 1). Their occupants are, therefore, likely to be families with relatively high incomes; and nonwhite families are under-represented among the higher income groups. For example, only 8 per cent of the families reporting incomes of $8,000 or more were nonwhite. These rough calculations suggest that the proportion of nonwhite occupancy in new dwellings is accounted for to a considerable extent, though not wholly, by economic factors.

Selected structural characteristics of the 1950 inventory and of demolished and newly constructed dwellings are shown in Table 3–2. One might suspect that the proportion of very old units would be high for demolitions on the assumption that housing quality deteriorates over time. The NHI data are not wholly appropriate for examining this proposition. The oldest group of units for which information is available is the group built in 1929 or earlier, i.e., units built at least twenty-five years ago. The proportion of older units generally is higher among demolitions than in the 1950 total inventory. Probably the differences would be more clear cut if we were comparing the proportions of dwellings fifty years of age or older. In general, however, the data suggest that demolition, as well as new construction, reduces the median age of the housing inventory.

Demolition and new construction, separately and jointly, increased the proportion of single-family dwellings in the housing inventory between 1950 and 1956. Relatively few one-unit structures were demolished; a relatively high proportion of the units added through new construction were in one-unit structures. Demolition and new construction, separately and jointly, reduced the proportion of one-and two-room units in the housing inventory. Relatively many small units are demolished; relatively few small units are constructed. However, with respect to large units, i.e., units with seven rooms or more, relatively few are demolished and relatively few are constructed. Demolition tends to increase the proportion of large dwellings, whereas new construction tends to reduce it. Considered jointly, the processes no doubt reduce the proportion of large dwellings because the volume of new construction so greatly exceeds the volume of demolition.

With respect to a number of the characteristics examined, the demolition and construction processes reinforce one another in producing compositional changes in the inventory. They tend to raise the proportion of home ownership and lower the proportion of renters; to increase the proportion standard and reduce the proportion substandard; to lower the median age of the inventory; to raise the proportion of single family dwellings and lower the proportion of units in multi-unit structures; and to reduce the proportions of small and large units and increase the proportion of units in the range of three to six rooms.

## CONVERSION AND MERGER

We now turn our attention to before-and-after views of converted and merged units. Typically, conversion entails the creation of two dwelling units from one existing dwelling; merger entails the creation of one dwelling unit from two existing units. Roughly 2 per cent of the 1950 inventory was converted between 1950 and 1956, and about 2 per cent of the 1950 inventory was merged between 1950 and 1956. The numbers of dwellings involved in conversion or merger generally are small. Again we caution the reader against attributing significance to rather small differences between areas or categories in the summary measures.

We first note with regard to the summary statistics in Table 3–3 that the vacancy rate after conversion, i.e., in 1956, consistently was higher than the vacancy rate before conversion, i.e., in 1950. In part, the higher after-conversion vacancy rates can be accounted for by the general loosening of the housing market. Conversion itself necessitates change in occupants, which probably also contributes to the higher after-conversion vacancy rates. In some areas, the after-merger vacancy rate was higher than the before-merger vacancy rate; in other areas, the reverse is observed. The patterns are not sharp enough to warrant generalization, but there is some suggestion that relationships between vacancy rates and the conversion and merger processes merit further investigation.

The before-conversion rate of home ownership is consistently higher than the after-conversion rate of home ownership. The before-merger rate of home ownership consistently is lower than the after-merger rate of home ownership. We can only speculate with regard to the factors underlying these observed changes. The reduction in home ownership which accompanies conversion may reflect decisions of home owners to subdivide their dwelling and rent one or both of the units obtained through conversion. The increase in home ownership which accompanies merger may reflect decisions of home owners to combine their unit with a rental unit in the same structure and continue owner occupancy in the merged unit; or perhaps the home owner, at the time he purchases the structure, chooses to merge two rental units within it for his own occupancy.

The proportion substandard is lower before conversion than after conversion, whereas the proportion substandard is higher before merger than after merger. We suspect that the unit which is subdivided often has only one bath; occupants of the units created through conversion must share a bath unless additional facilities are installed. The converse would be true in the case of merger, i.e., the bath formerly shared would become a bath for exclusive use. If this is the case, the downgrading which accompanies conversion and the upgrading which accompanies

## Table 3–3
## Occupancy Characteristics and Quality for Dwelling Units Converted or Merged between 1950 and 1956: Selected Standard Metropolitan Areas and Cities

| CHARACTERISTIC AND GROUP OF DWELLING UNITS | STANDARD METROPOLITAN AREA | | | | | | CITY | |
|---|---|---|---|---|---|---|---|---|
| | Boston | Chicago | Detroit | Los Angeles | New York | Phila-delphia | Chicago | Phila-delphia |
| **Occupancy status:** | | | | | | | | |
| Per cent vacant | | | | | | | | |
| Units before conversion | 2 | ... | 2 | ... | 6 | 4 | ... | 4 |
| Units after conversion | 7 | 6 | 14 | 5 | 7 | 12 | ... | 11 |
| Units before merger | 3 | 2 | 5 | 14 | 13 | 5 | 3 | 5 |
| Units after merger | 8 | ... | 13 | ... | 3 | 10 | ... | 13 |
| **Tenure:** | | | | | | | | |
| Per cent owner occupied | | | | | | | | |
| Units before conversion | 45 | 57 | 39 | 75 | 50 | 61 | 54 | 57 |
| Units after conversion | 32 | 39 | 15 | 39 | 23 | 36 | 29 | 34 |
| Units before merger | 31 | 23 | 26 | 23 | 39 | 28 | 20 | 24 |
| Units after merger | 73 | 56 | 35 | 50 | 71 | 59 | 50 | 47 |
| **Quality:** | | | | | | | | |
| Per cent substandard | | | | | | | | |
| Units before conversion | 7 | 18 | 19 | ... | 6 | 10 | 17 | 9 |
| Units after conversion | 9 | 25 | 27 | 16 | 14 | 10 | 32 | 14 |
| Units before merger | 43 | 59 | 57 | 42 | 28 | 52 | 62 | 54 |
| Units after merger | 9 | 21 | 23 | 14 | 11 | 12 | 21 | 14 |
| **Color of occupant:** | | | | | | | | |
| Per cent nonwhite | | | | | | | | |
| Units before conversion | 2 | 13 | 21 | 12 | 6 | 16 | 8 | 19 |
| Units after conversion | 5 | 35 | 37 | 6 | 9 | 28 | 39 | 36 |
| Units before merger | 6 | 26 | 20 | 17 | 10 | 26 | 29 | 38 |
| Units after merger | 9 | 22 | 27 | 17 | 18 | 40 | 29 | 55 |

... 0.5 per cent or less.
Source: 1956 NHI, Vol. I, Tables 1 and 2.

merger often stem from changes in the occupancy pattern rather than from any sort of structural alteration.

The proportion of units occupied by nonwhite households typically is higher after conversion than before conversion. In part, the increase in proportion nonwhite no doubt is accounted for by the fact that the nonwhite population has been growing more rapidly than the white population in these large metropolitan centers. However, it may well be that conversion is a common means of increasing the number of units for nonwhite occupancy. If so, the number of units occupied by nonwhites is growing more rapidly than the amount of shelter space occupied by nonwhites. The before-merger proportion nonwhite was about the same as or somewhat lower than the after-merger proportion nonwhite. Given the fact that dwellings infrequently revert from nonwhite to white occupancy, it is improbable the proportion nonwhite would decrease with merger.

The statistics on "year built," shown in Table 3–4, serve only to indicate that both conversion and merger are concentrated in older structures. In most areas, relatively high proportions of the conversions take place in single-family dwellings and relatively high proportions of the mergers result in single-family dwellings. The rate of conversion appears to be as high for single-family homes as for dwellings in multi-unit structures. The rate of merger appears to be as high for units in duplexes as for units in larger structures.

The statistics on size of unit before and after conversion and before and after merger are highly informative. Before conversion, the proportion of units with seven rooms or more is extremely high; after conversion, the proportion of one-and-two-room units is high. Before merger, the proportion of very small units is high; after merger, the proportion of units with seven rooms or more is high. This suggests that conversion often is undertaken as a solution for the "too-large" dwelling and

## Table 3–4
## Structural Characteristics for Dwelling Units Converted or Merged between 1950 and 1956: Selected Standard Metropolitan Areas and Cities

| CHARACTERISTIC AND GROUP OF DWELLING UNITS | STANDARD METROPOLITAN AREA | | | | | | CITY | |
|---|---|---|---|---|---|---|---|---|
| | Boston | Chicago | Detroit | Los Angeles | New York | Phila-delphia | Chicago | Phila-delphia |
| **Year built:** | | | | | | | | |
| Per cent built 1929 or earlier | | | | | | | | |
| Units before conversion | 98 | 90 | 82 | 71 | 90 | 97 | 91 | 99 |
| Units after conversion | 96 | 94 | 89 | 74 | 90 | 98 | 93 | 99 |
| Units before merger | 98 | 97 | 88 | 85 | 85 | 96 | 97 | 97 |
| Units after merger | 100 | 89 | 94 | 86 | 91 | 100 | 100 | 100 |
| **Size of structure:** | | | | | | | | |
| Per cent 1 dwelling unit | | | | | | | | |
| Units before conversion | 37 | 52 | 42 | 88 | 47 | 76 | 46 | 72 |
| Units after conversion | ... | ... | ... | ... | ... | ... | ... | ... |
| Units before merger | ... | ... | ... | ... | ... | ... | ... | ... |
| Units after merger | 51 | 37 | 29 | 57 | 60 | 65 | 29 | 53 |
| **Number of rooms:** | | | | | | | | |
| Per cent 1 and 2 rooms | | | | | | | | |
| Units before conversion | 1 | 5 | 9 | ... | 2 | 5 | 8 | 8 |
| Units after conversion | 13 | 21 | 32 | 47 | 35 | 19 | 25 | 25 |
| Units before merger | 22 | 54 | 40 | 58 | 17 | 32 | 60 | 39 |
| Units after merger | ... | 11 | 13 | ... | 3 | 2 | 14 | 3 |
| Per cent 7 rooms or more | | | | | | | | |
| Units before conversion | 57 | 36 | 24 | 38 | 31 | 57 | 31 | 52 |
| Units after conversion | 4 | ... | 1 | ... | 3 | 1 | ... | 2 |
| Units before merger | 9 | 3 | 5 | ... | 6 | 6 | ... | 5 |
| Units after merger | 56 | 26 | 24 | 14 | 49 | 44 | 29 | 31 |

... 0.5 per cent or less.
Source: 1956 NHI, Vol. I, Tables 1 and 2.

merger is undertaken as a solution for the "too-small" dwelling. We suspect that often the size or layout of a "too-large" dwelling is such that subdivision does not yield two satisfactory units. And we suspect that merger often results in a "too-large" dwelling.

The foregoing observations suggest that the effects of conversion and merger are quite orderly and, with fuller data, might be explained quite satisfactorily.

*4*

# The Current Housing
# Situation (1956)

ALTHOUGH WE HAVE EXPLORED the impact of the several change processes on the composition of the housing inventory in each area, only incidental attention has been given inter-area differences in the composition of the inventory as such. Here a set of comparisons among the areas is undertaken with respect to structural and financial characteristics of the inventory. It is necessarily a superficial description of the differences which obtain, for their "explanation" would call for far more intensive study than we can undertake. Readers well acquainted with one or more of these areas are almost certain to note that we have overlooked distinctive characteristics of the inventory in the local area. However, our major purpose is to give some indication of the diversity which obtains among the major metropolitan areas with respect to housing conditions. The final section concerns residential mobility in the central city and metropolitan ring of each of the six largest SMA's. The statistics on location of present residence in relation to location of previous residence made available in the NHI are likely to receive considerable attention although, as we will point out, their interpretation poses difficult problems.

## COMPOSITION OF THE INVENTORY

Occupancy-tenure status and quality of the inventory in each area were discussed briefly in Chapter 2 and are not considered here. In Table 4–1, the inventory in each area is characterized in terms of three structural characteristics—type of structure, size of unit, and year built. Detroit, Los Angeles, and Philadelphia stand out as areas of single-family homes. A relatively high proportion of the units in Boston are located in small multi-unit structures. Disproportionate numbers of the dwellings in Chicago and New York are in large multi-unit structures, particularly structures which include twenty units or more. On the basis of number of rooms or number of bedrooms, dwellings in the Philadelphia area typically were more spacious than those in the other areas. The "average" unit in Philadelphia had 5.7 rooms and 2.7 bedrooms. In the other SMA's, median size of unit ranged from 4.4 to 5.1 rooms or 2.0 to 2.4 bedrooms. In terms of "age," the housing inventory of the Boston, Chicago, New York, and Philadelphia areas might be characterized as older, the inventory of the Detroit and Los Angeles areas as younger.

Some indicators of housing conditions, particularly the intensity with which housing is used, are given in Table 4–2. No over-all measure of crowding, such as the persons-per-room ratio, is given in the NHI; nor can one be calculated readily. (The difficulties involved in such a calculation become apparent when one examines the size-of-household by size-of-dwelling tabulations of the 1956 NHI, Vol. III, Table 7.) The room crowding measure shown in Table 4–2 is the proportion of households with three members or more who occupy units so small that there are more than two household members per bedroom. The measure, which is insensitive to "crowding" among small households, cannot be regarded as a wholly satisfactory summary indicator. With respect to crowding of larger households, Chicago, Los Angeles, and New York rank relatively high. Boston, Detroit, and Philadelphia evidence substantially less crowding. The proportion of crowded larger households in the City of Chicago was more than double the proportion in the City of Philadelphia.

Also shown in Table 4–2 are the proportions of substandard units, dilapidated units, and non-dilapidated substandard units. Recall that substandard units comprise dilapidated units and units which are not dilapidated but lack adequate plumbing facilities. As noted earlier, substandard housing was most prevalent in the Chicago and New York areas. In Chicago, the high proportion substandard is accounted for primarily by non-dilapidated substandard housing rather than by dilapidated substandard housing. In New York, on the other hand, the non-dilapidated substandard and dilapidated substandard categories make roughly equal contributions to the proportion substandard. The high proportion substandard in Chicago reflects primarily

## Table 4–1
## Structural Characteristics: Selected Standard Metropolitan Areas and Cities, 1956

| ITEM | STANDARD METROPOLITAN AREA | | | | | | CITY | |
|---|---|---|---|---|---|---|---|---|
| | Boston | Chicago | Detroit | Los Angeles | New York | Phila-delphia | Chicago | Phila-delphia |
| | | | | percentage distribution | | | | |
| **Type of structure** | | | | | | | | |
| All units | 100 | 100 | 100 | 100 | 100 | 100 | 100 | 100 |
| 1 unit | 38 | 41 | 68 | 71 | 30 | 76 | 21 | 65 |
| 2 to 4 unit | 43 | 32 | 22 | 15 | 27 | 16 | 39 | 20 |
| 5 to 19 unit | 14 | 15 | 6 | 10 | 16 | 6 | 22 | 10 |
| 20 unit or more | 4 | 12 | 4 | 4 | 26 | 3 | 17 | 5 |
| **Number of rooms** | | | | | | | | |
| All units | 100 | 100 | 100 | 100 | 100 | 100 | 100 | 100 |
| 1 to 3 rooms | 15 | 20 | 12 | 26 | 29 | 15 | 26 | 22 |
| 4 rooms | 19 | 25 | 16 | 20 | 24 | 11 | 24 | 10 |
| 5 rooms | 26 | 27 | 36 | 29 | 19 | 16 | 26 | 14 |
| 6 rooms or more | 41 | 28 | 35 | 24 | 28 | 58 | 24 | 54 |
| Median number of rooms | 5.1 | 4.7 | 5.1 | 4.6 | 4.4 | 5.7 | 4.5 | 5.6 |
| **Number of bedrooms** | | | | | | | | |
| All units | 100 | 100 | 100 | 100 | 100 | 100 | 100 | 100 |
| 0 or 1 bedroom | 20 | 27 | 15 | 31 | 32 | 16 | 34 | 23 |
| 2 bedrooms | 36 | 41 | 41 | 39 | 37 | 24 | 41 | 21 |
| 3 bedrooms or more | 44 | 32 | 44 | 30 | 31 | 60 | 25 | 55 |
| Median number of bedrooms | 2.3 | 2.1 | 2.4 | 2.0 | 2.0 | 2.7 | 1.9 | 2.5 |
| **Year built** | | | | | | | | |
| All units | 100 | 100 | 100 | 100 | 100 | 100 | 100 | 100 |
| 1950 or later | 9 | 16 | 23 | 30 | 16 | 18 | 7 | 7 |
| 1930 to 1950 | 12 | 15 | 29 | 36 | 20 | 14 | 9 | 9 |
| Before 1930 | 79 | 69 | 48 | 34 | 64 | 67 | 84 | 84 |

Source: 1956 NHI, Vol. III, Table 1.

# Table 4–2
## Crowding and Quality of Housing Inventory: Selected Standard Metropolitan Areas and Cities, 1956

| CHARACTERISTIC | STANDARD METROPOLITAN AREA | | | | | | CITY | |
|---|---|---|---|---|---|---|---|---|
| | Boston | Chicago | Detroit | Los Angeles | New York | Phila-delphia | Chicago | Phila-delphia |
| Crowding (per cent of large households crowded)* | 12 | 23 | 16 | 22 | 25 | 9 | 28 | 12 |
| Substandard housing (per cent of units substandard) | 8 | 12 | 6 | 4 | 11 | 8 | 15 | 9 |
| Dilapidated housing (per cent of units dilapidated) | 4 | 3 | 2 | 1 | 5 | 3 | 4 | 3 |
| Non-dilapidated substandard housing (per cent of units not dilapidated but lacking private toilet, bath, or hot running water) | 4 | 10 | 5 | 3 | 6 | 4 | 11 | 6 |

* 3 or 4 persons with 0 or 1 bedroom and 5 persons or more with 0, 1, or 2 bedrooms as per cent of households with 3 persons or more reporting bedrooms.
Source: 1956 NHI, Vol. III, Tables 1 and 7.

overintensive use of physically sound housing, whereas over-intensive use and physical dilapidation are of roughly equal importance in New York.

Financial characteristics of the rental inventory in each area are presented in Table 4–3. On the average, units command higher rentals in Chicago than in any other area. The median gross monthly rental of dwellings in Chicago was $78. The Detroit inventory with a median rent of $74 ranked second. Median rent was about $68 in Boston and Los Angeles, $64 in New York, and only $59 in Philadelphia. It may be noted that although nearly three-fifths of the rental units in the New York SMA were "rent-controlled," rent levels in New York tended to be higher than in Philadelphia.

When inter-area comparisons are restricted to standard units, Chicago again ranks at the top with a median gross rent of $84 per month. The median rent in Chicago is $8 higher than in any other area and $21 higher than in Philadelphia. The average substandard unit in Chicago rented for $55 per month, as compared with $57 in Detroit, $53 in Boston, and not more than $45 in any other area. If comparisons are restricted to dwellings of the same size (i.e., with the same number of bedrooms), median gross monthly rent tends to be highest in Chicago and lowest in Philadelphia.

The median gross monthly rent paid by primary families and individuals in each of six rather broad income groups also is shown for each area in Table 4–3. The data suggest that renters in the Chicago area pay, on the average, rents equal to or greater than those paid by renters of equivalent income living in other areas. Philadelphia renters appear to pay rents no more than, or less than, those paid by renters of equivalent income living in other areas. We use the words "suggest" and "appear" advisedly, for within each broad income group Chicago-area

**Table 4–3**
**Gross Monthly Rent of Renter-Occupied Nonfarm Dwelling Units, by Quality, Number of Bedrooms, and Income of Occupant: Selected Standard Metropolitan Areas and Cities, 1956**

| ITEM | STANDARD METROPOLITAN AREA | | | | | | CITY | |
|---|---|---|---|---|---|---|---|---|
| | Boston | Chicago | Detroit | Los Angeles | New York | Phila-delphia | Chicago | Phila-delphia |
| Gross monthly rent (per cent distribution): | | | | | | | | |
| All units | 100 | 100 | 100 | 100 | 100 | 100 | 100 | 100 |
| Under $60 | 34 | 24 | 25 | 37 | 42 | 52 | 25 | 60 |
| $60 to $79 | 35 | 28 | 36 | 31 | 29 | 27 | 27 | 25 |
| $80 to $99 | 19 | 26 | 23 | 20 | 14 | 11 | 27 | 8 |
| $100 or more | 12 | 22 | 16 | 12 | 15 | 10 | 21 | 6 |
| Median gross monthly rent (dollars): | | | | | | | | |
| All units | 69 | 78 | 74 | 68 | 64 | 59 | 78 | 55 |
| Standard | 71 | 84 | 76 | 69 | 69 | 63 | 84 | 58 |
| Substandard | 53 | 55 | 57 | 44 | 45 | 43 | 55 | 42 |
| 0 or 1 bedroom | 65 | 73 | 65 | 59 | 65 | 53 | 72 | 51 |
| 2 bedrooms | 69 | 80 | 77 | 82 | 63 | 65 | 79 | 58 |
| 3 bedrooms or more | 74 | 93 | 90 | 91 | 69 | 67 | 93 | 62 |
| Income of primary family or individual: | | | | | | | | |
| Less than $2,000 | 53 | 57 | 63 | 54 | 48 | 46 | 58 | 45 |
| $2,000 to $3,999 | 63 | 68 | 68 | 61 | 57 | 53 | 67 | 51 |
| $4,000 to $5,999 | 71 | 79 | 77 | 71 | 68 | 64 | 79 | 60 |
| $6,000 to $7,999 | 77 | 85 | 78 | 78 | 72 | 71 | 85 | 58 |
| $8,000 to $9,999 | 89 | 92 | 83 | 88 | 82 | 79 | 93 | 73 |
| $10,000 or more | 100+ | 100+ | 96 | 96 | 100+ | 97 | 100+ | 100+ |

Source: 1956 NHI, Vol. III, Tables 3 and 12.

renters may be clustered toward the upper limit and Philadelphia-area renters clustered toward the lower limit.

An examination of the frequency and characteristics of available vacant units for rent suggests that the relatively high rent level prevailing in Chicago is associated with a relative shortage of desirable available rental vacancies. (Available rental vacancies are units which are suitable for year-round occupancy, are not dilapidated, and are being offered for rent.) Table 4–4 shows that in Chicago there were three available rental vacancies for every hundred renter-occupied units. Available rental vacancies per hundred renter-occupied units numbered two in the New York SMA, four in Los Angeles, and five or more in each other area. Equally, if not more important is the fact that at the time of the NHI less than 10 per cent of the available vacant units in Chicago had been vacant for as long as four months. By contrast, the duration of vacancy was four months or more for about 15 per cent of the available rental vacancies in Detroit and Los Angeles, 23 per cent of the vacancies in New York, and about 40 per cent of the vacancies in the Boston and Philadelphia SMA's. In each area, available rental vacancies included relatively large numbers of units which lacked adequate plumbing facilities, which were small in size, and which were located in older structures as compared with the occupied rental inventory. For example, in Chicago over 30 per cent of the available rental vacancies lacked adequate plumbing facilities, 60 per cent were units with no bedroom or one bedroom, and over 80 per cent were in structures built before 1930. With relevant statistics available for only six areas at a single point in time, it is impossible to determine whether rent level is directly related to a scarcity of desirable available rental vacancies on an area-by-area basis. However, there is some suggestion that this is the case.

Within the owner inventory, financial characteristics are

**Table 4-4**

**Characteristics of Available Vacancies for Rent: Selected Standard Metropolitan Areas and Cities, 1956**

| ITEM | STANDARD METROPOLITAN AREA | | | | | | CITY | |
|---|---|---|---|---|---|---|---|---|
| | Boston | Chicago | Detroit | Los Angeles | New York | Phila-delphia | Chicago | Phila-delphia |
| Vacancies per 100 renter-occupied units | 5 | 3 | 7 | 4 | 2 | 8 | 2 | 9 |
| Duration of vacancy (per cent distribution): | | | | | | | | |
| All units | 100 | 100 | 100 | 100 | 100 | 100 | 100 | 100 |
| Less than 1 month | 32 | 58 | 32 | 50 | 31 | 30 | 54 | 19 |
| 1 to 4 months | 26 | 35 | 53 | 36 | 46 | 30 | 36 | 34 |
| 4 months or more | 42 | 7 | 15 | 14 | 23 | 39 | 10 | 47 |
| Per cent lacking adequate plumbing facilities | 17 | 31 | 26 | 8 | 19 | 22 | 37 | 29 |
| Per cent with 0 or 1 bedroom | 34 | 60 | 64 | 77 | 67 | 65 | 63 | 68 |
| Per cent in structures built before 1930 | 94 | 83 | 79 | 54 | 73 | 86 | 87 | 95 |

Source: 1956 NHI, Vol. III, Tables 1 and 18.

available only for those owner-occupied units which are in one-unit properties without business. The available characteristic is the owner-occupant's estimate of the selling price of the structure and land under ordinary conditions. Shown below are the proportion of the owner sector covered by the value figure, i.e., the proportion of owner-occupied units which are located in one-unit properties without business, and the median value, or estimated selling price, of such properties. (The figures are from 1956 NHI, Vol. III, Table 3.)

| SMA | Per cent covered | Median value |
|---|---|---|
| Philadelphia | 90 | $10,700 |
| Los Angeles | 89 | $14,300 |
| Detroit | 88 | $13,100 |
| **Chicago** | 71 | $16,900 |
| New York | 69 | $15,800 |
| Boston | 67 | $15,000 |

About 90 per cent of the owner inventory in the Philadelphia, Los Angeles, and Detroit SMA's is covered by the value figures; median value ranges from $11,000 to $14,000. Around 70 per cent of the owner inventory in the Chicago, New York, and Boston SMA's is covered; median value ranges from $15,000 to $17,000. Although we would not want to assert that the inter-area variation in value simply reflects differential coverage, the differential coverage is a limiting factor on any interpretation. The two cities for which value figures are available fall into the foregoing pattern. In Philadelphia, a median value of $8,400 is reported for the 86 per cent of the owner-occupied units which are covered. In Chicago, a median value of $17,600 is reported for the 50 per cent of the owner-occupied units which are covered. No interpretation of the reported differences among areas in value of owner-occupied properties is undertaken here in large part because we cannot undertake the sorts of analyses called for in conjunction with the coverage problem.

RESIDENTIAL MOBILITY

Most of the comments in this section are of a methodological character. The NHI mobility data have certain limitations which may not be apparent immediately. Each household covered by the NHI was asked when the household moved into the dwelling which it occupied currently. If the household members moved into the dwelling at different times, the year in which the first household member moved in was recorded. Those households reporting that they had moved into their "present" dwelling in 1955 or 1956, i.e., within the preceding two years, were designated "recent-mover" households. For recent-mover households, an additional question was asked regarding the location of the "previous" dwelling, i.e., the dwelling in which they resided just prior to moving to their present dwelling. If the household had moved more than once during 1955–56, the previous dwelling was the one from which the household moved when it occupied the present dwelling. For recent-mover households in each of the six SMA's, the location of the present dwelling was classified as "inside the central city of this SMA" or "in the metropolitan ring of this SMA." The location of the previous dwelling of those recent-mover households which had the same household head in both the present and previous dwelling was classified as "inside the central city of this SMA," "in the metropolitan ring of this SMA," or "outside this SMA." (Tabulations of recent-mover households with the same household head by locations of present and previous dwellings are published as Table 14, Volume III of the 1956 NHI.)

Because of widespread interest in "suburbanization" and "back-to-the-city" movements, we suspect that many users of the NHI data will attempt to measure the volume or rate of movement from the city to the ring, or vice versa, from the tabulations of locations of present and previous dwellings for recent-mover households with the same head. Other users will attempt to measure the volume or rate of in-migration to a given SMA, its central city or metropolitan ring, from these statistics. Before undertaking such analyses, users would be well advised to take note of certain features of the NHI mobility data.

In contrast to the data on migration and mobility obtained in the 1940 and 1950 Censuses, the NHI data cannot be used to calculate gross or net migration rates or to measure streams of movement from one area to another. By volume of in-migration to a community we mean the number of persons or households moving to the community within a specified time period or those persons or households currently living in the community who resided elsewhere at a specified prior date. Volume of out-migration from a community is the number moving from the community within a specified time period or those currently living elsewhere who resided in the community at a specified prior date. Volume of net migration is obtained by subtracting the number of out-migrants from the number of in-migrants. A migration stream is defined as the number of persons or households moving from community A to community B within a specified period of time or the number currently residing in community A who were living in community B at a specified prior date. The mobility-migration question used in the Censuses was of the form: Where were you living one (or five) years ago? Thus, from the Census data, gross and net migration for given communities and migration streams between given communities could be obtained. As noted earlier, however, the mobility questions used in the NHI were of the form: How long have you lived in this dwelling? Where did you live just prior to moving into this dwelling?

The impossibility of measuring a migration stream from the NHI data can be illustrated with statistics for the Chicago area. The fact that 6,000 recent-mover households living in the City of Chicago at the close of 1956 reported their last previous residence in the Chicago metropolitan ring (Table 14, Vol. III, 1956 NHI) might tempt one to assert that a "back-to-the-city" movement of 6,000 households occurred in metropolitan Chicago during the two-year period 1955–56. This assertion implies that 6,000 households living in the city at the close of 1956 were living in the metropolitan ring in January 1955. If each household had moved only once during the two-year period 1955–56, the number of recent-mover households living in the city at the close of 1956 and reporting previous residence in the ring would equal the number of households living in the city at the close of 1956 who had been living in the ring in January 1955. However, a sizeable number of the recent-mover households will have moved more than once during the two-year period, and last previous residence is not necessarily the same as residence in January 1955 for these households. For example, a household which moved from outside the SMA to the metropolitan ring in 1955 and from the ring to the city in 1956 would appear in the NHI tabulation as "present residence in city, previous residence in ring" although the place of residence in January 1955 was outside the SMA. A household which moved from the ring to the city in 1955 and moved to a different dwelling within the city in 1956 would be reported as "present residence in city, previous residence in city" although the place of residence in January 1955 was in the metropolitan ring. Thus, we cannot determine whether the migration stream from the ring to the city over the two-year period 1955–56 was less than, equal to, or greater than 6,000. For the same types of reasons, the number of in-migrants to the city over the period cannot be ascertained from the NHI data.

On the other hand, a meaningful mobility rate can be calculated from the NHI data as well as from the statistics of the 1940 and 1950 Censuses. The percentage of the population or households currently living in the community who moved within the past two (or one or five) years can be computed. Communities in which the percentage of recent movers is relatively high might be characterized as "residentially mobile" communities; those in which the percentage of recent movers is relatively low might be characterized as "residentially stable" communities. From the NHI (Table 2, Vol. III), it can be ascertained that 284,000 of the 1,133,000 households living in the City of Chicago at the close of 1956 had moved at least once within the preceding two years or that 26 per cent of the households in the city were recent movers. However, we cannot break this mobility rate down into a component accounted for by in-migrants to the city and a component accounted for by intra-city movement of city residents for the reasons mentioned earlier.

Special note should be taken that the NHI concerns the "mobility of households" which is more difficult to conceptualize and measure than the more common "mobility of individuals." Household movement confounds the moves of intact households with the moves of households which are undergoing formation, dissolution, or change in composition. A good deal of household movement is of the latter type. A move to a new dwelling often is engendered by changes in the household itself. For example, upon the death of her spouse, a widow may seek new dwelling quarters. The birth of another child may lead the family to seek more spacious living quarters. The departure of children from the parental home may lead a married couple to seek smaller living quarters. In the NHI, recent-mover households were classified as "essentially the same" before and after the move provided the household head was the same at both locations; all other recent-mover households were grouped together. In other words, moves were dichotomized as those which involved no change in headship and those which involved a change in headship. This criterion of classification—change in headship—

seemingly results in some difficulty. Consider, for example, a couple who establish their household upon marriage in a dwelling not previously occupied by either spouse. If prior to marriage the husband was living as a primary individual, i.e., he maintained his own household, the move to the new dwelling entailed no change in headship and is classified as a move of an "essentially-the-same" household. If, prior to marriage, the wife was living as a primary individual and the husband lived, say, as a lodger, i.e., he did not maintain his own household, the move to the new dwelling entailed a change in headship and is classified as an "other type" of move. For at least some purposes, the common factor in these two cases—move engendered by marriage—is more important than their difference with regard to change in headship. As an additional complication, households were classified as recent movers or non-recent movers on the basis of when a member of the present household first moved to the dwelling rather than when the household head first moved to the dwelling. Thus, a couple who establish their household upon marriage in a dwelling previously occupied by the wife would not be designated recent movers although the head had lived in the dwelling less than two years.

It should be made clear, however, that the issue is not simply the consistency of definitions used in the NHI survey or the fact that classification in terms of one criterion obscures other relevant bases of classification. The notion of household mobility itself requires careful study. On the surface, the notion seems quite simple. A household moved from one dwelling to another. If a married couple with one child move from one dwelling to another, a move of an intact household clearly has occurred. However, if a married couple with one child move from one dwelling to another which they share with an elderly relative, has a household moved or has one household been dissolved and another formed? If the survivors of a married couple with one child move from one dwelling to another upon the death of the husband, has a household moved or has one household been dissolved and another formed? It is by no means clear how much change in composition a "household" can undergo and still be regarded as a continuing household. We do not even attempt to resolve these problems here, but we regard as critical the question: When is a household a household?

Leaving aside conceptual problems of the type just alluded to, the NHI data do permit the calculation of a meaningful mobility rate. Such a rate, which is computed by dividing the number of recent-mover households by the total number of households, can be calculated for each of the six SMA's. Although figures on recent-movers are published for central city and metropolitan ring respectively within each SMA, the total number of households in the respective areas is available only for Chicago and Philadelphia. The lack of appropriate bases to which to relate the recent-mover figures hampers comparison of central cities and metropolitan rings in terms of residential mobility.

The proportion of recent movers in each area is shown in Table 4–5. The rate of residential mobility is substantially higher in Los Angeles than in the other SMA's, 39 as compared with 22 to 28 per cent. Our conjecture is that the relatively high mobility rate in Los Angeles reflects a relatively high rate of in-migration to the Los Angeles SMA. The fact that the expansion of the Los Angeles housing inventory in the post-1950 period was more rapid than in the other SMA's is consistent with this supposition. On the basis of the data for Chicago and Philadelphia, it would appear that residential mobility is only slightly, if at all, lower in the cities than in their metropolitan rings. Following our earlier line of conjecture, this would imply that the rate of in-migration to the central city was about the same as the rate of in-migration to its suburban ring. This could be consistent with the relatively low growth rates observed in the central cities if their out-migration rates were substantially greater than those obtaining in the respective metropolitan rings. In any case, it seems clear that allowance must be made for inter-area variation in rates of in-migration before it can be inferred that movement within the area varies from one SMA or city to another.

The mobility rates for households who own their present dwelling are consistently lower than the rates for households who are renters. It may be that the relatively high mobility rate among renters is indicative of their relatively high intra-area movement; or perhaps disproportionate numbers of the in-migrants enter the rental market on arrival in the area. The SMA's vary markedly with respect to the tenure-specific mobility rates. Twelve per cent of the present owners in the Boston SMA as compared with 26 per cent of the present owners in the Los Angeles SMA have occupied their dwellings less than two years. Only 27 per cent of the present renters in the New York area as compared with 58 per cent of the present renters in Los Angeles are classified as recent movers.

In Table 4–5, distributions of households by length of residence in the present dwelling are shown for each area. In each area, the proportion of households reporting that they moved to their present dwelling in 1956, the most recent year, is higher than the proportion of households reporting that they moved to their present dwelling in the year 1955 or the year 1954. This should not be taken to mean that the rate of household mobility accelerated in the terminal year, 1956. Rather the finding is consistent with other evidence that there exists a highly mobile segment of the population which changes dwellings on a more or less annual basis and which always will appear among movers in the terminal year. Were a survey to be taken at the close of 1957, the proportion of households reporting that they

## Table 4-5
## Residential Mobility Rates: Selected Standard Metropolitan Areas and Cities, 1956 and 1950

| ITEM | STANDARD METROPOLITAN AREA | | | | | | CITY | |
| --- | --- | --- | --- | --- | --- | --- | --- | --- |
| | Boston | Chicago | Detroit | Los Angeles | New York | Phila-delphia | Chicago | Phila-delphia |
| **Percentage of households moving to present dwelling in 1955 or 1956** | | | | | | | | |
| All households | 22 | 27 | 28 | 39 | 23 | 23 | 26 | 21 |
| Owners | 12 | 20 | 19 | 26 | 16 | 14 | 14 | 11 |
| Renters | 32 | 34 | 49 | 58 | 27 | 44 | 32 | 38 |
| **Percentage increase in housing inventory, 1950 to 1957** | 10 | 17 | 26 | 40 | 17 | 22 | 5 | 7 |
| **Year moved to present (1956) dwelling (per cent distribution)** | | | | | | | | |
| All households | 100 | 100 | 100 | 100 | 100 | 100 | 100 | 100 |
| 1956 | 14 | 18 | 17 | 26 | 13 | 13 | 18 | 13 |
| 1955 | 8 | 9 | 11 | 14 | 10 | 10 | 8 | 8 |
| 1954 | 11 | 13 | 10 | 13 | 9 | 7 | 14 | 8 |
| 1950 to 1953 | 22 | 23 | 25 | 22 | 24 | 26 | 24 | 25 |
| 1949 or earlier | 44 | 37 | 37 | 26 | 44 | 44 | 36 | 47 |
| **Percentage movers, 1950 (Per cent of population 1 year old and over living in present dwelling less than one year)** | 13 | 16 | 17 | 26 | 12 | 13 | 15 | 12 |

Source: Table 2-2; 1956 NHI, Vol. III, Table 2; and 1950 Census of Population, Vol. II, Part I, Table 86.

moved to their present dwelling in 1956 probably would be about the same as the proportion reporting that they moved to their present dwelling in the year 1955 or the year 1954. A sizeable number of the households which moved in 1956 would have moved again in 1957 and, hence, would appear as movers in the terminal year, 1957. A comparison of the proportion of households reporting that they moved to their dwelling in 1956 with the proportion of the 1950 population reporting that they had lived in their present (1950) dwelling for less than a year provides further evidence that there has been no acceleration in area-specific mobility rates. The proportions are virtually identical on an area-by-area basis.

Of the recent-mover households with the same head at present and previous residences currently living in the central city or cities of the SMA's, a majority reported their previous residence within the same central city or cities. The proportion with present and previous residence in the same city (or cities) ranged from 67 per cent in Los Angeles City to 91 per cent in New York, Jersey City, and Newark, the central cities of the New York SMA (see Table 4–6). Of the recent movers currently residing in the metropolitan ring, a majority reported their previous residence as in the same metropolitan ring. The proportion with present and previous residence in the same ring ranged from 53 per cent in the ring of the Detroit SMA to 79 per cent in the ring of the Boston SMA. These findings suggest the existence of a "city housing market" and a "ring housing market" within the metropolitan market. Vacancies occurring in the city appear most likely to be filled by city residents, whereas vacancies occurring in the ring are more likely to be filled by ring residents. Although there is considerable variation from area to area, a city's suburban ring and the remainder of the nation are equally important sources of recent movers in the city. The central city of a suburban ring is only a slightly more important source of recent movers in the ring than is the remainder of the nation. Going somewhat beyond a strict interpretation of the data, it seems that the mobility patterns are far more complicated than is implied by the notion that in-migrants come to the central city and central city residents filter outward to the suburban ring. The proportion of recent movers reporting their last previous residence outside the SMA tends to be slightly higher in the ring than in the central city. The proportion of recent movers currently living in the central city who report their last previous residence in its suburban ring is relatively small, but nonetheless is evidence of a counter-flow to the publicized city-to-ring movement. The nature of the mobility statistics and the lack of appropriate bases to which to relate them make it impossible to unscramble the streams of movement toward and within the metropolitan areas with any precision.

From the mobility statistics of the NHI, we can infer that one of every five households in a metropolitan area will move at least once in a two-year period. On an annual basis, the rate of residential mobility is on the order of one out of eight households, or 12 per cent. There is no evidence of acceleration in the mobility rate since 1950. Our conjecture is that areas with relatively high mobility rates are experiencing a comparatively heavy in-migration from other parts of the nation although we cannot measure volume or rate of in-migration from the NHI data. Over four-fifths of the moves which terminate in a metropolitan area involve a change from one dwelling to another within the same area rather than in-movement from other parts of the nation; however, in part, the intra-area moves may be attributable to high mobility on the part of relatively recent in-migrants who are seeking suitable dwelling quarters. Patterns of movement within the metropolitan area cannot be discerned readily from the NHI statistics. However, a majority of the moves terminating in the central city involve change from one

## Table 4-6
### Locations of Present and Previous Residences for Recent-Mover Households: Selected Standard Metropolitan Areas and Cities, 1956

| ITEM | AREA | | | | | | |
|---|---|---|---|---|---|---|---|
| | Boston | Chicago | Detroit | Los Angeles | New York | Phila- delphia |
| Percentage of recent-mover households with same head in previous dwelling: | | | | | | |
| Present dwelling in SMA | 81 | 85 | 85 | 86 | 79 | 84 |
| Present dwelling in central city | 80 | 83 | 85 | 82 | 80 | 81 |
| Present dwelling in metropolitan ring | 82 | 88 | 85 | 89 | 77 | 86 |
| *Recent movers, same head:* | | | | | | |
| Percentage at present living in SMA with last previous residence in SMA | 90 | 88 | 88 | 83 | 91 | 87 |
| Percentage at present living in city with last previous residence: | | | | | | |
| In city | 79 | 87 | 83 | 67 | 81 | 91 |
| In ring | 14 | 3 | 7 | 19 | 11 | 3 |
| Outside SMA | 7 | 10 | 10 | 14 | 8 | 6 |
| Percentage at present living in ring with last previous residence: | | | | | | |
| In ring | 79 | 67 | 53 | 57 | 67 | 62 |
| In city | 10 | 19 | 33 | 25 | 21 | 19 |
| Outside SMA | 11 | 14 | 14 | 18 | 12 | 19 |

Source: 1956 NHI, Vol. III, Table 14.

dwelling to another within the city. A majority of the moves terminating in the metropolitan ring involve change from one dwelling to another within the ring. Although we cannot estimate the volumes of the city-to-ring and ring-to-city flows, it is clear that they are substantial. A tenth to a third of the moves terminating in the ring originated in the city. Three per cent to a fifth of the moves terminating in the city originated in the ring. Measurement of these streams of movement must await the results of the 1960 Censuses.

*Part II*

# HOUSING DIFFERENTIALS IN THE CITY OF CHICAGO

# Introduction to Part II

A UNIQUE BODY OF DATA on housing in the City of Chicago was obtained through the CSNHI (Chicago Supplement to the National Housing Inventory). At the outset, it was clear that we could not exhaust the analytical possibilities of these data within a reasonable time-cost budget. Our decision was to organize the data around three "problems" which seem to have received rather wide attention—differentials in the housing of lower-income and higher-income families, of white and nonwhite families, and of "younger" and "older" families.

Chapter 5 focuses on the housing of families with different income levels. Families with limited incomes are contrasted with higher-income families in terms of their characteristics and those of their dwellings. The impact of public housing on the housing conditions of lower-income families is sketched briefly. The chapter closes with an extended discussion of the relationship between income and housing expenditures, with particular emphasis on the interpretation of observed relationships.

Major attention is given the differences which obtain between the housing of white families and the housing of nonwhite families in Chapter 6. First, some of the ways in which the living arrangements and occupancy patterns of white families differ from those of nonwhite families are explored. The interrelations among quality of dwelling, rent paid for dwelling, and income of the occupant for white and nonwhite families then are investigated. Finally, variation in the housing conditions of white and nonwhite households residing in different parts of the city are examined.

The analyses of housing conditions in Chapter 7 are organized around the stages of the family life cycle. Comparisons are made among "young couples," "families with small children," "older families with children," and "older couples" with respect to such characteristics as frequency of home ownership and prevalence of substandard housing. The housing of persons sixty-five years of age or older is singled out for more extensive examination.

The reader will note that some topics are treated rather fully, whereas in other cases only a brief descriptive sketch is presented. This variability stems in part from differences in the amount of data available for analysis and in part from predilections of the authors. It perhaps is worth noting that the special tabulations were not designed solely for analytical use in frameworks of the type we have chosen. In fact, a major purpose of the Chicago supplementation was to obtain statistics which would be useful in the operations of local housing agencies. Perhaps the analyses reported in Part II will serve a multipurpose function as did the tabulation program.

# 5

# Housing Lower-Income Families

AT ONE TIME or another, most of us have spoken of "lower-income families" or "middle-income families" or "higher-income families." We have some general notion of the kinds of families to which we refer; but we probably would be hard put to specify the income range of, say, "lower-income families." Inasmuch as there is no clear cut, generally accepted definition of a lower-income family, it seems appropriate to consider alternative definitions.

One approach is to define as lower-income families all families with income of less than a specified amount. Concretely, suppose we say lower-income families are those reporting a family income of less than $2,000. Lower-income families then would comprise a sixth of all families in the United States in 1956. A twelfth of the families in the largest urbanized areas as compared with two-fifths of the rural-farm families would be lower-income. An eighth of the families living in the North Central region and a fourth of those in the South would be classified as lower-income (Bureau of the Census, 1958). Under this criterion, 6 per cent of the families living in Chicago at the beginning of 1957 would be classified as lower-income. Some 13 per cent of the families living in the City in 1950 and about 70 per cent of the families living in Chicago in 1935–36 (Department of Labor, 1939a, Tabular Summary, Section A, Table 3) would be classified as lower-income. Inasmuch as the cost of roughly equivalent goods and services varies through time and among areas, we can not assume that the relative economic position of lower-income families, so defined, is constant.

An alternative approach is to array the families in order of increasing income and designate the first fifth or other specified proportion of the distribution lower-income families. In this case, the proportion of families classified as lower-income is constant from area to area and from time to time although the maximum income of a lower-income family will vary. For example, let us define lower-income families as the lowest fifth of the distribution of families by income. The maximum income of a lower-income family is $2,500 in the nation as a whole, $3,500 in the largest urbanized areas, $1,000 in the rural-farm population; the maximum is $4,000 for families living in Chicago in 1956 as compared with $750 for families living in the City in 1935–36. We cannot assume that the real income of lower-income families, so defined, is invariant; but the economic disadvantage of lower-income families relative to other families would be more or less constant if the inequality of income distribution remained more or less constant.

For our special analyses, we have chosen a definition of the second type, although we recognize that the absolute and relative economic position of lower-income families will still differ somewhat among areas and through time. For analytical purposes, we will classify families in the lowest fifth of the income distribution as lower-income. For primary families living in Chicago at the beginning of 1957 this corresponds with families reporting family incomes of less than $4,000 for 1956. Families with incomes of $4,000 to $7,999, about three-fifths of all families, are classified as middle-income; and families with incomes of $8,000 or more, about a fifth of all families, are designated higher-income. Insofar as comparative materials for other areas or other time periods are used, lower-income will refer to the lowest fifth of the distribution of families by income, middle-income to the middle three-fifths, and higher-income to the highest fifth.

At the outset, some qualifications should be set forth. We are classifying families as lower-income, middle-income, or higher-income on the basis of their income in a single year, 1956. The family's income in 1956 may have been about the same in real dollars as their average income in say the years 1953–55; on the other hand, it may have been very different. Winnick (1957, p. 43) states:

> A family's income for any single year may sometimes be a deceptive indicator of its average economic position in the community over a longer period of time. This is why many students regard consumption expenditures rather than income to be a more reliable index of economic status, even though consumption (particularly rent) may adjust slowly to changing circumstances.

*124*

Drawing on the general theory of consumption presented by Friedman (1957), Dunsing and Reid (1958, p. 348) state:

> Family income in any one year is looked upon as having two components, described here as permanent and transitory. The permanent component can suitably be looked upon as the systematic component that families count upon to finance their consumption level. It seems highly probable that expenditures in any one year are more closely related to the permanent than to the transitory component.

Recent empirical investigations by Dunsing and Reid (1958) and Muth (1958) suggest that the relationship between housing expenditures and permanent income differs from the relationship between housing expenditures and current income.

At this point, we note that the classification of families by current income employed in these analyses is not the same as a classification of families by permanent income or average economic status. For example, our lower-income category will include families whose income has been relatively low for several years; it also will include families whose income has been higher in past years but dropped sharply in the most recent year. Further, of the families experiencing a reduction in income, some are faced with a temporary reduction brought about by short-term illness or unemployment of a wage earner or failure of a business venture, while others are faced with a longer run reduction such as that accompanying retirement of a wage earner from the labor force. If this decrease in income is temporary, or is regarded as temporary by the family, the family is unlikely to reorganize their pattern of expenditures to conform to their new and lower income level; instead they will become dis-savers, borrowing on their accumulated assets or from other sources to maintain their former pattern of expenditures.

## CHARACTERISTICS OF LOWER-INCOME FAMILIES

At the end of 1956, about 964,000 primary families were living in the City of Chicago. Almost 10 per cent, or 92,000 families, failed to report their family income for 1956. In terms of several of the family and housing characteristics examined here, the families which failed to report their income resemble the families which reported income; with respect to other characteristics, the non-respondents differ from the respondents. We can not exclude the possibility that the income distribution of the non-respondents differs significantly from that of the respondents; but we have little basis for inferring the magnitude or direction of the differential.

Of the primary families reporting income, some 200,000 (23 per cent) reported that their family income in 1956 was less than $4,000—the families here designated as lower-income families. About 488,000 families (56 per cent) reported incomes of $4,000 to $7,999; this is the group of families classified as middle-income. Higher income families include the 184,000 families (21 per cent) reporting incomes of $8,000 or more.

Selected comparisons of lower-income, middle-income, and higher-income families are shown in Table 5–1. Home owners are under-represented among the lower-income families. Lower-income families are more likely to occupy substandard housing. Nonwhites are over-represented among the lower-income families. Normal family groups are under-represented among lower-income families. A high proportion of the lower-income families are headed by older persons. Lower-income families include a child somewhat less often than do middle-income families; but the proportion including a child is about the same for lower-income and higher-income families. On the

126

## Table 5–1
## Selected Characteristics of Lower-Income, Middle-Income, and Higher-Income Families: City of Chicago, 1956

| CHARACTERISTIC | ALL PRIMARY FAMILIES | FAMILY INCOME IN 1956 | | | | | |
|---|---|---|---|---|---|---|---|
| | | LESS THAN $4,000 | | | $4,000 TO $7,999 | $8,000 OR MORE | NOT REPORTED |
| | | All | Less than $3,000 | $3,000 to $3,999 | | | |
| All primary families (in thousands) | 964 | 200 | 97 | 102 | 488 | 184 | 92 |
| Home ownership (per cent of occupied units owner-occupied) | 37 | 22 | 21 | 22 | 36 | 53 | 38 |
| Substandard housing (per cent of units substandard) | 11 | 27 | 32 | 22 | 9 | 3 | 9 |
| Nonwhite occupancy (per cent nonwhite) | 19 | 39 | 37 | 41 | 16 | 8 | 15 |
| Normal families (per cent husband-wife families, no nonrelatives) | 85 | 74 | 66 | 81 | 88 | 90 | 86 |
| Older heads (per cent heads 65 or more) | 12 | 21 | 27 | 15 | 9 | 8 | 14 |
| Children (per cent with own child[ren] under 18) | 53 | 48 | 43 | 52 | 58 | 50 | 40 |
| Family size (median number of persons in family) | 3.1 | 2.5 | 2.4 | 2.9 | 3.2 | 3.5 | 2.9 |

Source: CSNHI, Tables 4–3, 4–5, 8–1, 9–6, and unpublished tabulations.

average, lower-income families are smaller than middle-income or higher-income families.

Turning to characteristics of the lower-income families themselves, we observe that a fifth are home owners. About a fourth occupy dwellings which are dilapidated and/or have inadequate plumbing facilities. Two-fifths are nonwhite. Three-fourths consist of a married couple and their relatives, if any. A fifth are headed by a person sixty-five years old or over. Half include a child under eighteen who is related to the family head. Median family size is 2.5 persons.

From this brief overview, it is evident that home ownership occurs relatively infrequently among lower-income families. It also is clear that these families have somewhat limited access to standard housing. However, the available summary measures of family composition present a mixed picture.

If home owners and renters are examined separately, the picture becomes clearer. Some distinctive characteristics of lower-income owners and renters can be seen in Figure 5–1. As the data in Table 5–2 show, the proportion of lower-income home owners occupying substandard dwellings is relatively small, although it is greater than the proportion substandard among middle-income and higher-income home owners. About 6 per cent of the lower-income home owners occupied substandard dwellings as compared with 1 per cent for the other groups. When we turn to family characteristics, the lower-income families differ markedly from other families. The family head is sixty-five years old or over in 49 per cent of the lower-income families, 13 per cent of the middle-income families, and 11 per cent of the higher-income families. The proportion of families including at least one child is 30 per cent of the lower-income families, 59 per cent for the middle-income families, and 54 per cent for the higher-income families. The median number of persons in the family is 2.3 for lower-income families, 3.5

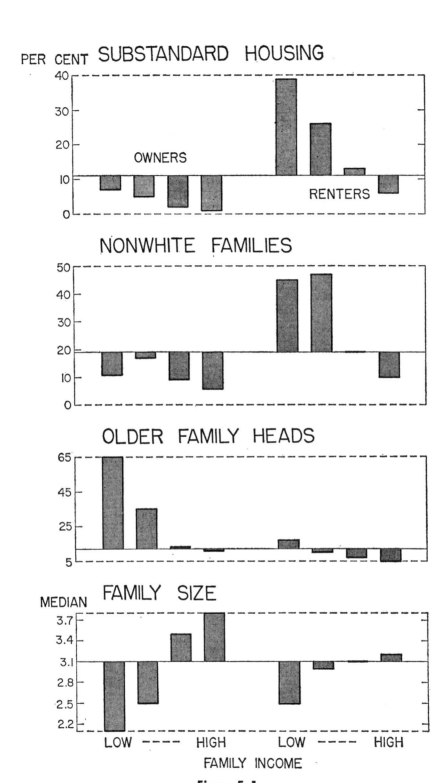

**Figure 5–1**

*Selected Characteristics of Families by Income and Tenure: City of Chicago, 1956. (Source: Tables 5–2 and 5–3) [Base line: per cent or median for all families.]*

## Table 5-2
## Selected Characteristics of Owner-Occupant Families by Income, City of Chicago, 1956

| CHARACTERISTIC | ALL PRIMARY FAMILIES | FAMILY INCOME IN 1956 | | | | | |
| --- | --- | --- | --- | --- | --- | --- | --- |
| | | LESS THAN $4,000 | | | $4,000 TO $7,999 | $8,000 OR MORE | NOT REPORTED |
| | | All | Less than $3,000 | $3,000 to $3,999 | | | |
| All owners (in thousands) | 353 | 43 | 21 | 22 | 178 | 98 | 35 |
| Substandard housing (per cent of units substandard) | 2 | 6 | 7 | 5 | 2 | 1 | ... |
| Nonwhite occupancy (per cent nonwhite) | 9 | 14 | 11 | 17 | 9 | 6 | 11 |
| Normal families (per cent husband-wife families, no nonrelatives) | 86 | 78 | 72 | 83 | 87 | 90 | 83 |
| Older heads (per cent heads 65 or more) | 17 | 49 | 65 | 35 | 13 | 11 | 12 |
| Children (per cent with own child[ren] under 18) | 53 | 30 | 18 | 41 | 59 | 54 | 46 |
| Family size (median number of persons in family) | 3.4 | 2.3 | 2.1 | 2.5 | 3.5 | 3.8 | 3.4 |

... 0.5 per cent or less.
Source: CSNHI, Tables 4–3, 4–4, 4–5, 8–1, 9–6, and unpublished tabulations.

for middle-income families, and 3.8 for higher-income families. In sum, the data suggest that within the owner sector, lower-income families are likely to consist of an older family head with one or two adult relatives; and the family infrequently occupies a substandard dwelling.

We have subclassified the lower-income families who are home owners into two groups—those with 1956 family incomes of less than $3,000 and those with incomes of $3,000 to $3,999. The major differences between the subgroups pertain to the proportion of older heads and the proportion of families with children. We already have noted that about half the lower-income families as compared with a tenth of the middle- and higher-income families are headed by persons sixty-five years old or over. Within the lower-income group, two-thirds of the families with incomes of less than $3,000 as compared with one-third of the families with incomes of $3,000 to $3,999 have older heads. We also pointed out that three-tenths of the lower-income families as compared with nearly six-tenths of the middle- and upper-income families include a minor child of the family head. Within the lower-income group, a fifth of the families with incomes of less than $3,000 as compared with two-fifths of the families with incomes of $3,000 to $3,999 include at least one child. The generalization that within the owner sector lower-income families are likely to consist of an older family head with one or two adult relatives is a particularly apt description of the group with incomes of less than $3,000.

It is primarily within the rental sector that lower-income families experience difficulty in securing standard housing; and the bulk of the lower-income families, four-fifths, are concentrated within the rental sector. About 32 per cent of the lower-income renter families as compared with 13 per cent of the middle-income and 6 per cent of the higher-income renter families occupy substandard housing. As was indicated earlier, less than 6 per cent of the home owners in each broad income group have substandard dwellings.

Selected characteristics of lower-income, middle-income, and higher-income families in the rental sector are shown in Table 5–3. The proportion nonwhite is considerably higher for lower-income renters than for middle-income or higher-income renters or for the home owners. Nearly half the lower-income renters (46 per cent) are nonwhite, as compared with a fifth of the middle-income renters, a tenth of the higher-income renters, and a tenth of the home owners. In fact, this difference in racial composition among the income groups is the most striking feature of Table 5–3.

In terms of family characteristics, we note that normal families are under-represented among the lower-income families. Normal families account for about 73 per cent of the lower-income renter families, as compared with about 89 per cent of the middle- and higher-income renter families. Older heads are somewhat over-represented among the lower-income families. On the average, family size is somewhat smaller for the lower-income families. Differences among income groups with respect to family characteristics are less marked in the rental sector than among home owners.

Subclassification of the lower-income renter families into those with incomes of less than $3,000 and those with incomes of $3,000 to $3,999 brings out the fact that the proportion of normal families is substantially lower in the former than in the latter group. Normal families account for only 64 per cent of the families with incomes of less than $3,000 as compared with 80 per cent of the families with incomes of $3,000 to $3,999; about 89 per cent of the middle- and upper-income families are normal families. Disproportionate numbers of the families with incomes of less than $3,000 are headed by older persons—17 per cent as compared with 10 per cent of the

## Table 5–3
### Selected Characteristics of Renter-Occupant Families by Income: City of Chicago, 1956

| CHARACTERISTIC | ALL PRIMARY FAMILIES | FAMILY INCOME IN 1956 | | | | | |
| --- | --- | --- | --- | --- | --- | --- | --- |
| | | LESS THAN $4,000 | | | $4,000 TO $7,999 | $8,000 OR MORE | NOT REPORTED |
| | | All | Less than $3,000 | $3,000 to $3,999 | | | |
| All renters (in thousands) | 611 | 157 | 77 | 80 | 310 | 86 | 58 |
| Substandard housing (per cent of units substandard) | 17 | 32 | 39 | 26 | 13 | 6 | 15 |
| Nonwhite occupancy (per cent nonwhite) | 25 | 46 | 45 | 47 | 19 | 10 | 18 |
| Normal families (per cent husband-wife families, no nonrelatives) | 84 | 73 | 64 | 80 | 88 | 90 | 88 |
| Older heads (per cent heads 65 or more) | 9 | 13 | 17 | 10 | 7 | 5 | 15 |
| Children (per cent with own child[ren] under 18) | 52 | 53 | 50 | 56 | 57 | 45 | 37 |
| Family size (median number of persons in family) | 3.0 | 2.7 | 2.5 | 3.0 | 3.1 | 3.2 | 2.7 |

Source: CSNHI, Tables 4–3, 4–4, 4–5, 8–1, 9–6, and unpublished tabulations.

families in the income group $3,000 to $3,999 and on the order of 7 per cent of the middle- and upper-income families. And disproportionate numbers of the families with incomes of less than $3,000 occupy substandard dwellings—39 per cent as compared with 26 per cent of the families with incomes of $3,000 to $3,999, 13 per cent of the middle-income families, and 6 per cent of the higher-income families.

Finally, we call attention to a series of differences between lower-income home owners and lower-income renters. Only 6 per cent of the lower-income home owners as compared with 32 per cent of the lower-income renters occupy substandard dwellings. Only 14 per cent of the owners as compared with 46 per cent of the renters are nonwhite. Only 30 per cent of the owner families as compared with 53 per cent of the renter families include a minor child of the family head. About 49 per cent of the owner-occupant families are headed by an older person whereas only 13 per cent of the renter-occupant families have older heads. These differences lead us to suspect that the lower-income home owners consist, in large part, of older families whose relative economic position was more favorable in the past. Many of these families can supplement their current income by drawing on accumulated savings. Their dwellings, by and large, are of standard quality. On the other hand, nearly nine-tenths of the lower-income renter families are headed by persons under sixty-five years of age and slightly over half include minor children. About a third of the lower-income renters occupy dwellings which are dilapidated or have inadequate plumbing facilities. The majority of families with low permanent income, or a persistent economic disadvantage, probably are found in the rental sector.

Detailed information on the composition of lower-income families and families with larger incomes in the rental sector is shown in Table 5–4. Lower-income renters include relatively few normal families and relatively many atypical family groups, i.e., families who share their dwelling with nonrelatives and/or families in which the spouse of the family head is absent. Among all lower-income renter families, 27 per cent are atypical —36 per cent of the families with incomes of less than $3,000 and 20 per cent of the families with incomes of $3,000 to $3,999; among the other renter families, only 11 per cent are atypical. We can subclassify the atypical families into two groups, atypical families with child(ren) and atypical families without children. The proportion of atypical families without children is more or less constant among the income groups, on the order of 10 per cent. But the proportion of atypical families with children decreases sharply as income rises. About 24 per cent of the families with incomes of less than $3,000 are atypical families with minor children; atypical families with a child account for 9 per cent of the families with incomes of $3,000 to $3,999 and 3 per cent of the families with incomes of $4,000 or more.

Table 5–5 shows the proportion of families in each income and type-of-household group in substandard housing. Recall that a third of all lower-income renters as compared with a tenth of all middle- and upper-income renters occupy substandard dwellings. Within each type-of-family group, the proportion substandard among lower-income families is two or three times as high as the proportion substandard among the other families. Looking at the data from a different standpoint, we note that among both lower-income families as well as other families the proportion substandard is considerably higher for atypical families with child(ren) than for any other type-of-family group. Half the lower-income atypical families with child(ren) and a fourth of the other atypical families with

## Table 5–4
## Percentage Distribution of Lower-Income and Other Renter-Occupant Families by Type of Family: City of Chicago, 1956

| TYPE OF FAMILY | ALL PRIMARY FAMILIES | FAMILY INCOME IN 1956 | | | | |
| --- | --- | --- | --- | --- | --- | --- |
| | | LESS THAN $4,000 | | | $4,000 OR MORE | NOT REPORTED |
| | | All | Less than $3,000 | $3,000 to $3,999 | | |
| All renters | 100 | 100 | 100 | 100 | 100 | 100 |
| Normal families (husband, wife, no nonrelatives) | 84 | 73 | 64 | 80 | 89 | 88 |
| Married couple (husband, wife) | 29 | 31 | 33 | 29 | 27 | 35 |
| Married couple with one child (couple, own child under 18) | 16 | 12 | 8 | 15 | 17 | 19 |
| Married couple with relatives including child (couple, child[ren], other relative[s], if any) | 30 | 25 | 18 | 32 | 34 | 15 |
| Married couple with relative[s] other than child (couple, relative[s] other than child) | 10 | 5 | 5 | 5 | 10 | 18 |
| Atypical families (family with nonrelative[s] or family with spouse of head absent) | 16 | 27 | 36 | 20 | 11 | 12 |
| Atypical family with child[ren] | 6 | 16 | 24 | 9 | 3 | 3 |
| Atypical family without child | 9 | 11 | 12 | 11 | 8 | 9 |

Source: CSNHI, Tables 4–3, 4–5, 8–1, 8–3, 8–4, and unpublished tabulations.

Table 5–5
## Percentage of Renter-Occupant Families Occupying Substandard Dwellings by Income Group and Type of Family: City of Chicago, 1956

| TYPE OF FAMILY† | ALL PRIMARY FAMILIES | FAMILY INCOME IN 1956 | | | | |
|---|---|---|---|---|---|---|
| | | LESS THAN $4,000 | | | $4,000 OR MORE | NOT REPORTED |
| | | All | Less than $3,000 | $3,000 to $3,999 | | |
| All renters | 17 | 32 | 39 | 26 | 11 | 15 |
| Normal families | 15 | 30 | 35 | 26 | 11 | 13 |
| Married couple | 18 | 34 | 38 | 30 | 11 | 17 |
| Married couple with one child | 11 | 21 | 18* | 22 | 8 | 13 |
| Married couple with relatives including child | 17 | 33 | 44 | 27 | 13 | 6* |
| Married couple with relative[s] other than child | 9 | 16* | 21* | 12* | 7 | 11 |
| Atypical families | 26 | 38 | 45 | 26 | 14 | 29* |
| Atypical family with child[ren] | 38 | 47 | 54 | 30* | 24 | 17* |
| Atypical family without child | 17 | 25 | 26* | 23* | 10 | 32* |

* Based on less than 50 sample cases.
† The types of families below are defined in Table 5–4.
Source: CSNHI, Tables 4–4, 4–6, 8–2, 8–6, 8–7, and unpublished tabulations.

child(ren) are in substandard housing. These analyses point to the lower-income atypical families with children as a group with most limited access to standard housing.

## LOWER-INCOME FAMILIES
## AND PUBLIC HOUSING

At the beginning of 1957, some 15,000 dwelling units were available in projects of the Chicago Housing Authority. About 97 per cent of these dwellings were occupied by family groups (Chicago Housing Authority, 1957, Table 31). Residence in CHA (Chicago Housing Authority) projects is restricted to lower-income groups; and dwellings in the projects are of standard quality. We now pose the question: to what extent do the housing conditions of the lower-income families, described in the preceding section, reflect housing in CHA projects?

The available relevant data are summarized in Table 5–6. Dwellings in CHA projects account for only 2.5 per cent of all rental units in the City. However, dwellings in CHA projects account for about 10 per cent of all units rented by families with incomes of less than $3,000, about 4 per cent of all units rented by families with incomes of $3,000 to $3,999, and 2 per cent of all units rented by families with an income of $4,000 to $4,999. The proportion of families with an income of $5,000 or more renting units in CHA projects is negligible. Although dwellings in CHA projects are a small percentage of the City's rental housing supply, the projects house a tenth of the renter families with incomes below $3,000.

Three per cent of all standard rental housing in the City is accounted for by housing in CHA projects. However, about 15 per cent of all standard housing rented by families with incomes of less than $3,000 is located in CHA projects. Dwellings in CHA projects account for 6 per cent of all standard housing rented by families with an income of $3,000 to $3,999 and 2 per cent of all standard units rented by families with an income of $4,000 to $4,999. Dwellings in CHA projects provide a sixth of the standard housing rented by families with incomes of less than $3,000 although they make up only 3 per cent of the City's supply of standard rental housing.

The proportion of families living in substandard dwellings is substantially higher for lower-income renters than for renters with larger incomes. For example, nearly 40 per cent of the renter families with incomes below $3,000 as compared with 8 per cent of the renter families with incomes of $5,000 or more were living in substandard units. If comparisons are made among families living outside CHA projects, the differences among income groups in proportion occupying substandard housing become sharper. Among families living outside CHA projects, 43 per cent of the renters with incomes below $3,000 as compared with 8 per cent of the renters within incomes of $5,000 or more occupied substandard units.

Nonwhite occupancy is more frequent in the CHA projects than in the lower-income rental sector as a whole. About 81 per cent of the units in CHA projects are occupied by nonwhites (Chicago Housing Authority, 1957, Table 15). By comparison, nonwhites account for 45 per cent of all families with incomes of less than $3,000 and 47 per cent of the families with incomes of $3,000 to $3,999.

On the average, family size is markedly larger for families occupying units in CHA projects than for all lower-income families in rental units. Median family size for the former group of families is 4.2 persons (Chicago Housing Authority, 1957, Table 21); median family size for all families with incomes of less

**Table 5-6**

**Summary Measures of the Influence of Chicago Housing Authority Projects on Housing Conditions of Renter-Occupant Families in Different Income Groups: City of Chicago, 1956**

| ITEM | All primary families | | FAMILY INCOME IN 1956 | | | | |
| --- | --- | --- | --- | --- | --- | --- | --- |
| | | Less than $2,000 | $2,000 to $2,999 | $3,000 to $3,999 | $4,000 to $4,999 | $5,000 or more |
| All renters (in thousands)* | 611 | 45 | 40 | 88 | 125 | 313 |
| In standard units† | 508 | 26 | 26 | 65 | 104 | 286 |
| In CHA projects‡ | 15.1 | 4.8 | 3.5 | 3.9 | 2.4 | 0.5 |
| Units in CHA projects as a percentage of— | | | | | | |
| All rental units | 2.5 | 10.7 | 8.7 | 4.4 | 1.9 | 0.1 |
| All standard rental units | 3.0 | 18.4 | 13.5 | 6.0 | 2.3 | 0.2 |
| Substandard units as a percentage of all units | 17 | 42 | 35 | 26 | 17 | 8 |
| Substandard units as a percentage of all units outside CHA projects | 17 | 47 | 39 | 28 | 17 | 8 |

* Assumes income distribution of 58,000 families not reporting income identical with that of respondents.

† Assumes income distribution of 49,000 families not reporting income identical with that of respondents; assumes 429 rental units with quality not available are standard.

‡ Families in occupancy 31 March 1957; approximately 500 one-person households included.

Source: CSNHI, Tables 4–3 and 4–4; Chicago Housing Authority, 1957, Table 25.

than $3,000 is 2.5 persons and for all families with incomes of $3,000 to $3,999 the median is 3.0 persons.

About half the families occupying units in CHA projects consist of a married couple with at least one child, whereas about two-fifths of all lower-income families in the rental sector are of this type. Nearly two-fifths of the families occupying units in CHA projects consist of a family head with spouse absent and at least one child, but not more than a sixth of all lower-income families in the rental sector are of this type. Altogether nearly nine-tenths of the families occupying units in CHA projects include at least one child (Chicago Housing Authority, 1957, Table 31), as compared with only half the lower-income families in the rental sector.

The bases of comparison are too few to permit any broad conclusions about selectivity of families occupying units in CHA projects. However, higher nonwhite occupancy, larger families, a higher proportion of families with children, and a higher proportion of atypical family groups appear to differentiate the CHA projects from the remainder of the rental sector.

## RENTS PAID BY LOWER-INCOME FAMILIES

Relationships between rent and income receive a good deal of attention. In fact, we often hear such "rules of thumb" as "a month's rent should not exceed a week's pay." The form of the rent-income relationship also has been generalized. The most frequent observation is that the proportion of income spent on rent decreases as income increases. Occasionally it is noted that the proportion of income spent on rent increases as rent increases. Less frequently it is pointed out that the correlation between a family's rent and their income is rather low.

*Correlation of rent and income on a household basis.* Winnick (1957, p. 43) has called attention to the looseness of relationship between a household's rent and its income. He cites a correlation coefficient of .41 between rent and income, presumably for the United States in 1950. The correlation coefficient is positive in sign, indicating that households paying lower rents have, on the average, lower incomes or, conversely, that households with lower incomes pay on the average lower rents. The square of the correlation coefficient, which can be interpreted as the proportion of total variation in rent among households accounted for by the association of rent and income, is only .17. Thus, only a sixth of the variation among households in rent paid is accounted for by variation among households in income.

We have computed the correlation between gross monthly rent of the dwelling unit and income in 1956 of the primary family or primary individual occupying the unit for the City of Chicago, based on the 641,000 units in the rental sector for which rent and income of occupant are available. The basic table from which we are working is a cross-tabulation of renter households by gross monthly rent (11 intervals ranging from less than $20 to $120 or more) and income in 1956 of the primary family or primary individual (8 intervals ranging from less than $2,000 to $10,000 or more). (The tabulation was included in the "regular" NHI program of the Bureau of the Census. It is more detailed than Table 12, Vol. III, 1956 NHI.) Where $R$ equals gross monthly rent and $I$ equals income in 1956, the coefficient of correlation ($r_{RI}$) equals .42; the square of the correlation coefficient ($r_{RI}^2$) equals .18. Our results are about the same as those reported by Winnick for the United States.

The correlation analysis shows that households paying lower rents have on the average lower incomes; but only a sixth of the total variation in rent among households is accounted for by the association of rent and income. In other words, families with the same income pay a wide range of rents and families paying the same rent vary substantially in their income.

*Rent-income relationships by income.* The positive correlation coefficient between rent and income shows an average tendency for households with lower incomes to pay lower rents. Although households with the same income differ substantially in rent paid, we find that the average rent paid by households with the same income increases as income increases. We first will examine the regression of rent on income graphically.

In Figure 5–2, we show the mean (average) gross monthly rent for households in each of the eight income intervals $(\overline{R}_I)$ with an open circle; for example, the mean gross monthly rent paid by households with incomes of less than $2,000 is $61. The intersection of the two solid lines indicates the mean rent ($79) and the mean income ($5,143) for all households. The solid lines are the least squares regression lines calculated from our cross-tabulation of households by rent and income. One of the solid lines is the "best fit" to the open circles (weighted by the number of cases each represents) plotted in the scattergram if our criterion of "best fit" is to minimize the squared deviations of all dots from the line. The open circles, representing the mean gross monthly rent of households in each of the eight income intervals, lie close to the regression line; this indicates that the regression relationship provides a "good" estimate of the *average* rent paid by households of a given income level. In fact, average rent estimated from the regression line differs by less than $4 from the actual average rent paid by households in each of the eight income intervals. But the relatively low correlation coefficient cited earlier indicates that there is a sub-

*143*

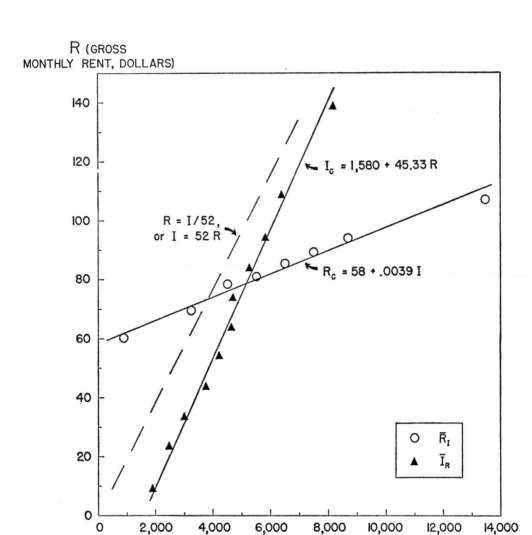

R (GROSS MONTHLY RENT, DOLLARS)

I (ANNUAL INCOME, DOLLARS)

$I_c = 1,580 + 45.33\,R$

$R = I/52$, or $I = 52\,R$

$R_c = 58 + .0039\,I$

○  $\bar{R}_I$
▲  $\bar{I}_R$

**Figure 5–2**
*Scattergrams Depicting the Regressions of Rent on Income and Income on Rent for Renter Households: City of Chicago, 1956. (Source: Tables 5–7 and 5–8)*

stantial dispersion of rents paid by households of a given income about the average rent for households of that income level.

The equation which describes this least squares regression line is $R_c = 58 + .0039I$, where $R$ equals gross monthly rent and $I$ equals annual income. On the basis of the regression relationship, we expect households with no current income ($I = 0$) to pay a gross monthly rent of \$58 and households with a current income of \$1,000 ($I = \$1,000$) to pay a gross monthly rent of \$62, i.e., \$58 + (.0039) (\$1,000), or \$58 + \$4. On the basis of this relationship, we expect an increase of \$1,000 in income to be accompanied by an increase of \$4 (or more precisely \$3.94) in gross monthly rent.

A modification of the "rule of thumb" alluded to earlier also is shown in Figure 5-2: specifically, that "a month's rent should equal a week's pay." Under this rule, gross monthly rent equals annual income divided by fifty-two, the number of weeks per year. The dashed line is a graphic representation of the rule; the equation for the "rule-of-thumb" line is $R = I/52$. On the basis of this relationship, we expect households with no current income to pay a gross monthly rent of \$0 and households with a current income of \$1,000 to pay a gross monthly rent of \$19 (\$1,000/52). In other words, we expect an increase of \$1,000 in income to be accompanied by an increase of \$19 in gross monthly rent. This particular rent/income relationship assumes that at each income level 23 per cent of the annual income is spent for gross rent over a period of a year. It is evident from the scattergram that the "rule of thumb" is an extremely poor description of the relationship which actually obtains between rent and income. We now can consider some reasons why this rule—or more generally any rule which assumes a constant rent/income ratio over all income levels—has low descriptive value.

Let us first introduce the notion of total expenditures. We

define expenditures as income minus savings. Expenditures can be greater than, equal to, or less than income. Savings then can be negative (dis-saving or borrowing), zero, or positive. Within each income group, expenditures will exceed income for some families; however, the proportion of families having a deficit (expenditures exceed income) decreases as the income level increases. And the average net deficit per family decreases as the income level increases. For example, in Chicago in 1935–36, about 70 per cent of the families with an income of $500 to $749 reported a deficit; and the average net deficit for families in this income group amounted to $204. Only 28 per cent of the families with an income of $1,500 to $1,749 reported a deficit, and the average net deficit per family at this income level amounted to $3. (See Department of Labor, 1939b, Table 5; figures cited are for nonrelief native white families.)

To simplify the discussion, let us assume that rent is a constant proportion of total expenditures at each income level. Probably rent tends to constitute a decreasing proportion of total expenditures as income level increases (Department of Labor, 1939b, Table 15), but the general argument remains the same. We now identify: $E$, expenditures; $R'$, annual gross rent (as distinct from $R$, gross monthly rent); $S$, savings; $I$, income. We then assume the following relationships among variables:

$E = I - S$ (by definition);

$R' = KE$, where $K$ is a constant proportion, positive in sign, and less than unity;

$S = d + eI$, where d is negative in sign and e is a constant proportion, positive in sign, and less than unity.

Then, by substitution,

$R' = -Kd + K(1 - e)I$.

Since $K$ and $d$ are constants by hypothesis, the product, $-Kd$, is a constant; we will call it $a$. The term $a$ is necessarily positive because we assumed that $K$ was positive in sign and $d$ was negative in sign. The term $K(1-e)$ also is a constant since $K$ and $e$ are constants by hypothesis; we will call this term $b$. The term $b$ is necessarily positive in sign and less than unity because we assumed that $K$ and $e$ were constant proportions, positive in sign, and less than unity. Given the foregoing relationships between rent and expenditures and between savings and income, the relationship between rent and income is described by an equation of the type $R' = a + bI$. The rent/income ratio, then, decreases as income increases; for we can show that, by substitution,

$$R'/I = (a + bI) / I = (a/I) + b.$$

This exercise in deductive logic is presented to show why we need to take account of income level when we compare rent/income ratios for groups of families classified by other characteristics. Although a family may receive no income in a given year, it continues to make expenditures; to do so it borrows on accumulated assets or from other sources. Among its expenditures will be payments of rental for the dwelling it occupies. Inasmuch as this is the case, rent cannot be a constant proportion of income at all income levels because a constant rent/income ratio implies that families with no current income pay no rent. The foregoing exercise shows that given the types of relationship which obtain between rent and expenditures and between savings and income, the rent/income ratio will decrease as income increases.

It is somewhat difficult to grasp the relationship of the rent/income ratio to income from the scattergram in Figure 5–2. Some readers may find it more convenient to examine the rent-income relationship itself in tabular form. The relevant data are shown in Table 5–7. At the lowest income level (less than $2,000), it appears that gross rent accounts for 80 per cent of income over a period of a year; however, recall that total expenditures are substantially greater than income in the lowest

Table 5–7
**Summary of Regression of Gross Monthly Rent on Annual Income,**
**for Renter-Occupants: City of Chicago, 1956**

| INCOME OF PRIMARY FAMILY OR INDIVIDUAL IN 1956 (I)† | MEAN GROSS MONTHLY RENT | | MEAN RENT/INCOME RATIO | |
|---|---|---|---|---|
| | Observed | Calculated* | Observed | Calculated* |
| | $\bar{R}$ | $\bar{R}_c$ | $12\bar{R}/I$ | $12\bar{R}_c/I$ |
| Less than $2,000 ($906) | $61 | $62 | 80 | 82 |
| $2,000 to $3,999 ($3,243) | $69 | $71 | 26 | 26 |
| $4,000 to $4,999 ($4,500) | $78 | $76 | 21 | 20 |
| $5,000 to $5,999 ($5,500) | $81 | $80 | 18 | 17 |
| $6,000 to $6,999 ($6,500) | $86 | $84 | 16 | 16 |
| $7,000 to $7,999 ($7,500) | $89 | $88 | 14 | 14 |
| $8,000 to $9,999 ($8,692) | $94 | $93 | 13 | 13 |
| $10,000 or more ($13,465) | $107 | $111 | 10 | 10 |

* Calculated from the least squares regression equation $R_c = \$58 + .0039\,I$.
† Income interval and assumed "mid-point."

income groups and, hence, gross rent accounts for considerably less than 80 per cent of total expenditures. For the group with incomes of $2,000 to $3,999, gross rent accounts for some 26 per cent of annual income. The rent/income ratio continues to decrease as income level increases. At the highest income level ($10,000 or more), annual gross rent is only ten per cent of annual gross income.

*Rent-income relationships by rent.* Probably we more often think about rent in relation to income, as is suggested by interest in the rent/income ratio, then about income in relation to rent. Income is by no means the sole determinant of rent, but a household's income does limit the amount of rent it can pay. We cannot think of rent determining, or limiting, income in the same sense. Nonetheless, we may be interested in the relationship of income to rent. For example, what is the average income of households which occupy units with a gross monthly rent of $40 to $49? What proportion of their income is accounted for by gross rent? The correlation analysis has shown that households paying lower rents have on the average lower incomes; but we

*148*

have not yet examined the rent/income ratio in relation to rent.

In Figure 5–2, we show the mean annual income of households in each of the eleven monthly rent groups $(\overline{I}_R)$ with a triangle. For example, the mean income of households occupying units with a gross monthly rent of less than $20 is $1,905. One of the solid lines is the "best fit" to the triangles (weighted by the number of cases each represents) plotted in the scattergram if our criterion of "best fit" is to minimize the squared deviations of all dots from the line. Note that this line which describes the regression of income on rent differs from the least squares regression line of rent on income; this difference will be considered in more detail in the next section. The triangles representing the mean income of households in each of the eleven rent groups lie close to the regression line; this indicates that the regression relationship of income on rent provides a "good" estimate of the *average* income of households occupying units with a given rental. The dashed line is a graphic representation of our modified "rule of thumb" which assumes that the rent/income ratio is constant over all rent intervals. Again it provides a poor fit to the actual data.

The regression of income on gross rent is summarized in tabular form in Table 5–8. Average annual income estimated from the regression line differs by less than $300 from the actual average annual income of households in each of the eleven gross monthly rent intervals; however, recall the relatively low correlation coefficient between rent and income which indicates that households which pay the same rent differ substantially in their income. We also see that the rent/income ratio increases as rent increases. Households occupying units with the lowest gross monthly rent (less than $20) have a rent/income ratio of only 6 per cent; in the rent interval $20 to $29, gross rent accounts for 12 per cent of income over a period of a year. In the highest gross rent intervals ($100 to $119 and

## Table 5–8
### Summary of Regression of Annual Income on Gross Monthly Rent, for Renter-Occupants: City of Chicago, 1956

| GROSS MONTHLY RENT(R)† | | MEAN INCOME OF PRIMARY FAMILY OR INDIVIDUAL IN 1956 | | MEAN RENT/INCOME RATIO | |
|---|---|---|---|---|---|
| | | Observed | Calculated* | Observed | Calculated* |
| | | $\bar{I}$ | $\bar{I}_c$ | $12R/\bar{I}$ | $12R/\bar{I}_c$ |
| Less than $20 | ($10.00) | $1,905 | $2,033 | 6 | 6 |
| $20 to $29 | ($24.50) | $2,479 | $2,690 | 12 | 11 |
| $30 to $39 | ($34.50) | $3,017 | $3,143 | 14 | 13 |
| $40 to $49 | ($44.50) | $3,746 | $3,597 | 14 | 15 |
| $50 to $59 | ($54.50) | $4,262 | $4,050 | 15 | 16 |
| $60 to $69 | ($64.50) | $4,651 | $4,503 | 17 | 17 |
| $70 to $79 | ($74.50) | $4,699 | $4,957 | 19 | 18 |
| $80 to $89 | ($84.50) | $5,320 | $5,410 | 19 | 19 |
| $90 to $99 | ($94.50) | $5,852 | $5,863 | 19 | 19 |
| $100 to $119 | ($109.50) | $6,398 | $6,543 | 21 | 20 |
| $120 or more | ($139.50) | $8,192 | $7,903 | 20 | 21 |

\* Calculated from the least squares regression equation $I_c = \$1,580 + 45.33 R$.
† Rent interval and assumed "mid-point."

$120 or more), households have a rent/income ratio of about 20 per cent.

It may seem somewhat puzzling that rent increased as income increased, the rent/income ratio decreased as income increased, and the rent/income ratio increased as rent increased. To be sure, if rent and income were perfectly correlated, and if the rent/income ratio decreased as income increased, the rent/income ratio also would decrease as rent increased. But recall that only a sixth of the differences in gross rent paid by households living in Chicago was accounted for by differences in income among these households ($r^2_{RI} = .18$). The models with which we have been working greatly simplify the relationship which exists between rent and income on a household-by-household basis. We have described the relationship of rent to income with an equation of the type $R' = a + bI$. Actually an equation describing the relationship of rent to income would be of the type $R' = a + bI + fZ$, where $Z$ represents a whole complex of

*150*

factors, such as size of family, number of children, style of life, family tastes or preferences, which in combination with income determine how much rent the family pays. In addition, of course, we have errors in the measurement of both rent and income. Given the imperfect correlation of rent and income, the regression of rent on income, and the nature of the data with which we are working, we find that the rent/income ratio will necessarily increase as rent increases.

There are two regression equations with which we are concerned. The first, $R_c = a + bI$, is the regression of rent on income; the second, $I_c = A + BR$, is the regression of income on rent. Now $R_c/I$, the rent/income ratio calculated from the regression of rent on income, can be written as $(a/I) + b$; the rent/income ratio, therefore, decreases as income increases. The rent/income ratio calculated from the regression of income on rent, $R/I_c$, can be written as $R/(A + BR)$ or as $1/[(A/R) + B]$. Inasmuch as $bB = r_{RI}^2$ and $b$ is positive in sign, $B$ is positive in sign. If $A$ also is positive in sign, the term $R/I_c$ increases as rent increases. The basic data with which we are working (our 8 by 11 table of households by income in 1956 and gross monthly rent—not reproduced here) show rent and income in positive terms, i.e., we have no category of negative income or negative rent; therefore, given the data, $A$ must be positive in value.

This suggests that our observations that the rent/income ratio decreases with income and the rent/income ratio increases with rent are not independent. In strictly mathematical terms, one does not imply the other. But if (1) the correlation between rent and income is imperfect, (2) the regressions of rent on income and income on rent are linear, (3) one of the foregoing regressions is positive, and (4) rent and income can assume only positive values, then the rent/income ratio will decrease as income increases and the rent/income ratio will increase as rent increases.

*Permanent versus transitory income and rent-income relationships.* From our analyses of rent-income relationships, we conclude: first, the relationship between rent and income is loose on a household basis; second, there is, however, an average tendency for rent to increase as income increases or, conversely, for income to increase as rent increases; third, on the average, the rent/income ratio decreases as income increases; and fourth, on the average, the rent/income ratio increases as rent increases.

In the first part of this chapter, the notion of permanent versus transitory income was introduced. In any given year a family's income can be regarded as the sum of their permanent and transitory incomes. Transitory income can assume either negative (bad luck) or positive (windfall) values; hence, income in a given year can be greater than or less than permanent income. It also was suggested that family expenditures, including expenditures for housing, were geared to the permanent income component rather than to current income (income in a given year). The major generalizations drawn from the foregoing correlation and regression analyses are consistent with propositions deduced from this theory of consumption.

To facilitate discussion, the hypothesized relationship among current income, permanent income, and rent are shown below in schematic form.

| Current income | Permanent income | Rent | Rent/permanent income | Rent/current income |
|---|---|---|---|---|
| Lower | Lower | Lower | Normal | Normal |
| Lower | Middle | Middle | Normal | Higher |
| Lower | Higher | Higher | Normal | Higher |
| Middle | Lower | Lower | Normal | Lower |
| Middle | Middle | Middle | Normal | Normal |
| Middle | Higher | Higher | Normal | Higher |
| Higher | Lower | Lower | Normal | Lower |
| Higher | Middle | Middle | Normal | Lower |
| Higher | Higher | Higher | Normal | Normal |

We first note that the association between current income and rent is imperfect even if we assume the association between permanent income and rent is perfect. For example, the second line in the scheme above is the category "lower current income, middle permanent income, middle rent." A concrete case might be: In the current year, the main earner has a serious illness which causes a temporary drop in income; because the decrease is regarded as temporary, the household does not move to a less expensive dwelling. Or, consider the eighth line, the category "higher current income, middle permanent income, middle rent." A case might be: In the current year, the main earner had an unusually profitable year in the operation of his business; because he does not anticipate that his income will be as high in future years, the household does not move to a more expensive dwelling. We then would expect to find households with the same current income paying different rentals even if we assume no differences among households in size, tastes, and the like. However, if for the majority of households current income is about the same as permanent income, there would be an average tendency for rent to increase as current income increases. The scheme above also shows that the mean rent/income ratio tends to be greater for families with current lower incomes than for families with current higher incomes. Assuming a "normal" ratio of rent to permanent income within each permanent income group we note an upward bias in the rent/income ratios for the lower-current-income groups and a downward bias in the rent/income ratios for the higher-current-income groups. For the middle-current-income groups, the downward and upward biases tend to counteract one another.

Furthermore, the same set of propositions implies that the mean rent/income ratio is lower for families occupying units with lower rentals than for families occupying units with higher

*153*

rentals. A rearrangement of the cells in the scheme shown above brings out this point.

| Rent | Permanent income | Current income | Rent/permanent income | Rent/current income |
|---|---|---|---|---|
| Lower | Lower | Lower | Normal | Normal |
| Lower | Lower | Middle | Normal | Lower |
| Lower | Lower | Higher | Normal | Lower |
| Middle | Middle | Lower | Normal | Higher |
| Middle | Middle | Middle | Normal | Normal |
| Middle | Middle | Higher | Normal | Lower |
| Higher | Higher | Lower | Normal | Higher |
| Higher | Higher | Middle | Normal | Higher |
| Higher | Higher | Higher | Normal | Normal |

We note a downward bias in the rent/income ratios for the households in lower-rent dwellings and an upward bias in the rent/income ratios for the households in higher-rent dwellings. Again the downward and upward biases tend to counteract one another for the households in middle-rent dwellings.

The foregoing discussion does not purport to be a systematic exposition of the implications of Friedman's theory of consumption for rent-income relations on a household basis. It is intended only to suggest that the relationships between rent and income observed in the City of Chicago are consistent with theoretical formulations of expenditure-income patterns.

*Dispersion of rents within income groups.* Up to this point, we have been focusing on mean (average) rent/income ratios for groups of households classified by income, i.e., we have been calculating the ratio of the average rent of households in a given income group to the average income of households in that income group. However, we have called attention to the fact that households in a given income group pay a wide range of rents and consequently spend different proportions of their income on rent. Within a given income group, some households pay rents considerably higher than the group average, some pay rents about the same as the average rent for the group, and others pay rents well below the group average. Rapkin *et al.* (1953, p. 66) have stated:

> . . . an average proportion of income spent on rent can only have meaning if the average describes a true behavior pattern, that is, if the rent expenditures of families in any income class describe a real central tendency in the distribution of rent ratios for that class.

The statement appears in an exposition of theory and methods in housing market analysis; and we should not assume that the authors regard the mean rent or the mean rent/income ratio for households of a given income as useless in all contexts even though there is considerable dispersion about the mean. However, their caution regarding the use of mean rent or mean rent/income ratio suggests that we should look at dispersion about the mean.

It is by no means clear what Rapkin *et al.* would regard as sufficient evidence of a "real central tendency." One of their examples for evaluating central tendency concerns the spread of quartiles of rent distribution for families in a given income group; in the case discussed by them, $(Q_2 - Q_1)/Q_2$ and $(Q_3 - Q_2)/Q_2$ typically were less than 15 per cent. Or, in other words, the first and third quartiles were usually within 15 per cent of the median. Examining our data for renter households in Chicago, we find that the relative deviation of the quartiles from the median is substantially greater, ranging from 16 to 35 per cent (Table 5–9) over the eight income groups. There appears to be a tendency toward greater dispersion of rents at the lower income levels; this may be associated with greater heterogeneity of household type and size or greater dispersion by income within the income interval, but we do not have data available for exploring such associations.

Whether there is evidence of "real central tendency" or not, the reader should be aware that households of a given income differ substantially in terms of rent. Among Chicago households with incomes of less than $2,000 in 1956, a fourth paid a gross monthly rent of less than $41, a fourth paid $41 to $57, a fourth paid $57 to $77, and a fourth paid $77 or more. Among households with incomes of $2,000 to $3,999, a fourth paid a gross monthly rent of less than $52, a fourth paid $52 to $68, a fourth paid $68 to $83, and a fourth paid $83 or more. This, of course, suggests the desirability of examining the entire rent distribution of households with a given income as opposed to considering only the median rent.

**Table 5–9**
**Summary Measures of the Gross Monthly Rent Distribution of Renter Households by 1956 Income of Primary Family or Individual: City of Chicago, 1956**

| INCOME OF PRIMARY FAMILY OR INDIVIDUAL IN 1956 | QUARTILES | | | PER CENT DEVIATION FROM MEDIAN | |
|---|---|---|---|---|---|
| | First $Q_1$ | Median $Q_2$ | Third $Q_3$ | $(Q_2 - Q_1)/Q_2$ | $(Q_3 - Q_2)/Q_2$ |
| Less than $2,000 | $41 | $57 | $77 | 28 | 35 |
| $2,000 to $3,999 | $52 | $68 | $83 | 24 | 22 |
| $4,000 to $4,999 | $63 | $77 | $90 | 18 | 17 |
| $5,000 to $5,999 | $64 | $81 | $94 | 21 | 16 |
| $6,000 to $6,999 | $67 | $84 | $98 | 20 | 17 |
| $7,000 to $7,999 | $68 | $86 | $105 | 21 | 22 |
| $8,000 to $9,999 | $74 | $93 | $112 | 20 | 20 |
| $10,000 or more | $86 | $107 | >$120 | 20 | ... |

*Rent/income ratios for households compared with ratios for families.* The only data available for an analysis of rent-income relationships of primary families living in Chicago at the beginning of 1957 are in the form of rent/income ratios by

*156*

income. Rent/income ratios are available for 489,000 of the 611,000 primary families in the rental sector. Ratios are not available for the 40,000 families with incomes of $10,000 or more, the 58,000 families which failed to report income, and 25,000 families which failed to report rent, occupied rent-free units or units with a gross rent of $1,000 or more, or had an income of less than $100. Rent/income ratios were obtained by multiplying gross monthly rent by 12 to convert it to an annual basis and then dividing annual gross rent by family income in 1956; the ratio was calculated separately for each family. Families then were grouped in terms of family income in 1956; and the distribution of families in each income group by the rent/income ratio is presented. Six rent/income ratio intervals were employed in tabulation, ranging from less than 10 per cent to 30 per cent or more.

Insofar as we can tell, the mean rent/income ratios for all renter households, which were cited earlier, are very close to the median rent/income ratios calculated from the distribution of renter primary families by the rent/income ratio. The following comparison makes the point:

| Income group | Mean, all households | Median, primary families |
|---|---|---|
| $4,000–4,999 | 21 | 22 |
| $5,000–5,999 | 18 | 18 |
| $6,000–7,999 | 15 | 15 |
| $8,000–9,999 | 13 | 13 |

Unfortunately we cannot make rigorous comparisons for the lower-income groups. The mean ratio of rent to current income for all renter households was 80 per cent for households with incomes of less than $2,000 and 26 per cent for households with incomes of $2,000 to $3,999. The median rent/income ratio for renter primary families with incomes of less than $3,000 was greater than 30 per cent, but because it falls in the upper, open-ended interval we do not know its magnitude. The median rent/income ratio for renter primary families with incomes of $3,000 to $3,999 was 24 per cent; this is fairly close to the mean rent/income ratio of 26 per cent for all households with incomes of $2,000 to $3,999.

We can only suggest that the dispersion of families of a given income by the rent/income ratio is about the same as the dispersion of households of a given income by rent. It was shown, in Table 5–9, that for households with an income of $4,000 to $4,999 the first quartile of rent was 18 per cent below the median rent and the third quartile was 17 per cent above the median; for primary families in this income group, the first quartile of the rent/income ratio is 20 per cent below the median rent/income ratio and the third quartile is 21 per cent above the median. For the income group $5,000 to $5,999, the first quartile of rent was 21 per cent below the median and the third quartile was 16 per cent above the median for all households; for primary families, the first quartile of the rent/income ratio is 21 per cent below the median and the third quartile is 23 per cent above the median.

Insofar as we can tell, the rent-income relationships described for all households probably are a fairly realistic description of rent-income relationships for primary families. First, the correlation between rent and income on a household-by-household basis is imperfect. About a sixth of the differences among households in rent paid is accounted for by differences among them in income. The looseness of relationship between rent and income means that households paying the same rent vary substantially in their income and households with the same income pay a wide range of rents. Second, there is, nonetheless, a strong average tendency for rent to increase as income increases and, conversely, for income to increase as rent increases.

The average tendencies for the rent/income ratio to decrease as income increases and for the rent/income ratio to increase as rent increases follow from these rent-income relationships and the nature of the basic data.

Among lower-income families, the ratio of gross rent to current income is high as compared with rent/income ratios for middle- and upper-income families. Very possibly gross rent accounts for a higher proportion of the total expenditures of lower-income families than of middle- and upper-income families, although the rent/expenditure ratio varies less with income than does the rent/income ratio. In the middle-income range, our analyses based on all households yield results which differ little from results of analyses based on primary families. In the lower-income range, we are unable to make systematic comparisons between results based on all households and those based on primary families only; and it is in the lower-income range, in which substantial numbers of primary individuals are found, that we might expect the results based on all households to differ somewhat from the results based on primary families only. Nonetheless, it is probable that the rentals of lower-income primary families are of roughly the same magnitude as those of all lower-income households.

*Rent-income relationships in earlier years.* The association of rent and income for renter households can be examined with data of the 1950 Census of Housing. (A cross-tabulation of renter households by gross monthly rent and income in 1949 for the City of Chicago appears in Table B-3, Vol. II, Part 2, Chapter 36.) In 1950, as in 1956, the relationship between rent and income was loose although, on the average, lower-income households paid relatively low rents.

The regression analyses for 1950 and 1956 are compared below. Recall that $R =$ gross monthly rent and $I =$ annual income.

|  1950 | 1956 |
|---|---|

$$R_c = 38 + .0031I \qquad\qquad R_c = 58 + .0039I$$
$$I_c = 1{,}505 + 47.61R \qquad\qquad I_c = 1{,}580 + 45.33R$$
$$r_{RI} = .38 \qquad\qquad\qquad r_{RI} = .42$$
$$r^2_{RI} = .14 \qquad\qquad\qquad r^2_{RI} = .18$$
$$\bar{R} = 50; \bar{I} = 3{,}901 \qquad\qquad \bar{R} = 79; \bar{I} = 5{,}143$$

In both years, the regression analysis was based on data grouped in broad intervals, and the intervals used in the 1950 tabulation differed from those used in 1956. The "midvalues" of class intervals used in the computation—in particular that of the open-ended upper interval—may have been inappropriate in one or both years. Thus, the apparent changes in the nature of the relationship should be interpreted with caution.

In both 1950 and 1956, the computed linear regression provides a good estimate of the average rent paid by households at each income level and a close estimate of the average income of households occupying units in a given rental group. (The close fit of the regression line in 1956 can be seen in Figure 5–2.) Here, we focus on the relationship of gross monthly rent to annual income. In 1950, on the basis of the regression analysis, we expect an increase of $1,000 in annual income to be accompanied by an increase of about $3 in monthly rent. In 1956, it appears that an increase of about $4 in monthly rent accompanies an increase of $1,000 in annual income. This apparent change in the nature of the relationship may be an artifact of the use of partially estimated data, but it is probably safe to conclude that the increase in rent associated with an increase of $1,000 in income was no less in 1956 than in 1950. The nature of the relationship between rent and income on a household basis observed in 1950, thus, resembles that previously described in greater detail for 1956.

We now turn to an examination of the changes in rent and income which occurred between 1950 and 1956. First, consider the shifts in average rent and average income for all households which occurred between the two years. Average rent for all renters increased by $29, from $50 in 1950 to $79 in 1956— a proportional increase of 58 per cent. During the same period, average income for renter households increased by $1,242, from $3,901 to $5,143—a proportional increase of only 32 per cent. This information, considered in conjunction with the regression equation, means that households at each income level were paying substantially higher rents in 1956 than in 1950 and that rent constituted a larger proportion of current income for households at each income level in 1956 than it had in 1950.

In absolute, or numerical, terms, the increase in average monthly rent between 1950 and 1956 was no more for households with a low income than for households with a high income. In fact, on the basis of the regression equations, it appears that the absolute increase in rent was a few dollars less for the households with below-average incomes than for those with higher incomes. However, the relative, or percentage, increases in rent between 1950 and 1956 quite clearly were greater for households with below-average incomes than for those with above-average incomes.

The rent/income ratios for households with low incomes estimated from the regression of rent on income in 1950 are quite close to those reported for 1950 in the recent "Study of Consumer Expenditures" (Bureau of Labor Statistics, 1956, Table 3–4). For a small sample of some 400 households in Chicago, housing expenditures were 73 per cent of net money income in 1950 for the group with incomes of less than $1,000, 31 per cent for the group with incomes of $1,000 to $1,999, and 21 per cent for the group with incomes of $2,000 to $2,999. The average rent/income ratio estimated from the regression equation is 96 per cent when income is $500, 50 per cent when income is $1,000, 34 per cent when income is $1,500, and 22 per cent when income is $2,500. It should be noted that the data of the 1950 Census of Housing are not fully comparable with those of the "Study of Consumer Expenditures." In the latter survey, net money income includes the value of food and housing received as pay and excludes personal taxes and occupational expenses. The housing expenditure figure was obtained by summing expenditures for housing and for fuel, light, and refrigeration. The figures are for home owners and renters combined. However, the comparison suggests that the rent/income ratios estimated from the regression of rent on income can be used with some confidence in describing rent-income relationships for lower-income families.

As we pointed out earlier, the average rent/income ratio was higher in 1956 than in 1950 for households at a given income level. For example, the rent/income ratio estimated from the regression of rent on income for 1956 was about 51 per cent when income was $1,500 and 33 per cent when income was $2,500. By comparison, the estimated rent/income ratio in 1950 was 34 per cent when income was $1,500 and 22 per cent when income was $2,500. However, these comparisons do not tell us whether rent/income ratios increased for households with the same relative position in the income distribution, for it will be recalled that an upward shift in mean income occurred between 1950 and 1956.

When we compare the rent/income ratio at a given decile of the 1950 income distribution with the rent/income ratio at the same decile of the 1956 income distribution, it appears that the rent/income ratios increased slightly between 1950 and 1956 for households with the same relative position in the income distribution. Rent/income ratios estimated from the regression of rent on income at the quintiles of the 1950 and 1956 distributions of renter households by income are:

| QUINTILE | RENT/INCOME RATIO | |
| --- | --- | --- |
| | 1950 | 1956 |
| Lowest | 27 | 31 |
| Second | 19 | 22 |
| Third | 15 | 18 |
| Highest | 12 | 15 |

On the basis of these results, we are fairly confident that rent/ income ratios in 1956 were at least as high as in 1950 for households with the same relative position in the income distribution, if not actually higher.

It also has been reported (Department of Labor, 1939a, p. 94) that rent/income ratios ranging from 50 to 150 per cent were observed among Chicago households with incomes of less than $500 in 1935–36, which at that time constituted about 14 per cent of all Chicago households. An average rent/income ratio of 64 per cent for nonrelief households with incomes of $250 to $499 is reported, and mean rent/income ratios of 41 per cent for the income group $500 to $749 and 31 per cent for the income group $750 to $999 are shown (Department of Labor, 1939a, Table 56). Again the definition of income is not wholly comparable with the NHI and 1950 Census of Housing definition, and the rent figures refer to contract rather than gross rent. Lack of comparability precludes any sort of inference about changes in rent/income ratios for lower-income households over time. However, it is clear that high ratios of rent to current income have characterized lower-income households in Chicago, as in other areas, for many years.

*Quality of dwelling and rent/income ratio for lower-income families.* The data in Table 5–10 show clearly that the rent/income ratio is typically higher among lower-income families in standard dwellings than among lower-income families in substandard dwellings. Of course, on the average, the rent/income ratios for lower-income families in substandard dwellings are

*163*

themselves high as compared with the ratios for middle- and higher-income families.

In one sense the observed standard-substandard differential in the rent/income ratio at a given income level can be "explained" quite readily. We strongly suspect that one can infer from this differential that lower-income families in standard

**Table 5–10**
**Percentage Distributions by Rent/Income Ratio of Lower-Income, Renter-Occupant Families, in Standard and Substandard Dwellings: City of Chicago, 1956**

| Income in 1956 and ratio of annual gross rent to annual income | All primary families | Families in standard dwellings | Families in substandard dwellings |
|---|---|---|---|
| Income less than $3,000 | | | |
| All renters (in thousands) | 77 | 47 | 30 |
| Number reporting ratio (in thousands) | 69 | 41 | 28 |
| Per cent distribution: | | | |
| Total reporting ratio | 100 | 100 | 100 |
| Less than 10 per cent | ... | ... | 1 |
| 10 to 14 per cent | 1 | ... | 1 |
| 15 to 19 per cent | 5 | 3 | 8 |
| 20 to 24 per cent | 8 | 5 | 12 |
| 25 to 29 per cent | 8 | 8 | 9 |
| 30 per cent or more | 78 | 84 | 69 |
| Income $3,000 to $3,999 | | | |
| All renters (in thousands) | 80 | 59 | 21 |
| Number reporting ratio (in thousands) | 77 | 57 | 20 |
| Per cent distribution: | | | |
| Total reporting ratio | 100 | 100 | 100 |
| Less than 10 per cent | ... | ... | 1 |
| 10 to 14 per cent | 5 | 4 | 11 |
| 15 to 19 per cent | 19 | 18 | 21 |
| 20 to 24 per cent | 30 | 27 | 40 |
| 25 to 29 per cent | 20 | 21 | 19 |
| 30 per cent or more | 25 | 30 | 10 |

... 0.5 per cent or less.
Source: CSNHI, Tables 5–8 and 5–9.

units tend to pay more rent than do lower-income families in substandard dwellings. The inference would be correct unless within each income interval families in standard units are concentrated toward the lower limit of income and families in substandard units are concentrated toward the upper limit of income; we regard this within-income-interval distribution as improbable. If our inference is correct, the standard-substandard differential can be restated as: lower-income families in standard dwellings typically pay more rent than do lower-income families in substandard dwellings. The fact that standard dwellings typically command higher rentals than substandard dwellings then would "explain" the observed difference.

On the other hand, it is more difficult to "explain" why families in standard units spend, on the average, a higher proportion of income on rent than do families in substandard units when the income of the two groups is roughly equal, i.e., how do we account for the fact that one group of families spends a higher proportion of income on rent than does another group of families with like income. One possible explanation would hinge on differences in family composition between the two groups of families. The data summarized in Table 5–11, however, suggest that the standard-substandard differential cannot be accounted for by family size and type. We use the word "suggest" because the number of cases often is very small and the controls on family type and size are broad. The rent/income ratios tend to be higher for families in standard dwellings than for families in substandard dwellings for married couples living alone, for normal families, for 2-person atypical families, and for larger atypical families. If the distribution of families in each size- and type-of-family group by rent/income ratio was the same for families in standard units as for families in substandard units, the distributions of families in standard units and of

## Table 5-11

**Percentage Distributions by Rent/Income Ratio of Lower-Income, Renter-Occupant Families by Type and Size of Family and Quality of Dwelling: City of Chicago, 1956**

| FAMILY INCOME IN 1956 AND RATIO OF ANNUAL GROSS RENT TO ANNUAL INCOME | NORMAL FAMILIES | | | | ATYPICAL FAMILIES | | | |
|---|---|---|---|---|---|---|---|---|
| | 2 PERSONS | | 3 PERSONS OR MORE | | 2 PERSONS | | 3 PERSONS OR MORE | |
| | Standard | Sub-standard | Standard | Sub-standard | Standard | Sub-standard | Standard | Sub-standard |
| **Income less than $3,000** | | | | | | | | |
| All renters (in thousands) | 16 | 10 | 16 | 8 | 8 | 6 | 7 | 6 |
| Per cent distribution: | | | | | | | | |
| Total reporting ratio | 100 | 100 | 100 | 100 | 100* | 100* | 100* | 100* |
| Less than 15 per cent | ... | 2 | ... | ... | ... | ... | 2 | 4 |
| 15 to 19 per cent | 3 | 10 | 2 | 16 | 4 | 3 | 7 | ... |
| 20 to 24 per cent | 2 | 14 | 7 | 13 | 3 | 16 | 7 | 6 |
| 25 to 29 per cent | 12 | 6 | 8 | 19 | ... | ... | 8 | 9 |
| 30 per cent or more | 83 | 68 | 82 | 53 | 93 | 82 | 77 | 80 |
| **Income $3,000 to $3,999** | | | | | | | | |
| All renters (in thousands) | 16 | 7 | 31 | 10 | 6 | 2 | 5 | 2 |
| Per cent distribution: | | | | | | | | |
| Total reporting ratio | 100 | 100* | 100 | 100 | 100* | 100* | 100* | 100* |
| Less than 15 per cent | 4 | 16 | 3 | 8 | 7 | 8 | ... | 15 |
| 15 to 19 per cent | 22 | 25 | 14 | 15 | 8 | 38 | 40 | 18 |
| 20 to 24 per cent | 24 | 43 | 30 | 43 | 32 | 24 | 13 | 32 |
| 25 to 29 per cent | 16 | 10 | 24 | 21 | 27 | 21 | 15 | 36 |
| 30 per cent or more | 32 | 6 | 30 | 14 | 25 | 9 | 32 | ... |

* Based on less than 50 sample cases.
... 0.5 per cent or less.
Source: CSNHI, Tables 5-9 and 5-11.

families in substandard units by rent/income ratio would be virtually identical.

We have no tabulations of families by income and quality of dwelling unit by other family or housing characteristics. Perhaps the families in substandard units have heavier demands on their income arising from, say, medical expenses; or perhaps the families in substandard units prefer to use a higher proportion of their limited incomes for other goods or services. To revert to the notion of permanent income versus current income, disproportionate numbers of the families in substandard units may be families with low permanent incomes to which their housing expenditures are geared.

# 6

# White-Nonwhite Differentials in Housing

SEVERAL STUDIES of Chicago's population have noted the high incidence of family disorganization in the nonwhite population (e.g., Frazier, 1932; Duncan and Duncan, 1957). One manifestation is the frequency of irregular living arrangements. Nonwhite families are more likely than white families to have nonrelatives sharing their dwellings. Broken families are more common in the nonwhite population. A concomitant, and possibly a cause, of this family disorganization is severe room crowding; the "persons per room" ratio typically is much higher for nonwhite households than for white households. Our statistics on type and size of household and shelter space per person will be interpreted within this broader framework of white-nonwhite differentials in living patterns.

From time to time it has been observed that: (a) the quality of dwellings occupied by nonwhites is, on the average, inferior to the quality of dwellings with white occupants; (b) rentals paid by nonwhites, on the average, are only slightly less than, if not equal to rentals paid by whites; and (c) income received by nonwhite families is, on the average, less than income received by white families. We are confident that these three observations are related, but with the sorts of data usually available, it has been difficult to answer questions of the following types. At a given income level, do nonwhite families spend as much for rental as do white families? At a given rental level, are the dwellings occupied by nonwhites as spacious and of as good a quality as the dwellings occupied by whites? Although data of the CSNHI do not yield conclusive answers to these questions, they permit a somewhat more thorough exploration than has been possible in the past.

In the final part of this chapter, we consider differences in the housing conditions of the white and nonwhite populations living in the central and outlying parts of the City of Chicago. Certain comparisons also can be made between housing conditions in the areas in which sizeable numbers of nonwhites have resided for a number of years and housing conditions in the areas of more recent nonwhite occupancy.

GROWTH OF HOUSEHOLDS

Before undertaking an examination of white-nonwhite differences in household composition and housing characteristics, we present some summary statistics on changes in the numbers of white and nonwhite households which occurred between 1940 and 1956. The data are given in Tables 6–1 and 6–2.

The reported numbers of households by color in 1940, 1950, and 1956 and the numbers of households by color expected on the basis of the size and age composition of the respective population in each year are shown in the first two panels of Table 6–1. Usually comparisons are made between the reported number of households and the number of households expected on the basis of population size. For example, the increase in households is compared with the increase in population between two dates or the proportion of the households accounted for by nonwhites is compared with the proportion nonwhite in the population at a given date. Actually, the number of households depends on the age composition of the population as well as on population size. Children under 15 are virtually never heads of households; hence, an increase in the child population does not imply an increase in the number of households. Persons 15 to 24 years of age are rather unlikely to be household heads; only 8 per cent of this age group in the Chicago SMA were reported as household heads in 1950, whereas about 34 per cent of the persons aged 25 to 34, 43 per cent of the persons aged 35 to 44, and 48 to 52 per cent of the persons aged 45 to 54, 55 to 64, and 65 or more headed households. When these age-specific headship rates are applied to the reported population by age and color in 1940 and 1950 and to the estimated population by age and color in 1956, the "expected" numbers of households by color are obtained. (The schedule of age-specific headship rates for the total population in the Chicago SMA in 1950 was calculated from Tables 53 and 58 of the 1950 Census of Population, Vol. II, Part 13. To adjust for the SMA-City difference in rates, a constant multiplier of 1.01 was applied to the schedule so that "expected" households

**Table 6–1**
**Number of Households by Color, Reported and Expected on
the Basis of Population Size and Age Composition:
City of Chicago, 1956, 1950, and 1940**

| Item | 1956 | 1950 | 1940 |
|---|---|---|---|
| | households in thousands | | |
| Households reported | | | |
| All | 1,133 | 1,087 | 950 |
| White | 919 | 956 | 873 |
| Nonwhite | 214 | 131 | 76 |
| Households expected on basis of population size and age | | | |
| All | 1,085 | 1,087 | 993 |
| White | 886 | 949 | 912 |
| Nonwhite | 199 | 139 | 81 |
| Ratio of reported to expected households (base: 1950 total) | | | |
| All | 104 | 100 | 96 |
| White | 104 | 101 | 96 |
| Nonwhite | 108 | 95 | 95 |
| | population in thousands | | |
| Total population | | | |
| All | 3,749* | 3,621 | 3,397 |
| White | 2,944* | 3,112 | 3,115 |
| Nonwhite | 805* | 509 | 282 |

\* Population in households estimated from distributions of households by size in CSNHI;
  population outside households assumed to be the same as in 1950.
Note: See text for explanation of expected number of households.
Source: CSNHI, Table 1–2; Hauser and Kitagawa (1953), Table 1.

would equal reported households in the City of Chicago in
1950.) The estimates of 1956 population by color were obtained
as follows: the white and nonwhite populations living in households were estimated from statistics on households by size and
color reported in the CSNHI; white and nonwhite populations
living outside households were assumed to be the same in 1956
and in 1950. The age composition of each population was assumed to be the same as the age composition of that population
estimated by the composite technique (Chicago Community Inventory, University of Chicago, 1958a). Because the 1956 popu-

*171*

lation figures are estimates and subject to errors which cannot be specified, they should be treated with caution. However, we regard them as satisfactory for the uses to which they are put in this analysis.

If within each age group the proportion of household heads had been the same throughout the period 1940 to 1956, the ratio of reported to expected households would be 100 in each year. Actually, the ratio is 96 in 1940, 100 in 1950, 104 in 1956. This means that, in part, the growth in households was due to factors other than population size and age composition. The summary measures in Table 6–2 bring out this point somewhat more clearly. Between 1950 and 1956, households in the City

**Table 6–2**
**Change in Number of Households by Color, Reported and Expected on the Basis of Population Size and Age Composition: City of Chicago, 1950–56, 1940–50, and 1940–56**

| ITEM | NUMERICAL CHANGE | | | PERCENTAGE CHANGE | | |
|---|---|---|---|---|---|---|
| | 1950–1956 | 1940–1950 | 1940–1956 | 1950–1956 | 1940–1950 | 1940–1956 |
| | *in thousands* | | | | | |
| All households | | | | | | |
| Total change | 45 | 138 | 183 | 4 | 15 | 19 |
| Due to population size and age | −2 | 94 | 92 | . . . | 10 | 10 |
| Due to other factors | 47 | 44 | 91 | 4 | 5 | 9 |
| White households | | | | | | |
| Total change | −37 | 82 | 45 | −4 | 9 | 5 |
| Due to population size and age | −62 | 36 | −26 | −7 | 4 | −3 |
| Due to other factors | 25 | 46 | 71 | 3 | 5 | 8 |
| Nonwhite households | | | | | | |
| Total change | 83 | 55 | 138 | 63 | 72 | 181 |
| Due to population size and age | 60 | 58 | 118 | 46 | 76 | 155 |
| Due to other factors | 23 | −3 | 20 | 17 | −4 | 26 |

. . . 0.5 per cent or less.
Source: Table 6–1.

of Chicago increased by 45,000. If there had been no change in the age-specific headship rates, then the changes which took place in the size and age composition of the City's population would have resulted in a decrease of 2,000 households. Consequently, an increase of 47,000 households can be attributed to factors other than population size and age composition. Between 1940 and 1950, an increase of 138,000 households occurred; an increase of 94,000 households is attributable to change in population size and age composition and an increase of 44,000 households is attributable to other factors.

What sorts of things are the "other factors"? The median age at marriage has been falling, and an increasing proportion of young adults head families. With improving economic conditions and an easing of the housing shortage, the proportion of young families setting up their own households, as opposed to sharing the dwelling of their parents or other relatives, has increased. The proportion of older persons maintaining their own households increased as benefits from public and private old-age security measures rose and improvements in mortality retarded dissolution of the family. "Doubling up" of married couples, a response to prewar depression and wartime housing shortages, has been reduced. (See Glick, 1957, Chapter 9 for a discussion of household formation.) Somewhat as an aside, the analysis makes it clear that forecasts of household formation must reckon with "other factors" as well as with prospective population changes.

Turning now to the figures for white and nonwhite households separately, we observe quite different patterns of both reported and "expected" growth for the two populations. In the decade 1940 to 1950, white households increased by 82,000, or nine per cent, and nonwhite households increased by 55,000 or 72 per cent. In part, the changes in households reflect changes in the size and age composition of the white and nonwhite populations. They also reflect changes in age-specific headship rates, which for convenience we call changes due to "other factors." When we focus on the changes due to other factors, we note an increase of 5 per cent for white households as opposed to a decrease of 4 per cent for nonwhite households. It appears—though this is conjectural—that the rapid in-migration of non-whites during the 1940's coupled with a housing shortage encouraged doubling up of nonwhite families and other somewhat irregular living arrangements. At the beginning of the decade, the population/household ratio was about the same in the white and nonwhite populations when allowance is made for their age compositions; note that the ratio of actual to expected households (Table 6–1) is about the same for whites and non-whites in 1940. The rate of household formation in the nonwhite population was depressed during the decade 1940 to 1950 relative to the rate for the white population. By 1950, the age-standardized ratio of actual to expected households was some-what lower for nonwhites than for whites. In the post-1950 period, however, the nonwhite population appears to have "caught up" in terms of household formation. White households decreased by 37,000, or 4 per cent, between 1950 and 1956; nonwhite households increased by 83,000 or 63 per cent, during the same period. The increase in households due to other factors amounted to 3 per cent for white households and 17 per cent for nonwhite households. In 1956, the ratio of actual to expected households may have been somewhat higher for non-whites than for whites.

Although the 1956 figures on size and age composition of the white and nonwhite populations are estimates, we think that it is safe to infer that the age-specific headship rates were on the average as high in the nonwhite population as in the white population by 1956. This similarity in white and nonwhite age-specific headship rates does not necessarily imply that the white and nonwhite populations are similar with respect to frequency of irregular living arrangements, crowding, or access to standard housing. We now turn to an examination of white-nonwhite differentials with respect to household composition and housing characteristics.

## HOUSEHOLD COMPOSITION

One of the few items for which we can compile fairly comparable data for whites and nonwhites separately over a period of years is size of household or number of persons sharing the dwelling. In both 1940 and 1950, disproportionate numbers of nonwhite households consisted of persons living alone and of relatively large households—five and six or seven or more persons. Disproportionate numbers of white households consisted of two, three, and four persons. Median household size was about the same for the two groups, but the clustering about the median was less for nonwhite than for white households. The dissimilarity of the white and nonwhite distributions by size of household is indicated by the fact that 13 per cent of the nonwhite households would have to be shifted to a different size category to make their household-size distribution coincide with that of white households. A rather different pattern of white-nonwhite differences in household size is observed in 1956. Table 6–3 shows that disproportionate numbers of nonwhite households appear only in the larger size-of-household categories—five and six persons or seven persons or more; disproportionate numbers of white households are found in each smaller size category, including persons living alone. Median household size is a little larger for the nonwhite than for the white group,

3.1 persons as compared with 2.9 persons. However, the difference in the over-all distributions of white and nonwhite households by size appears slightly less than in earlier years. In 1956, only 10 per cent of the nonwhite households would have to be shifted to a different size category to make their household-size distribution coincide with that of white households.

The most striking change in pattern is the sharp reduction in the proportion of nonwhite households which consist of a person living alone. One-person households accounted for 14 per cent of all nonwhite households in 1940, 16 per cent in 1950, but only 10 per cent in 1956; among white households, persons living alone accounted for 8 per cent in 1940, 11 per cent in 1950, and 13 per cent in 1956. Although the data on household size by color for the three years are not fully comparable, it is improbable that the change in pattern can be accounted for by differences in definition and coverage. (Lodging houses with five to ten lodgers were counted as dwelling units or households in 1940; in 1950 and 1956, they were classified as non-dwelling-unit quarters and do not appear in the count of households. The reclassification effects only the largest size-of-household categories, however. The nonwhite category in 1950 includes only nonwhite households in census tracts with 250 or more nonwhite residents; however, these comprise 97 per cent of all nonwhite households.)

An unmistakable convergence in the proportion of household heads who are primary individuals also is observed in the white and nonwhite populations for the period 1950 to 1956. Primary individuals include persons living alone in a dwelling unit (one-person households) and persons who share a dwelling with one or more nonrelatives but no relatives. The proportion of primary individuals among white households increased from 10 per cent in 1940, to 13 per cent in 1950, to 15 per cent in 1956. Among nonwhite households the proportion of primary

*176*

**Table 6–3**

**Percentage Distribution of Households by Number of Persons in Household, by Color: City of Chicago, 1956, 1950, and 1940**

| NUMBER OF PERSONS IN HOUSEHOLD | 1956 | | | 1950* | | | 1940 | | |
|---|---|---|---|---|---|---|---|---|---|
| | All | White | Non-white | All | White | Non-white | All | White | Non-white |
| All households | 100 | 100 | 100 | 100 | 100 | 100 | 100 | 100 | 100 |
| 1 person | 12 | 13 | 10 | 12 | 11 | 16 | 8 | 8 | 14 |
| 2 persons | 28 | 29 | 27 | 30 | 30 | 27 | 26 | 26 | 26 |
| 3 persons | 23 | 24 | 21 | 23 | 24 | 18 | 23 | 24 | 18 |
| 4 persons | 18 | 18 | 16 | 18 | 19 | 14 | 19 | 20 | 14 |
| 5 and 6 persons | 14 | 14 | 18 | 14 | 14 | 16 | 17 | 17 | 17 |
| 7 persons or more | 4 | 2 | 8 | 4 | 3 | 9 | 6 | 5 | 12 |
| Median number of persons | 2.9 | 2.9 | 3.1 | 2.9 | 2.9 | 2.9 | 3.2 | 3.2 | 3.1 |

* Nonwhite category includes nonwhite households in census tracts with 250 or more nonwhite residents (97 per cent of all nonwhite households); other nonwhite households included in white category.

Source: CSNHI, Table 3–2; Duncan and Duncan (1957), Table 21.

individuals decreased from 23 per cent in 1940, to 21 per cent in 1950, to 15 per cent in 1956.

Because the proportion of persons who head households and the proportion of household heads who are primary individuals vary with age, it is important to take into account changes in the age composition of the white and nonwhite populations in assessing the observed changes in proportion of primary individuals. Recall that the age-specific headship rates tended to increase as age increased; roughly one-twelfth of the persons 15 to 24, a third of the persons 25 to 34, two-fifths of the persons 35 to 44, and half the persons 45 or more headed households in the Chicago SMA in 1950. The proportion of household heads who are primary individuals is highest at the younger and older ages; its relationship to age is U-shaped. Whereas 19 per cent of the household heads aged 14 to 24 were primary individuals, 9 per cent of the heads aged 25 to 44 were primary individuals. Primary individuals accounted for 15 per cent of the heads aged 45 to 64 and 27 per cent of the heads aged 65 or more. The foregoing figures relate to the City of Chicago in 1950. (Table B–4, Chicago Community Inventory, 1954; they are based on a 3 1/3 per cent sample of the returns of the 1950 Census of Population.) A comparison of the reported and age-standardized proportions of primary individuals shown in Table 6–4 indicates that the increase in the proportion for whites was greater than that expected on the basis of changing age composition while the proportion for nonwhites decreased, contrary to the increase expected, given their changing age composition. This rules out age as an explanation of convergence.

Between 1940 and 1956, an increase of only one percentage point in the proportion of primary individuals among white household heads would be expected, given the changing age composition of the white population. Actually, an increase from

10 to 13 per cent occurred between 1940 and 1950. Between 1950 and 1956, the proportion increased from 13 to 15 per cent. Comparison of the proportions of primary individuals and of one-person households among white households shows that the increase has been in persons living alone rather than in persons sharing their dwelling with nonrelatives. One might speculate that improved economic conditions, including greater financial security at the older ages, had been conducive to the formation or maintenance of households for an individual living alone. The picture is quite different in the nonwhite population. Between 1940 and 1956, given the changing age composition of

**Table 6–4**
**Primary Individuals as a Percentage of All Household Heads, by Color: City of Chicago, 1956, 1950, and 1940**

| Item | 1956 | 1950 | 1940 |
|---|---|---|---|
| Reported | | | |
| All | 15 | 14 | 11 |
| White | 15 | 13 | 10 |
| Nonwhite | 15 | 21 | 23 |
| Expected on basis of age composition | | | |
| All | 15 | 14 | 14 |
| White | 15 | 14 | 14 |
| Nonwhite | 14 | 13 | 13 |

Note: See text for explanation of expected percentages.
Source: CSNHI, Table 3–2; Chicago Community Inventory (1954), Table B–4; *1940 Census of Population and Housing, Families, General Characteristics, Tables 52 and 65.*

the nonwhite population, the proportion of primary individuals might be expected to increase slightly. Actually, the proportion fell from 23 per cent in 1940, to 21 per cent in 1950, to 15 per cent in 1956. Throughout the period 1940 to 1956, some factor(s) other than age composition has been operating toward a reduction in the proportion of primary individuals among nonwhite household heads. The factor(s) underlying the 1940–50 decrease probably differed from those underlying the 1950–

56 decrease. In the former period, the proportion living alone increased by two percentage points, whereas the proportion sharing their dwelling with nonrelatives fell four points. Between 1950 and 1956, the proportion living alone decreased by six percentage points, and the proportion sharing their dwelling remained unchanged.

Although there is some evidence that white and nonwhite households are becoming more alike in terms of their distributions by size and type, substantial differences remain. The distributions of white and nonwhite households in the City of Chicago in 1956 are shown by a very detailed size- and type-of-household classification in Table 6–5. Disproportionate numbers of small normal families (husband, wife, and not more than three relatives) are found among white households; disproportionate numbers of large normal families (husband, wife, and five or more relatives) and of atypical family groups( family head without spouse and relatives and/or nonrelatives; husband, wife, and nonrelatives and/or relatives) are found among nonwhite households. Disproportionate numbers of persons living alone in a dwelling are found among white households; disproportionate numbers of persons sharing their dwelling with nonrelatives only are found among nonwhite households. It is worth noting that white-nonwhite differences in type of household are greater than white-nonwhite differences in size of household. Normal families account for 75 per cent of the white households as compared with 62 per cent of the nonwhite households. Families in which the spouse of the head is absent account for only 9 per cent of the white households as opposed to 16 per cent of the nonwhite households. Families which share their dwelling with nonrelatives account for only 1 per cent of the white households as opposed to 8 per cent of the nonwhite households. The following figures provide a convenient summary: 20 per cent of the nonwhite households would have to be

**Table 6–5**
**Percentage Distribution of Households by Type and Size, by Color:**
**City of Chicago, 1956**

| Type and size of household | All | White | Nonwhite |
|---|---|---|---|
| All households | 100 | 100 | 100 |
| Normal families | 72 | 75 | 62 |
| Husband, wife only | 22 | 23 | 21 |
| Husband, wife, 1 relative | 19 | 20 | 13 |
| Husband, wife, 2 relatives | 16 | 17 | 11 |
| Husband, wife, 3 relatives | 8 | 9 | 7 |
| Husband, wife, 4 relatives | 4 | 4 | 4 |
| Husband, wife, 5 relatives | 2 | 2 | 3 |
| Husband, wife, 6 relatives or more | 1 | 1 | 4 |
| Atypical families with no nonrelatives | 10 | 9 | 16 |
| Family head, 1 relative | 5 | 5 | 5 |
| Family head, 2 relatives | 3 | 2 | 4 |
| Family head, 3 relatives | 1 | 1 | 2 |
| Family head, 4 relatives | 1 | 1 | 1 |
| Family head, 5 relatives or more | 1 | ... | 4 |
| Atypical families with nonrelatives | 3 | 1 | 8 |
| Family head, 2 persons (1 nonrelative) | 1 | 1 | 3 |
| Family head, 3 persons (at least 1 nonrelative) | 1 | ... | 2 |
| Family head, 4 persons (at least 1 nonrelative) | ... | ... | 1 |
| Family head, 5 persons or more (at least 1 nonrelative) | ... | ... | 2 |
| Primary individuals living alone | 12 | 13 | 10 |
| Primary individuals with nonrelatives | 2 | 2 | 5 |
| Primary individual, 1 nonrelative | 1 | 1 | 2 |
| Primary individual, 2 nonrelatives | 1 | 1 | 1 |
| Primary individual, 3 nonrelatives or more | ... | ... | 2 |

... 0.5 per cent or less.

Source: CSNHI, Table 3–2.

shifted to another type and size of household category to make their distribution by type and size of household identical with that of white households; 16 per cent of the nonwhite households would have to be shifted to another type-of-household category to make their distribution by type of household identical with that of white households; 10 per cent of the nonwhite households would have to be shifted to another size-of-household category to make their distribution by size of household identical with that of white households.

Crowding typically is measured in terms of the persons-per-room ratio, i.e., the number of persons in the household divided by the number of rooms in their dwelling. It is by no means clear what an appropriate criterion of "crowded" is in terms of the persons-per-room ratio. However, by and large, any household with a persons-per-room ratio of 1.51 or more can be regarded as crowded. This ratio implies two persons or more in a one-room unit, four persons or more in a two-room unit, five persons or more in a three-room unit, seven persons or more in a four-room unit, and so forth. By definition, a one-person household cannot be crowded; hence, the following analyses are restricted to multi-person households. The proportion of crowded multi-person households increased slightly from 1940 to 1950—from 6 to 7 per cent—and then decreased somewhat between 1950 and 1956—from 7 to 5 per cent. About 5 per cent of the white multi-person households were crowded both in 1940 and 1950; an estimated 2 to 3 per cent were crowded in 1956. The proportion crowded among nonwhite households increased from 22 to 28 per cent between 1940 and 1950 and then fell to an estimated 12 to 16 per cent in 1956. There is evidence of an over-all decrease in crowding for both white and nonwhite households in the post-1950 period; however, the proportion crowded for nonwhites remains at least four times as great as the proportion crowded for whites. The figures on crowding are shown in Table 6–6.

In the CSNHI, a persons-per-bedroom ratio rather than a

**Table 6–6**
**Percentage of Multi-Person Households with Persons-Per-Room**
**Ratios of 1.51 or More, by Color: City of Chicago,**
**1956, 1950, and 1940**

| Year | All | White | Nonwhite |
|---|---|---|---|
| 1956 (estimate) | 5 | 2 to 3 | 12 to 16 |
| 1950 | 7 | 5 | 28 |
| 1940 | 6 | 5 | 22 |

Source: estimates based on unpublished tabulations of household size (1 to 6 or more persons) by number of rooms (1 to 9 or more rooms) obtained from the 1956 NHI of the Bureau of the Census; Duncan and Duncan (1957), Tables 21 and 22.

persons-per-room ratio was reported. Because comparable data are not available for earlier years, we cannot trace changes in crowding as measured by the persons-per-bedroom ratio. In 1956, 3 per cent of the multi-person households in Chicago were occupying units which included no bedroom at the time of original construction. The proportion occupying no-bedroom units was the same for white and nonwhite households. Twenty per cent of the households in Chicago had persons-per-bedroom ratios of 2.01 or more—17 per cent of the white households and 31 per cent of the nonwhite households. These data, summarized in Table 6–7, indicate substantially more crowding among non-white households than among white households.

**Table 6–7**
**Percentage Distribution by Persons-Per-Bedroom Ratio of**
**Multi-Person Households, by Color: City of Chicago, 1956**

| Persons-per-bedroom ratio | All | White | Nonwhite |
|---|---|---|---|
| Households with 2 persons or more | 100 | 100 | 100 |
| No bedroom | 3 | 3 | 3 |
| 1 bedroom or more | 97 | 97 | 97 |
| Persons per bedroom: | | | |
| 2.01 or more | 20 | 17 | 31 |
| Less than 2.01 | 77 | 80 | 66 |

Source: CSNHI, Table 3–5.

We now turn to white-nonwhite differentials in quality of dwelling, rental, and income of occupant. In the main, the analyses are restricted to the renter sector for which data are more abundant. As Table 6–8 shows, the proportion of renters among both white and nonwhite households has been decreasing during the period 1940 to 1956; at the latter date, 62 per cent of the white households and 83 per cent of the nonwhite households were renters.

**Table 6–8**
**Percentage of Households Renting Their Dwelling, by Color:**
**City of Chicago, 1956, 1950, and 1940**

| Year | All | White | Nonwhite |
|------|-----|-------|----------|
| 1956 | 66  | 62    | 83       |
| 1950 | 70  | 67    | 88       |
| 1940 | 76  | 74    | 92       |

Source: CSNHI, Table 1–2; Duncan and Duncan (1957), Table 23.

The proportion of renter households occupying substandard dwellings decreased substantially between 1950 and 1956— from 29 to 21 per cent. The decrease in substandard housing was somewhat greater among nonwhite households (60 to 35 per cent) than among white households (24 to 17 per cent). However, in 1956, the proportion substandard for nonwhites was still more than double the proportion substandard for whites. In the 1940 Census of Housing, the concept "needing major repairs" was employed rather than the concept "dilapidated" which was introduced in the 1950 Census and used again in the NHI. Furthermore, the 1956 and 1950 data recognize "hot running water on a year-round basis" as an indicator of quality whereas the 1940 data do not. Unfortunately, we do not know whether the proportion of units classified as "needing major repairs or lacking private bath and/or toilet" in 1940 is greater or less

*184*

than the proportion of units which would have been classified "substandard" in that year. The 1940 proportions are shown in Table 6–9 along with the proportions substandard in 1950 and 1956. A sizeable white-nonwhite differential in quality of housing obtained even before the heavy in-migration of nonwhites during the housing shortage of the 1940's. Noncomparability precludes any estimate of the absolute amount or even direction of changes in the proportion of substandard housing between 1940 and 1950, i.e., it is impossible to tell whether substandard housing increased or decreased between 1940 and 1950. It is fairly clear, however, that any changes that did occur must have been no more favorable for nonwhites than for whites.

Although the proportion substandard among dwellings occupied by nonwhites is more than double the proportion substandard among dwellings occupied by whites, rentals paid by nonwhites are, on the average, only slightly lower than rentals paid by whites. In 1956, the median gross monthly rent for all

**Table 6–9**
**Percentage of Renter Households Occupying Substandard Dwellings, by Color: City of Chicago, 1956, 1950, and 1940**

| Year | All | White | Nonwhite |
|---|---|---|---|
| 1956 (Substandard) | 21 | 17 | 35 |
| 1950 (Substandard) | 29 | 24 | 60 |
| 1940 (Needing major repairs or lacking private bath and toilet) | 25 | 22 | 57 |

Note: 1940 not comparable with 1950 and 1956; see text.
Source: CSNHI, Table 1–2; 1940 Census of Housing, Vol. III, Illinois, Table B–3 and B–5a.

rental units in Chicago City was $78. The median rental for units occupied by nonwhites was $76; the median rental for units occupied by whites was $78. As indicated earlier, 35 per cent of the units rented by nonwhites were substandard as compared with 17 per cent of the units rented by whites.

Analysis of changes through time in white-nonwhite differentials with respect to rent is difficult because two concepts of rental have been used. The first, contract rent, is the rental contracted for; it may include or exclude utilities and fuels and may be for a furnished or unfurnished unit. The second, gross rent, is contract rent plus the cost of utilities and fuels if these are not included in the contract rent minus the estimated portion of the contract rent charged for furniture in the case of furnished units. Presumably, gross rent—in which inter-unit differences in the inclusion of utilities, fuels, and furniture in the contract rent are eliminated—is the more desirable measure for comparisons among groups where the perquisites may vary. In Table 6–10, the available statistics on rentals paid by white and nonwhite renters are summarized.

In terms of contract rent, the white-nonwhite differential was reduced between 1940 and 1950. Median contract monthly rentals of $33 for white households and $24 for nonwhite households are reported in 1940. In 1950, the median rental was $45 for white households and $41 for nonwhite households. Incidentally, differences in rental between standard and substandard units were markedly larger than differences in rental between units with white occupants and units with nonwhite occupants. In 1940, median contract monthly rental for units "needing no major repairs and with private bath and toilet" was $37 as compared with a median of $17 for other units; median gross monthly rental for standard units in 1950 was $53 as compared with a median of $34 for substandard units. In 1956, statistics on gross rent are available both for households by color and dwellings by quality. Median gross monthly rentals of $78 for white households and $76 for nonwhite households are reported. Median gross monthly rentals of $83 for standard units and $55 for substandard units are reported.

Before considering the interrelations between quality of dwelling and rental for white and nonwhite renters, we present some statistics on the incomes of white and nonwhite families;

# Table 6-10
## Percentage Distribution of Renter-Occupied Dwelling Units by Rent, by Color of Occupant: City of Chicago, 1956, 1950, and 1940

| MONTHLY RENT | 1956 | | | 1950 | | | 1940 | | |
|---|---|---|---|---|---|---|---|---|---|
| | All | White | Non-white | All | White | Non-white | All | White | Non-white |
| **Contract rent:** | | | | | | | | | |
| All | 100 | (n.a.) | (n.a.) | 100 | 100 | 100 | 100 | 100 | 100 |
| Less than $20 | 1 | | | 9 | 9 | 7 | 25 | 23 | 35 |
| $20 to $39 | 11 | | | 31 | 30 | 39 | 41 | 41 | 44 |
| $40 to $49 | 10 | | | 21 | 21 | 21 | 19 | 20 | 12 |
| $50 to $59 | 11 | | | 16 | 16 | 16 | 8 | 8 | 6 |
| $60 to $99 | 51 | | | 18 | 19 | 16 | 6 | 6 | 2 |
| $100 or more | 17 | | | 4 | 4 | 1 | 1 | 2 | ... |
| Median | $72 | | | $44 | $45 | $41 | $32 | $33 | $24 |
| **Gross rent:** | | | | | | | | | |
| All | 100 | 100 | 100 | 100 | (n.a.) | (n.a.) | 100 | (n.a.) | (n.a.) |
| Less than $40 | 6 | 6 | 5 | 30 | | | 58 | | |
| $40 to $49 | 8 | 8 | 9 | 22 | | | 22 | | |
| $50 to $59 | 11 | 11 | 12 | 21 | | | 11 | | |
| $60 to $99 | 54 | 54 | 54 | 22 | | | 8 | | |
| $100 or more | 21 | 21 | 20 | 4 | | | 1 | | |
| Median | $78 | $78 | $76 | $48 | | | $36 | | |

... 0.5 per cent or less.
(n.a.) Data not available.

Source: CSNHI, Table 5–3; 1956 NHI, Vol III, Table 3; Duncan and Duncan (1957), Table 24; 1950 Census of Housing, Vol. II, Chap. 36, Table B–3; 1940 Census of Housing, Vol. III, Illinois, Table B–3.

the figures are for owners and renters combined. The median 1956 family income for all primary families in Chicago was $5,590. For white primary families, the median was $5,910, and for nonwhite primary families the median was $4,192. Disproportionate numbers of white families are found at each income level above $5,000; disproportionate numbers of nonwhite families are found at each income level below $5,000. The average family living in Chicago in 1950 received an income of $3,956 in 1949; the median income was $4,189 for white families and $2,526 for nonwhite families. Disproportionate numbers of white families are found at each income level above $3,000; disproportionate numbers of nonwhite families are found at each income level below $3,000.

Probably the incomes of white and nonwhite families were no more alike in 1956 than in 1950. The median income for nonwhite families was about $1,700 less than the median income for white families both in 1949 and 1956. The ratio of nonwhite to white median income may have been slightly lower in 1949 than in 1956. The difficulty in assessing the change in the white-nonwhite differential with respect to income over the seven-year period stems from the fact that the 1956 statistics are restricted to primary families (families comprising a household head with relatives who share the dwelling) whereas the 1950 statistics pertain to all families (primary families and secondary families who live in a household headed by a nonrelative or in a quasi-household). Primary families accounted for about 97 per cent of all white families and 90 per cent of all nonwhite families in 1950 (Chicago Community Inventory, 1954, Table B–4 and Hauser and Kitagawa, 1953, Table 7). It seems likely that primary families would tend to have higher incomes than secondary families; if so, the white-nonwhite difference in 1949 income of primary families would have been slightly less than the observed difference for all families. Therefore, it seems safe to conclude

**Table 6–11**
**Percentage Distribution of Families by Family Income, by Color:**
**City of Chicago, 1956 and 1950**

| FAMILY INCOME | PRIMARY FAMILIES, 1956 (1956 INCOME) | | | ALL FAMILIES, 1950 (1949 INCOME)* | | |
|---|---|---|---|---|---|---|
| | All | White | Nonwhite | All | White | Nonwhite |
| All families reporting | 100 | 100 | 100 | 100 | 100 | 100 |
| Less than $2,000 | 6 | 5 | 10 | 14 | 12 | 34 |
| $2,000 to $2,999 | 5 | 4 | 11 | 15 | 13 | 29 |
| $3,000 to $3,999 | 12 | 9 | 25 | 22 | 22 | 19 |
| $4,000 to $4,999 | 17 | 17 | 20 | 16 | 17 | 9 |
| $5,000 to $5,999 | 16 | 17 | 13 | 12 | 13 | 4 |
| $6,000 or more | 43 | 48 | 22 | 21 | 23 | 4 |
| Median | $5,590 | $5,910 | $4,192 | $3,956 | $4,189 | $2,526 |
| Median income for renters only | $5,078 | $5,517 | $3,947 | | | |

* Nonwhite category includes nonwhite families in census tracts with 250 or more nonwhite residents; other nonwhite households included in white category.
Note: 1950 not comparable with 1956; see text.
Source: CSNHI, Tables 4–3 and 4–4; Duncan and Duncan (1957), Tables 19 and 20; Hauser and Kitagawa (1953), Table 7.

that the income differential between white and nonwhite families was not reduced between 1950 and 1956.

Income statistics for renter families separately are available only in 1956. The median income for all renter families was $5,078 in 1956, some $500 below the median for all families. The median income for white renters was $5,517, as compared with a median of $3,947 for nonwhite renters. The white-nonwhite difference in median income, thus, is about $1,600 for renters, or about the same as for all families.

The data just presented have shown that: (1) the housing of nonwhites is, on the average, inferior in quality to the housing of whites; (2) rentals paid by nonwhites are, on the average, nearly as great as rentals paid by whites; and (3) incomes received by nonwhites are, on the average, substantially lower than incomes received by whites. To compete in the housing market nonwhites must pay rentals more or less equivalent to those paid by whites and can do so only by allocating larger proportions of their income to housing. However, even though the nonwhite families pay rentals equivalent to those paid by white families, they are more likely to obtain substandard housing. More detailed analyses of the relationships among housing quality, income, rentals, size of unit, and type of family in 1956 follow.

*Quality, rent, and income.* The data in Table 6–12 show that disproportionate numbers of nonwhite renter families received incomes of less than $4,000 in 1956 and that the proportion of

### Table 6–12
**Percentage of Renter Families in Substandard Dwellings, by Color and Income: City of Chicago, 1956**

| FAMILY INCOME IN 1956 | PERCENTAGE OF FAMILIES IN SUBSTANDARD UNITS | | | PERCENTAGE DISTRIBUTION OF FAMILIES BY INCOME | | |
|---|---|---|---|---|---|---|
| | All | White | Nonwhite | All | White | Nonwhite |
| All families reporting | 17 | 12 | 33 | 100 | 100 | 100 |
| Less than $2,000 | 42 | 29 | 60 | 7 | 6 | 12 |
| $2,000 to $2,999 | 35 | 31 | 39 | 6 | 4 | 12 |
| $3,000 to $3,999 | 26 | 22 | 31 | 14 | 10 | 27 |
| $4,000 to $4,999 | 17 | 13 | 30 | 20 | 21 | 20 |
| $5,000 to $5,999 | 12 | 9 | 23 | 16 | 17 | 12 |
| $6,000 to $6,999 | 8 | 4 | 25 | 12 | 13 | 7 |
| $7,000 to $7,999 | 10 | 7 | 26 | 8 | 10 | 4 |
| $8,000 to $8,999 | 7 | 5 | 22 | 6 | 7 | 2 |
| $9,000 to $9,999 | 4 | 2 | 16 | 2 | 3 | 1 |
| $10,000 or more | 5 | 5 | 7 | 7 | 9 | 2 |

Source: CSNHI, Tables 4–3 and 4–4 and unpublished tabulation.

families occupying substandard dwellings decreases as income increases. Thus, one would expect the proportion substandard to be somewhat higher among nonwhite than among white families because of the relatively low incomes received by nonwhite families. However, when white and nonwhite families with the same income are compared, the proportion of families in substandard dwellings is consistently higher for nonwhites than for whites. See Figure 6–1. In part, then, the higher proportion substandard

*190*

for all nonwhite families is accounted for by the fact that the income-specific proportions substandard are higher for nonwhite than for white families. An analytical technique known as "components of a difference between two rates" (Kitagawa, 1955) permits one to determine how much of the white-nonwhite difference in proportion substandard is due to the difference between white and nonwhite families in their income distributions and how much of the difference is due to differences between white and nonwhite families in their income-specific proportions substandard.

Twelve per cent of the white families as compared with 33 per cent of the nonwhite families who reported their 1956 family income were living in substandard units. Of the observed difference in proportion substandard, 28 per cent is accounted for by the difference between white and nonwhite families in their income distributions and 72 per cent is due to differences between white and nonwhite families in their income-specific proportions substandard. The observed difference and its "components," are as follows:

|  | Difference (nonwhite minus white) |
|---|---|
| Observed difference (33 minus 12) | 21 percentage points |
| Due to income distributions | 6 percentage points |
| Due to income-specific proportions | 15 percentage points |

(Calculation of the components is as follows: Let $S =$ the proportion substandard for whites in a given income group; $s =$ the proportion substandard for nonwhites in that income group; $W =$ the proportion of white families in that income group; and $N =$ the proportion of nonwhite families in that income group. Compute the product of $(s + S)/2$ times $(N - W)$ for each income group, and sum the products for all income groups. The sum is the difference accounted for by white-nonwhite differences

*191*

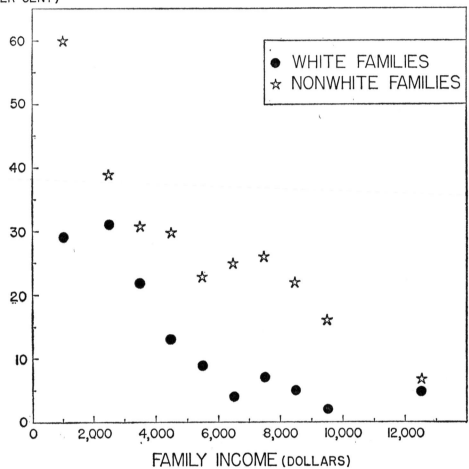

**Figure 6–1**

*Percentage of Renter Families in Substandard Dwellings, by Color and Income: City of Chicago, 1956. (Source: Table 6–12)*

in income distribution, or in the foregoing case, six percentage points. Then, compute the product of $(N + W)/2$ times $(s - S)$ for each income group, and sum the products for all income groups. The sum is the difference accounted for by white-nonwhite differences in income-specific proportions substandard, or in the foregoing case, fifteen percentage points.)

Table 6–13 shows that differences between white and non-white families with respect to gross rent are negligible. Thus, although the proportion substandard decreases as rent increases, white-nonwhite differences in rentals paid cannot account for much of the white-nonwhite difference in substandard housing. When white and nonwhite families paying the same rent are compared, the nonwhite families consistently have higher proportions substandard than do the white families. The pattern can be seen readily in Figure 6–2. The components analysis shows that only 5 per cent of the white-nonwhite differential in housing quality is accounted for by white-nonwhite differences in rentals; 95 per cent is accounted for by white-nonwhite differences in the rent-specific proportions substandard. The observed difference and its components are:

|  | Difference (Nonwhite minus white) |
|---|---|
| Observed difference (32 minus 12) | 20 percentage points |
| Due to rent distributions | 1 percentage point |
| Due to rent-specific proportions | 19 percentage points |

In sum, it is clear that nonwhite families receive less "quality" per dollar spent on housing than do white families; and the relatively high proportion of nonwhite families in substandard housing can be attributed only in small part to their relative economic disadvantage.

*Quality, rent, and size of unit.* The possibility that nonwhite families obtain larger dwellings than do white families paying like rentals is investigated in this section. In a sense, the question

**Table 6–13**
**Percentage of Renter Families in Substandard Dwellings, by Color and Rent: City of Chicago, 1956**

| GROS MONTHLY RENT | PERCENTAGE OF FAMILIES IN SUBSTANDARD UNITS | | | PERCENTAGE DISTRIBUTION OF FAMILIES BY RENT | | |
|---|---|---|---|---|---|---|
| | All | White | Nonwhite | All | White | Nonwhite |
| All families reporting | 17 | 12 | 32 | 100 | 100 | 100 |
| Less than $40 | 55 | 54 | 58 | 4 | 4 | 3 |
| $40 to $49 | 41 | 36 | 54 | 6 | 6 | 7 |
| $50 to $59 | 32 | 30 | 39 | 10 | 10 | 11 |
| $60 to $69 | 24 | 13 | 50 | 14 | 13 | 16 |
| $70 to $79 | 21 | 13 | 40 | 15 | 15 | 16 |
| $80 to $89 | 10 | 5 | 25 | 16 | 17 | 14 |
| $90 to $99 | 4 | ... | 15 | 12 | 12 | 11 |
| $100 to $109 | 5 | ... | 15 | 8 | 8 | 10 |
| $110 to $119 | 4 | 1 | 13 | 4 | 4 | 5 |
| $120 to $139 | 1 | ... | 5 | 5 | 5 | 6 |
| $140 or more | 1 | ... | 7 | 5 | 6 | 1 |

... 0.5 per cent or less.
Source: CSNHI, Table 5–4.

can be formulated as: Do nonwhite families sacrifice quality for space?

The available measure of dwelling-unit size is number of bedrooms in the unit. (Only rooms intended for use as bedrooms were to be reported; however, some respondents may have reported rooms designed for other use which are temporarily or secondarily being used as bedrooms in addition.) No statistically significant difference between the size of units occupied by white families and the size of units occupied by nonwhite families is found; the distributions of the respective groups by size of unit (unpublished tabulation, CSNHI) are:

| | Total | White | Nonwhite |
|---|---|---|---|
| All units | 100 | 100 | 100 |
| No bedroom | 5 | 5 | 3 |
| 1 bedroom | 35 | 34 | 38 |
| 2 bedrooms | 43 | 43 | 40 |
| 3 bedrooms | 15 | 15 | 15 |
| 4 bedrooms or more | 2 | 2 | 4 |

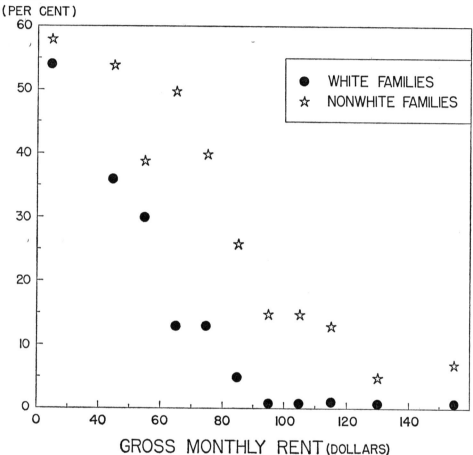

**Figure 6–2**

*Percentage of Renter Families in Substandard Dwellings, by Color and Rent: City of Chicago, 1956. (Source: Table 6–13)*

It was shown earlier that the over-all white and nonwhite distributions by rent were similar. Within each size-of-unit group, the rental distributions for white and nonwhite families are more or less the same. However, there is some tendency for nonwhite families to pay less than white families for small units (no bedroom or one bedroom) and more than white families for large units (three bedrooms or more). This may reflect more intense competition for large units inasmuch as the available vacancy rate (2.3 per cent for all rental units) was 3.6 per cent for units with one to three rooms and 1.5 per cent for units with four rooms or more (CSNHI, Table 1–4). (The statistics for available vacant units for rent pertain to number of rooms rather than number of bedrooms.)

The proportion substandard decreases as the size of unit increases for both white and nonwhite families; however, Table 6–14 shows that the proportion substandard is two or three times as great for nonwhite families as for white families within each size-of-unit group. When white and nonwhite families occupying units of the same size and with the same rental are compared, the proportion substandard consistently is higher for nonwhite families than for white families. The white-nonwhite differential in proportion substandard tends to be less for units with low rentals than for units with high rentals within each size-of-unit group. Although there is no direct evidence, this pattern may be related to the fact that dwellings in Chicago Housing Authority projects, none of which is substandard, are concentrated in the lowest rental groups and are occupied in the main by nonwhite families. (According to the CHA Annual Report for 1957, average rental per unit per month in CHA projects was $54; as noted earlier, four-fifths of the occupants were nonwhite.)

Nonwhite families apparently obtain no more space per housing dollar than do white families, but the space which they obtain is likely to be of poorer quality. The answer to our rhetor-

**Table 6–14**
**Percentage of Renter Families in Substandard Dwellings, by Color, Rent, and Size of Unit: City of Chicago, 1956**

| NUMBER OF BEDROOMS AND GROSS MONTHLY RENT | PERCENTAGE OF FAMILIES IN SUBSTANDARD UNITS | | | PERCENTAGE DISTRIBUTION OF FAMILIES BY RENT | | |
|---|---|---|---|---|---|---|
| | All | White | Nonwhite | All | White | Nonwhite |
| All families reporting: | 17 | 12 | 32 | 100 | 100 | 100 |
| Less than $60 | 39 | 36 | 47 | 20 | 20 | 21 |
| $60 to $79 | 22 | 13 | 45 | 28 | 28 | 32 |
| $80 to $99 | 7 | 3 | 21 | 28 | 30 | 25 |
| $100 or more | 3 | ... | 11 | 23 | 23 | 22 |
| 0 or 1 bedroom: | 24 | 16 | 50 | 100 | 100 | 100 |
| Less than $60 | 56 | 50 | 67 | 22 | 19 | 29 |
| $60 to $79 | 30 | 16 | 60 | 33 | 30 | 40 |
| $80 to $89 | 11 | 7 | 28 | 19 | 21 | 13 |
| $90 or more | 3 | ... | 17 | 27 | 30 | 18 |
| 2 bedrooms: | 13 | 11 | 20 | 100 | 100 | 100 |
| Less than $60 | 26 | 27 | 23 | 24 | 25 | 20 |
| $60 to $79 | 17 | 13 | 28 | 26 | 26 | 28 |
| $80 to $99 | 7 | 3 | 17 | 26 | 25 | 30 |
| $100 or more | 2 | ... | 8 | 24 | 25 | 23 |
| 3 bedrooms or more: | 9 | 6 | 18 | 100 | 100 | 100 |
| Less than $70 | 17 | 17 | 19* | 20 | 21 | 16 |
| $70 to $89 | 10 | 5 | 26 | 27 | 28 | 24 |
| $90 to $109 | 8 | 1 | 20 | 23 | 21 | 28 |
| $110 or more | 4 | 1 | 10 | 30 | 29 | 32 |

* Based on less than 50 sample cases.
... 0.5 per cent or less.
Source: CSNHI, Table 5–4.

ical question is clear: Nonwhite families get less desirable housing but no more space for a given rental than do white families.

*Quality, family type and size, and income.* Disproportionate numbers of white families comprise the husband, wife, and their relatives whereas in a relatively high proportion of the nonwhite families the spouse of the family head is absent and/or nonrelatives share the dwelling. White families also tend to be smaller than nonwhite families. (For statistics on type and size of family, see Table 6–5.)

Table 6–15 shows that when white and nonwhite families of the same type and size are compared, the proportion substandard is consistently higher for nonwhite families than for white families. If the proportions substandard are standardized for income, the white-nonwhite differential in housing quality for each type-and-size of family group is reduced by a tenth to a fourth; but nonwhite families are more likely to occupy substandard dwellings than are white families of the same size and type and with the same income. Inasmuch as nonwhite families tend to allocate greater proportions of their income to rent than do white families with equivalent incomes, standardization for rent probably would reduce the white-nonwhite housing quality differential even less than standardization for income. (No tabulation of families by size and type of family, rent and quality of dwelling is available.)

### Table 6–15
#### Percentage of Renter Families in Substandard Dwellings, by Color, Type, and Size, Observed and Standardized for Income: City of Chicago, 1956

| TYPE AND SIZE OF FAMILY | PERCENTAGE OF FAMILIES IN SUBSTANDARD UNITS | | | | |
|---|---|---|---|---|---|
| | | OBSERVED | | STANDARDIZED FOR INCOME* | |
| | All | White | Nonwhite | White | Nonwhite |
| All families | 17 | 12 | 32 | 12 | 28 |
| Normal families | 15 | 11 | 32 | 11 | 28 |
| 2 persons | 18 | 13 | 38 | 12 | 34 |
| 3 persons | 10 | 7 | 28 | 8 | 25 |
| 4 persons | 14 | 12 | 23 | 13 | 21 |
| 5 persons or more | 19 | 13 | 32 | 14 | 29 |
| Other families with no nonrelatives | 29 | 21 | 41 | 17 | 33 |
| 2 persons | 28 | 20 | 52 | 15 | 44 |
| 3 persons | 21 | 11 | 35 | 10 | 27 |
| 4 persons or more | 36 | 37† | 36 | 34† | 29 |
| Families with nonrelatives | 15 | 8† | 19 | 9† | 14 |

* Indirect standardization using income-specific proportions substandard of all white families.
† Based on less than 50 sample cases.
Source: CSNHI, Table 3–3.

Thus we conclude that the white-nonwhite differential in substandard housing is not accounted for by differences between white and nonwhite families in their composition and economic status.

The proportion of white and nonwhite families occupying substandard dwellings at each income level was shown in Table 6–12. Standardization for type and size of family reduces the white-nonwhite differential in substandard housing only a small amount. The proportion substandard for nonwhite families was twenty-one percentage points greater than the proportion substandard for white families; after standardization for size and type of family the proportion substandard for nonwhite families was eighteen percentage points greater than the proportion substandard for white families. The differences between observed and standardized proportions substandard are shown below at selected income levels:

| FAMILY INCOME | DIFFERENCE (NONWHITE MINUS WHITE) | |
|---|---|---|
| | Observed | Standardized |
| Less than $2,000 | 31 | 29 |
| $2,000 to $2,999 | 8 | 5 |
| $3,000 to $3,999 | 9 | 9 |
| $4,000 to $4,999 | 17 | 16 |
| $5,000 to $5,999 | 14 | 10 |
| $6,000 to $6,999 | 21 | 17 |

Each of the preceding analyses has brought out the fact that the white-nonwhite difference in housing quality is accounted for in only small part by differences between white and nonwhite families in their family characteristics, economic characteristics, or the rental and size of their dwellings. When comparisons are made between families of the same type and income or between families paying the same rents for dwellings of like size, the proportion substandard is substantially higher for nonwhite families than for white families.

*Rentals of standard and substandard units.* The statistics on rent, quality, and size of unit by color of occupant now are re-arranged to answer a somewhat different question: Can landlords get a "bonus" for renting to nonwhite households? The data shown in Figure 6–3 and Table 6–16 provide the answer.

Consider first the rentals for substandard dwellings. Half the substandard dwellings in the City of Chicago had gross monthly rentals of less than $55 in 1956. The median rental for white households in substandard units was $50 as compared with a median rental of $65 for nonwhite households in substandard units. On the average, then, a $15 "bonus" is found.

If comparisons are restricted to substandard dwellings of the same size, i.e., with the same number of bedrooms, nonwhites consistently pay higher rents than whites; and the differential apparently increases as size of unit increases. For example, the average one-bedroom, substandard unit with white occupants rented for $51 whereas the average one-bedroom, substandard unit with nonwhite occupants rented for $63. The average two-bedroom, substandard unit with white occupants rented for $52, whereas the average two-bedroom, substandard unit with non-white occupants rented for $72.

With regard to standard dwellings, the median rental for units occupied by whites, $83, was about the same as the median rental for units occupied by nonwhites, $84. We strongly suspect, although there is no direct evidence on the point, that if the stand-ard dwellings were classified into more detailed quality groups such as "sound" and "deteriorating," a "bonus" for renting to nonwhites again would appear.

The average one-bedroom, standard unit with white occupants rented for $84, as compared with $76 for the average one-bed-room, standard unit with nonwhite occupants. The average two-bedroom, standard unit with white occupants rented for $82, as compared with $84 for the average two-bedroom, standard unit with nonwhite occupants. However, the median rental of a stand-

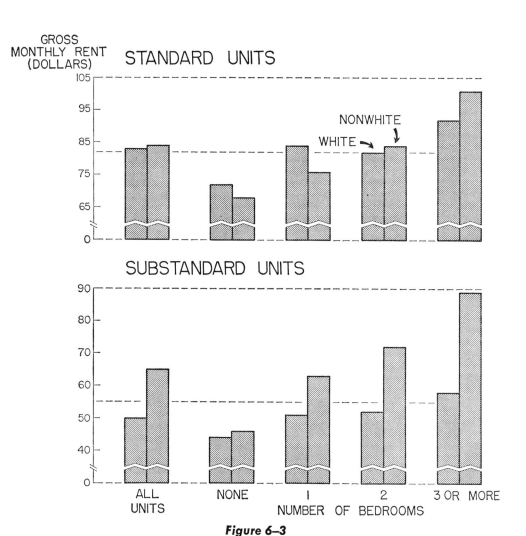

**Figure 6–3**

Median Gross Monthly Rent for Rental Units, by Quality and Size of Unit and Color of Occupant: City of Chicago, 1956. (Source: Table 6–16)

**Table 6–16**
**Quartiles of Gross Monthly Rent for Dwelling Units by Quality
and Color of Occupant: City of Chicago, 1956**

| QUARTILES OF GROSS MONTHLY RENT | STANDARD UNITS | | | SUBSTANDARD UNITS | | |
|---|---|---|---|---|---|---|
| | All | White | Non-white | All | White | Non-white |
| All renter occupied units: | | | *dollars* | | | |
| $Q_1$ | 66 | 67 | 65 | 42 | <40 | 51 |
| $Q_2$ (median) | 83 | 83 | 84 | 55 | 50 | 65 |
| $Q_3$ | 100 | 99 | 101 | 70 | 62 | 78 |
| No bedroom: | | | | | | |
| $Q_1$ | 63 | 63 | | <40 | <40 | |
| $Q_2$ (median) | 72 | 72 | 68* | 45 | 44 | 46* |
| $Q_3$ | 82 | 82 | | 55 | 55 | |
| 1 bedroom: | | | | | | |
| $Q_1$ | 68 | 70 | 58 | 42 | <40 | 49 |
| $Q_2$ (median) | 83 | 84 | 76 | 56 | 51 | 63 |
| $Q_3$ | 96 | 96 | 92 | 69 | 64 | 73 |
| 2 bedrooms: | | | | | | |
| $Q_1$ | 63 | 63 | 66 | 46 | 43 | 59 |
| $Q_2$ (median) | 83 | 82 | 84 | 58 | 52 | 72 |
| $Q_3$ | 102 | 103 | 100 | 74 | 65 | 84 |
| 3 bedrooms or more: | | | | | | |
| $Q_1$ | 76 | 75 | 79 | 57 | | |
| $Q_2$ (median) | 94 | 92 | 101 | 73 | 58* | 89* |
| $Q_3$ | 123 | 126 | 120 | 100 | | |

* Based on less than 50 sample cases.
Source: CSNHI, Table 5–3.

ard unit with three bedrooms or more was $92 if the occupants were white as compared with $101 if the occupants were nonwhite.

If comparisons between white and nonwhite households are made at the first or third quartile of rent rather than the median (second quartile), the pattern of differences is much the same. Nonwhite occupants pay more rent for substandard dwellings than do white occupants; rentals of standard units are about the same for white and nonwhite households.

The foregoing might be interpreted as evidence of "residential discrimination" as the term is used by Becker. Becker (1957, p. 60) states:

> Negroes still (1957) appear to pay significantly more than whites for equivalent housing in cities like Chicago, where rent control and restrictive covenants have been abolished for several years. This can be interpreted as an equilibrium difference that will be maintained until public policies or individual tastes change. Another interpretation is possible: that the very rapid influx of Negroes into Chicago during the last fifteen years has led to *temporary* differences between rents paid by Negroes and whites which would be eliminated a few years after the influx ceased.

Becker himself leans toward the latter interpretation and conjectures (p. 129) that "the residential discrimination observed in many northern cities is a consequence of the in-migration of Negroes and the residential segregation in these cities."

It may be that Becker's conjecture is right. However, it is worth noting that in 1940, following a decade of relatively slow in-migration of Negroes, residential discrimination was in evidence. The median monthly contract rent for a dwelling of inferior quality (needing major repairs and/or lacking facilities) was $17 if the occupants were white and $20 if the occupants were nonwhite (1940 Census of Housing, Vol. III, Illinois, Tables B–3 and B–5a). Although the "bonus" for renting to nonwhites was only on the order of $3, the median rental for nonwhites was 20 per cent greater than the median rental for whites. In 1956, the "bonus" appears to be about $15 and the median rental for nonwhites is some 30 per cent greater than the median rental for whites.

A somewhat different description of the situation might be offered. It can be conjectured that given the high degree of residential segregation which obtains in the City of Chicago, white and nonwhite households are not competing in the same housing market. Instead, white households are competing in a white housing market and nonwhite households are competing in a nonwhite housing market. If this were the case, supply and demand factors in the white housing market would be more or less independent of supply and demand factors in the nonwhite housing market; and relationships among quality, size, and rent might be quite different in the two markets.

*Quality and rental for recent in-migrants.* Separate tabulations of the CSNHI were prepared for households which reported that they had moved into their present dwelling and into the Chicago SMA within the two-year period preceding the survey, i.e., during 1955 or 1956. Some 43,000 households were reported as recent in-migrants—36,000 white households and 7,000 nonwhite households. Nonreporting was high on the mobility questions, and there is some reason to think that recent in-migrant households were underreported. (No independently derived statistics are available for comparison. The estimate of in-migrant households cannot be related to estimates of net in-migration of nonwhite population because the proportion of recent migrants living in households is unknown. However, Duncan and Duncan, 1957, pp. 40 and 43, cite evidence that in-migrants probably were underreported in the 1940 and 1950 Censuses.) Despite probable underreporting of migrants, examination of the housing characteristics of households who identified themselves as recent in-migrants seems warranted.

Recent in-migrant households are compared with households which have lived in the Chicago SMA for more than two years in Table 6–17. (An unknown number of recent in-migrant households may be included in the non-migrant group; however, they are households which failed to identify themselves as recent migrants.) About 94 per cent of the recent-migrant households, both white and nonwhite, are renters. By comparison only 65 per cent of the non-migrant households rented their dwellings, 60 per cent of the white households and 83 per cent of the nonwhite households. The following observations are restricted to the rental sector, in which virtually all of the recent migrants and about two-thirds of the non-migrants are found.

Renters who are recent migrants are occupying substandard units twice as often as are non-migrants. The proportion substandard is 40 per cent among recent migrants as compared with 20 per cent among non-migrants. The average dwelling unit occupied by a recent-migrant household rents for $68. By comparison the median rent paid by non-migrant households is $78, or about $10 more. When the recent-migrant *vs.* non-migrant comparison is restricted to units of the same quality, the differential tends to disappear. The average standard unit occupied by recent migrants rents for $78, as compared with a median rental of $84 for units rented by non-migrants. The average substandard unit occupied by recent migrants rents for $54, as compared with a median rental of $55 for units rented by non-migrants. On the average, units rented by recent migrants are of roughly the same size as units rented by non-migrants.

Apparently, then, recent migrants receive about as much space and housing "quality" per rental dollar as do the non-migrants. There is little to suggest that recent migrants are "taken advantage of" in the housing market. The relatively high proportion of recent migrants in substandard housing is accounted for in large part by the fact that they occupy relatively inexpensive dwellings. It may well be the case that many recent migrants are allocating high proportions of a very limited income to housing, but the rentals which they pay are low as compared with the rentals of non-migrants.

The proportion substandard for nonwhite households is about double the proportion substandard for white households among both recent migrants and non-migrants. Sixty per cent of the recent-migrant nonwhite renters as compared with 35 per cent of the recent-migrant white renters have substandard housing;

### Table 6–17
### Housing Characteristics of Recent-Migrant and Non-Migrant Households, by Color: City of Chicago, 1956

| CHARACTERISTIC | HOUSEHOLDS WHICH HAVE LIVED IN THE CHICAGO SMA— | | | | | |
|---|---|---|---|---|---|---|
| | NOT MORE THAN TWO YEARS | | | MORE THAN TWO YEARS* | | |
| | All | White | Nonwhite | All | White | Nonwhite |
| Number of households (in thousands) | 43 | 36 | 7 | 1,064 | 864 | 200 |
| Percentage renting | 94 | 94 | 93 | 65 | 60 | 83 |
| *Renters only:* | | | | | | |
| Substandard housing (per cent substandard) | 40 | 35 | 60 | 20 | 15 | 33 |
| Median gross monthly rent | | | | | | |
| All units | $68 | $69 | $64 | $78 | $79 | $76 |
| Standard | $78 | $77 | $82† | $84 | $84 | $85 |
| Substandard | $54 | $54 | $52† | $55 | $49 | $66 |
| Median number of bedrooms | | | | | | |
| All units | 1.4 | 1.4 | 1.3 | 1.6 | 1.5 | 1.6 |

\* Includes unknown number of households living in SMA not more than two years who did not report year moved into present dwelling.
† Based on less than 50 sample cases.
Source: CSNHI, Tables 5–3, 7–1, 7–2, 7–5, 7–7, and unpublished tabulation.

33 per cent of the non-migrant nonwhite renters as compared with 15 per cent of the non-migrant white renters are living in substandard units. However, among both recent migrants and non-migrants, rentals averaged only slightly less for nonwhite than for white households. Median rentals for recent migrants were $64 for nonwhites and $69 for whites; for the non-migrants, median rentals were $76 for nonwhites and $79 for whites. When quality of dwelling is controlled, nonwhite households appear to pay at least as much as white households for equivalent housing.

Note that among non-migrant renters living in substandard units, the nonwhite households pay a median rental of $66 whereas the white households pay a median rental of $49. On the average, the units occupied by nonwhite households are of about the same size as the units occupied by white households. The relative disadvantage of nonwhites in the housing market appears to be as great for households which have lived in the Chicago area for at least two years as for households which have moved to Chicago recently.

If Becker's conjecture is correct, i.e., if residential discrimination against nonwhites stems in part from their relatively heavy in-migration, the relationship is indirect rather than direct. There is no evidence that the in-migrants themselves are taken advantage of in the housing market. Rentals paid by recent migrants for dwellings of a given quality and size apparently are about the same as rentals paid by non-migrants for like dwellings. However, the relatively heavy in-migration of nonwhites and consequent rapid growth of nonwhite population may well underlie the "piling-up" process described by Duncan and Duncan (1957). Such rapid population growth may result in residential discrimination when it is not balanced by a proportional expansion of the available housing supply.

*White and nonwhite home owners.* About 34 per cent of the households in Chicago owned (or were purchasing) the dwelling which they occupied in 1956. Home ownership occurred twice as often among white households (38 per cent home owners) as among nonwhite households (17 per cent home owners).

The proportion substandard was six times as high for units with nonwhite owner-occupants as for units with white owner-occupants. Table 6–18 shows that 3 per cent of all owner-occupied dwellings were of substandard quality. Two per cent of the units with white owner-occupants as compared with 12 per cent of the units with nonwhite owner-occupants were dilapidated or lacked adequate facilities.

The average nonwhite owner-occupant family had an income of $5,500 in 1956—$1,000 less than the average white owner-occupant family. The number of nonwhite home owners is too small to permit any detailed analysis of differences in housing quality between white and nonwhite home owners with equivalent incomes. It seems probable, however, that the relative economic disadvantage of nonwhite home owners does not account fully for the observed white-nonwhite differential in quality of dwelling.

Value of property is the owner occupant's estimate of the selling price of his property, including both structure and land; and it is available only for one-dwelling-unit properties without business. Only half the owner-occupied dwellings in Chicago fall into this category—52 per cent of the units with white owner-occupants and 28 per cent of the units with nonwhite owner-occupants. The low proportions of owner-occupied units in one-unit properties without business in Chicago is of substantive interest, and the lesser frequency with which nonwhite home owners have

**Table 6–18**
**Selected Characteristics of Home Owners, by Color:**
**City of Chicago, 1956**

| Characteristic | All | White | Nonwhite |
|---|---|---|---|
| Number of households (in thousands) | 384 | 349 | 36 |
| Substandard housing (per cent of units substandard) | 3 | 2 | 12 |
| Median income of primary families | $5,590 | $6,549 | $5,544 |
| One-unit properties (per cent of units in 1-unit properties w/o business) | 50 | 52 | 28 |
| Median value of one-unit properties | $17,800 | $17,900 | $14,400 |

Source: CSNHI, Tables 1–2, 4–4, and 5–14.

one-unit properties without business suggests a white-nonwhite differential in the pattern of home ownership. However, the low proportions also limit the usefulness of the statistics on value. The median value of all owner-occupied, one-unit properties without business was $17,800. White occupants valued such properties at $17,900 and nonwhite occupants valued such properties at $14,400. The value statistics do not seem to provide an adequate basis for generalization about white-nonwhite differentials in financial characteristics of owner-occupied dwellings.

*Housing conditions: a summary*. In *Where Shall We Live?*, the Commission on Race and Housing asserts (1958, pp. 4–5):

> In no area of life are the disadvantages of minority groups more visible than in housing . . . The visible disparity between white and minority housing conditions is confirmed by Census statistics . . . In quality, space, and value, . . . the homes of minority families rank far below the general standard of housing in the United States.

With certain important qualifications, their assertion is descriptive of the situation in the City of Chicago. In Chicago, nonwhites are more than twice as likely as whites to be living in substandard housing if they are renters, six times as likely if they are home owners. However, the dwellings which the nonwhites occupy are of about the same size and command about the same rents as the dwellings occupied by whites.

Undesirable levels of crowding are more prevalent among nonwhites than among whites. However, in the case of Chicago, the relatively high level of crowding observed among nonwhite households comes about not because nonwhites occupy relatively small dwellings but because their households are relatively large in size. Doubling-up of families and sharing the dwelling with nonrelatives probably account for the relatively large household size in the nonwhite population; and such doubling-up and sharing of dwellings are themselves probably means by which nonwhites pool incomes in order to compete for housing.

Within the owner sector, the statistics obtained through the CSNHI do not provide a sufficient basis for generalization about differences in the values of homes occupied by whites and nonwhites respectively. Within the rental sector, units occupied by nonwhites have rentals more or less equivalent to those of units occupied by whites. Inasmuch as the incomes of nonwhites typically are lower than those of whites, it can be inferred that, on the average, rent constitutes a larger proportion of current income for nonwhites than for whites at each income level. (See also the rent/income ratios published in the CSNHI, Tables 5–8 and 5–10.) This observation seemingly is contrary to the conclusion reached by the Commission on Race and Housing (1958, p. 11): "The housing demand of nonwhites is further limited by their tendency to spend a smaller part of their resources for housing than do whites, regardless of income . . . Whatever the explanation, it seems evident that nonwhites as a group compete less strongly for housing than even their limited incomes would permit." Whether Chicago is a special case is open to question. However, it has been observed that in Chicago in 1935–36 (Department of Labor, 1939a, pp. 95–96) "At almost every income level the native white families generally paid a higher rent, and hence a higher proportion of their incomes for housing, than did the foreign born . . . The general tendency was for Negroes to pay approximately the same rents in proportion to their income as did the native whites." Thus, it appears that for many years nonwhites in Chicago have been competing for housing as strongly as their limited incomes permit.

The Commission on Race and Housing (1958, p. 36) formulates the residential discrimination problem in much the same way that Becker does, i.e., "The restriction of minority groups to limited areas and, in cities of the North and West, the accompanying increase of minority populations, together result in chronic, severe scarcity of housing available to segregated groups. . . . A striking consequence is that segregated groups receive less housing value for their dollars spent than do whites, by a wide margin." The CSNHI provides ample evidence that in 1956 nonwhites in Chicago were more likely to receive substandard housing for a given rental than were whites; it also is clear that nonwhites were paying more than whites for substandard dwellings of equivalent size and that nonwhites were paying about as much as whites for standard units of equivalent size. Owners of substandard dwellings apparently receive a "bonus" for renting to nonwhites; owners of dwellings in other "quality" categories also may receive a "bonus," for there is substantial variation in "quality" among standard units.

## AREAL VARIATION IN HOUSING

For purposes of the CSNHI, the City of Chicago was divided into five areas; i.e., the 935 census tracts making up the City were grouped into five areas. The subareas, delineated by the Chicago Housing Authority in consultation with the Chicago Land Clearance Commission, were selected in view of needs of local housing agencies rather than for general analytical purposes. Four factors were given explicit attention in their delineation: (1) the availability of vacancies for Negroes; (2) the proportion of Negroes living in the area; (3) the proportion of substandard housing in the area; and (4) characteristics of contiguous areas.

For general analytical purposes, the delineated areas can be characterized in the following way:

Area 1: Deteriorated Central Nonwhite Residential Area

Area 2: Deteriorated Central White Residential Area

Area 3: Mixed Residential Area

Area 4a: Outer Residential Area, North

Area 4b: Outer Residential Area, South.

The designations were selected after examining the 1950 and 1956 characteristics of the several areas.

SUBAREAS BY HOUSING QUALITY
AND COLOR COMPOSITION

Before examining patterns of areal variation in housing conditions, we present in summary form some information about housing quality and color composition in each subarea. Housing quality and color composition were the major criteria used in the delineation of the subareas. Thus, the areas differ substantially with respect to these characteristics.

*Deteriorated Central Nonwhite Residential Area.* Of the 935 census tracts making up the City of Chicago, 91 were grouped into an area which we designate the Deteriorated Central Nonwhite Residential Area. More than half the dwellings were substandard and more than half the residents were nonwhite as of 1950 in nearly three-fourths of these tracts. In a fifth of these tracts, more than half the dwellings were substandard in 1950 although less than half the residents were nonwhite. (See Table 6–19. For convenience, we refer to the 1950 proportion of units "with no private bath or dilapidated" as the 1950 proportion substandard for census tracts, although it does not include units substandard by virtue of lacking hot running water.) There seems to be ample basis for identifying this area as a deteriorated nonwhite residential area, and as Figure 6–4 shows, the area lies relatively close to the City center.

**Table 6–19**

**Housing Quality and Color Composition in Census Tracts Making Up the Deteriorated Central Nonwhite Residential Area: City of Chicago, 1950**

| PERCENTAGE OF POPULATION NONWHITE | ALL TRACTS | PERCENTAGE OF UNITS LACKING PRIVATE BATH AND/OR DILAPIDATED | |
|---|---|---|---|
| | | 50 or more | Under 50 |
| All tracts | 91* | 83 | 7 |
| 50 or more | 69 | 65 | 4 |
| 25 to 49 | 10 | 9 | 1 |
| 10 to 25 | 3 | 3 | 0 |
| Under 10 | 8 | 6 | 2 |

\* Includes one tract with no dwelling units in 1950.
Source: CSNHI, No. 6, p. 1, and Hauser and Kitagawa (1953), Table 5.

In the area as a whole (the aggregate of the 91 census tracts), the proportion substandard was 67 per cent in 1950 and 53 per cent in 1956. Nonwhites occupied 80 per cent of the dwellings in the area in 1950, 87 per cent of the dwellings in the area in 1956. These figures, which are shown in Table 6–22, will be examined in more detail later.

*Deteriorated Central White Residential Area.* This area is made up of 197 census tracts. A third of the tracts had proportions substandard of 25 per cent or more and proportions nonwhite of less than 1 per cent in 1950. About a fourth had proportions substandard of 10 per cent or more and proportions nonwhite of 1 to 9 per cent. (See Table 6–20.) Although substandard housing is much less prevalent than in the Deteriorated Central Nonwhite Residential Area, it occurs much more frequently than in the other white residential areas. In other words, with respect to housing quality, the worst white residential areas are markedly better than the worst nonwhite

*213*

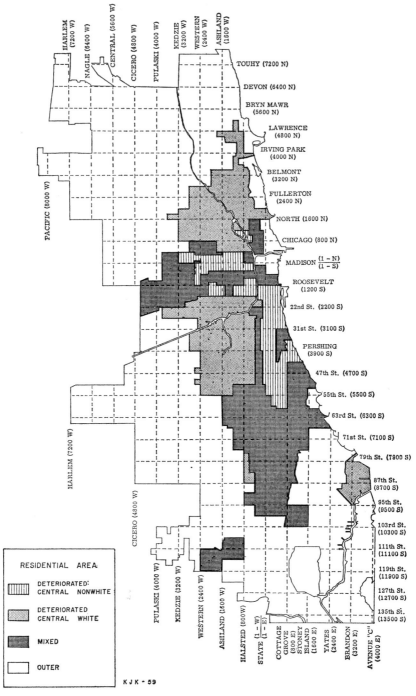

**Figure 6—4**

Subareas of the City Delineated for the Chicago Supplement to the
National Housing Inventory, 1956.

residential areas. Nonetheless, the designation Deteriorated Central White Residential Area seems appropriate.

**Table 6–20**
**Housing Quality and Color Composition in Census Tracts Making**
**Up the Deteriorated Central White Residential Area:**
**City of Chicago, 1950**

| PERCENTAGE OF POPULATION NONWHITE | ALL TRACTS | PERCENTAGE OF UNITS LACKING PRIVATE BATH AND/OR DILAPIDATED | | | |
|---|---|---|---|---|---|
| | | 50 or more | 25 to 49 | 10 to 24 | Under 10 |
| All tracts | 197* | 43 | 66 | 70 | 17 |
| 25 or more | 3 | 3 | 0 | 0 | 0 |
| 10 to 24 | 4 | 3 | 1 | 0 | 0 |
| 1 to 9 | 54 | 14 | 19 | 19 | 2 |
| Under 1 | 135 | 23 | 46 | 51 | 15 |

* Includes one tract with no dwelling units in 1950.
Source: CSNHI, No. 6, p. 1, and Hauser and Kitagawa (1953), Table 5.

In the area as a whole, 42 per cent of the dwellings were reported substandard in 1950; 28 per cent of the dwellings were classified substandard in 1956. Virtually all dwellings were occupied by whites in both years—99 per cent in 1950 and 97 per cent in 1956.

*Mixed Residential Area.* The 221 tracts making up the Mixed Residential Area vary considerably in their 1950 proportions substandard and proportions nonwhite. Half or more of the dwellings were substandard in a tenth of the tracts; three-tenths of the tracts had proportions substandard of 25 to 49 per cent; three-tenths had proportions substandard of 10 to 24 per cent; and less than 10 per cent of the dwellings were substandard in three-tenths of the tracts. In a fifth of the tracts, half or more of the 1950 residents were nonwhite; in a fifth, the proportion nonwhite was 10 to 49 per cent; nonwhites made up 1 to 9 per cent of the population in three-tenths of the tracts; and in three-tenths of the tracts, less than 1 per cent of the residents were nonwhite. Table 6–21 shows that, on the average, tracts with a relatively high proportion substandard had a relatively high proportion nonwhite and tracts with a relatively low proportion substandard had a relatively low proportion nonwhite. In 1950, then, the tracts falling in this area were "mixed" both in terms of proportion substandard and in terms of proportion nonwhite. The tracts also are "mixed" in terms of centralization—some lie near the City center, others are located at considerable distances from the center.

### Table 6–21
*Housing Quality and Color Composition in Census Tracts Making Up the Mixed Residential Area: City of Chicago, 1950*

| PERCENTAGE OF POPULATION NONWHITE | ALL TRACTS | PERCENTAGE OF UNITS LACKING PRIVATE BATH AND/OR DILAPIDATED | | | |
|---|---|---|---|---|---|
| | | 50 or more | 25 to 49 | 10 to 24 | Under 10 |
| All tracts | 221* | 25 | 68 | 58 | 65 |
| 50 or more | 45 | 13 | 19 | 8 | 5 |
| 25 to 49 | 19 | 3 | 8 | 4 | 4 |
| 10 to 24 | 26 | 3 | 13 | 7 | 3 |
| 1 to 9 | 59 | 4 | 21 | 18 | 16 |
| Under 1 | 67 | 2 | 7 | 21 | 37 |

\* Includes five tracts with no dwelling units in 1950.
Source: CSNHI, No. 6, p. 1, and Hauser and Kitagawa (1953), Table 5.

About 26 per cent of the dwellings in the area were substandard in 1950; 20 per cent were substandard in 1956. The proportion nonwhite increased substantially between 1950 and 1956, from 22 to 53 per cent. In general, then, this area includes those parts of the City which are in transition from white to nonwhite occupancy. In the judgment of responsible persons in the Chicago Housing Authority and Chicago Land Clearance Commission, at least some vacancies in each part of the Mixed Residential Area were available to nonwhites. (The judgment was reached after examining want-ads in the *Chicago Defender*.) It seems probable that by 1956 some parts of the area were occupied almost exclusively by nonwhites, whereas other parts were occupied almost exclusively by whites.

*Outer Residential Area.* All census tracts not assigned to one of the three foregoing areas fall in a residual category which we have designated the Outer Residential Area. Considering the area as a whole, it is clear that housing quality is high. Seven per cent of the dwellings were reported substandard in 1950. In 1956, 4 per cent of the dwellings in the northern portion of the area and 1 per cent of the dwellings in the southern portion of the area were substandard. The area is occupied almost exclusively by whites. Over 99 per cent of the dwellings in the northern part were occupied by whites both in 1950 and 1956. In the southern part, whites occupied 99 per cent of the dwellings in 1950 and 98 per cent of the dwellings in 1956. Of course an occasional tract falling in this area has a relatively high proportion of substandard dwellings, a central location, or a relatively high proportion of nonwhite residents. An example is the centrally-located tract 136 in which 87 per cent of the dwellings were substandard in 1950. Another example is tract 717, site of the Altgeld Gardens project of the Chicago Housing Authority, in which 84 per cent of the residents were nonwhite in 1950.

*Comparison of areas.* It is evident from the figures in Tables 6–19 through 6–21, as well as from the preceding discussion, that within each area there is considerable variation in housing conditions and in the color composition of the resident population. However, it also is clear that considered in their entirety the areas are quite distinct in their characteristics.

Table 6–22 summarizes the inter-area differences in proportion substandard and proportion nonwhite which were mentioned earlier. Substandard housing was reduced in each area between 1950 and 1956. In both years, substandard housing was most prevalent in the Deteriorated Central Area and least prevalent in the Outer Area. Nonwhite occupancy became more frequent in each area between 1950 and 1956. In both years, the Deteriorated Central Nonwhite Area was occupied in the main by nonwhites. The Mixed Area experienced a marked increase in proportion nonwhite between 1950 and 1956. The Deteriorated Central White Area and the Outer Area were occupied almost exclusively by whites both in 1956 and in 1950.

Attention is called to change in the total housing inventory in the several areas. In the Deteriorated Central Area, the number of dwellings actually decreased by about 6,000 between 1950 and 1956; given the statistics on new construction, we

**Table 6–22**
**Total Housing Inventory, Housing Quality, and Color Composition: Five Areas of the City of Chicago, 1956 and 1950**

| ITEM | CITY OF CHICAGO | DETERIORATED CENTRAL AREA Nonwhite | White | MIXED AREA | OUTER AREA North | South |
|---|---|---|---|---|---|---|
| Number of dwelling units (in thousands) | | | | | | |
| 1956 | 1,165 | 94 | 213 | 241 | 398 | 219 |
| 1950 | 1,106 | 97 | 216 | 237 | 367 | 189 |
| Substandard housing (per cent of units substandard) | | | | | | |
| 1956 | 15 | 53 | 28 | 20 | 4 | 1 |
| 1950 | 23 | 67 | 42 | 26 | 7 | 7 |
| Nonwhite occupancy (per cent nonwhite) | | | | | | |
| 1956 | 19 | 87 | 3 | 53 | 1 | 2 |
| 1950 | 12 | 80 | 1 | 22 | . . . | 1 |
| Change in number of dwelling units, 1950–56 (in thousands) | 59 | −3 | −3 | 4 | 31 | 30 |
| Units added by new construction, 1950–56 (in thousands)* | 78 | 5 | <1 | 8 | 32 | 34 |

. . . 0.5 per cent or less.
* Occupied units only.
Source: CSNHI, Tables 6–1 and 6–8.

infer that not less than 11,000 of the dwellings found in the area in 1950 were removed from the housing inventory between 1950 and 1956. Some 5,000 dwellings were built in the area between 1950 and 1956. This reflects the fact that in the Deteriorated Central Area more or less concerted renewal efforts are underway which involve the removal and replacement of a sizeable fraction of the housing inventory. In the Mixed Area, dwellings increased by 4,000 between 1950 and 1956. Inasmuch as 8,000 units were built in the area during that period, not less than 4,000 of the dwellings found in the area in 1950 were removed from the housing inventory between 1950 and 1956. One might conjecture that efforts are underway at least to maintain the overall housing quality in this area. Substantial increases in the housing inventory are observed only in the Outer Area, where 61,000 units were added to the housing supply between 1950 and 1956. New construction in the area is sufficient to account for the increase.

Unfortunately, statistics on the components of these observed changes in the housing inventory of each area, such as were analyzed in Chapter 2 for the City as a whole, are not available. From the fragmentary data just presented, we suggest that: (1) in the Deteriorated Central Area, there is at least a transitory reduction in the housing inventory stemming from the fact that new construction must lag demolition; (2) in the Mixed Area, the housing inventory is more or less static in size with new construction keeping apace of demolition; (3) in the Outer Area, the housing inventory is expanding by means of new construction.

*Expansion of nonwhite occupancy.* The areal data make it fairly clear that by and large nonwhites obtain additional housing space by taking up occupancy in dwellings which formerly had white occupants rather than by taking up occupancy in new dwellings. Recall that there was relatively little growth of the housing inventory in the Mixed Residential Area although the proportion nonwhite increased markedly. Table 6–23 shows that the number of dwellings with white occupants in the Mixed Area decreased by 72,000 whereas the number of dwellings with nonwhite occupants in the Mixed Area increased by 73,000 between 1950 and 1956. Large numbers of dwellings were "turning over" from white to nonwhite occupancy.

**Table 6–23**
**Change in the Housing Inventory, by Occupancy Status and Color of Occupant, 1950–56: Five Areas of the City of Chicago**

| ITEM | CITY OF CHICAGO | DETERIORATED CENTRAL AREA | | MIXED AREA | OUTER AREA | |
|---|---|---|---|---|---|---|
| | | Nonwhite | White | | North | South |
| | | | *thousands of units* | | | |
| Number of dwelling | | | | | | |
| units, 1956 | 1,165 | 94 | 213 | 241 | 398 | 219 |
| With white occupants | 919 | 12 | 199 | 110 | 388 | 210 |
| With nonwhite occupants | 214 | 77 | 7 | 123 | 3 | 4 |
| Vacant | 32 | 5 | 7 | 8 | 8 | 5 |
| Number of dwelling | | | | | | |
| units, 1950 | 1,106 | 97 | 216 | 237 | 367 | 189 |
| With white occupants | 956 | 19 | 209 | 183 | 361 | 184 |
| With nonwhite occupants | 131 | 76 | 3 | 50 | 1 | 2 |
| Vacant | 19 | 2 | 4 | 4 | 6 | 3 |
| Change, 1950 to 1956 | | | | | | |
| All dwelling units | 59 | −3 | −3 | 4 | 31 | 30 |
| With white occupants | −37 | −7 | −10 | −72 | 27 | 26 |
| With nonwhite occupants | 83 | 2 | 4 | 73 | 2 | 2 |
| Vacant | 13 | 3 | 3 | 3 | 2 | 3 |

Source: CSNHI, Table 6–1.

In the City as a whole, we can examine this turnover in color of occupant in more detail. Between 1950 and 1956, the number of dwellings occupied by whites decreased by 37,000, the number of dwellings occupied by nonwhites increased by 83,000, and the number of vacant dwellings increased by 13,000. Table 6–24 shows that the decrease of 37,000 white-occupied units

*220*

resulted from a decrease of about 29,000 units stemming from demolition, the conversion and merger processes, and other losses, an increase of 77,000 from new construction and other additions, and a decrease of 85,000 units stemming from net occupancy and color shifts. The increase of 83,000 nonwhite-occupied units resulted from a decrease of 11,000 units stemming from demolition, the conversion and merger processes, and other losses, an increase of 18,000 from new construction and other additions, and an increase of 76,000 units stemming from net occupancy-color shifts. Analysis of gross occupancy and color shifts shows that dwellings turn over from white to nonwhite occupancy quite frequently but rarely does a dwelling revert from nonwhite to white occupancy. Shown below are the occupancy status and color of occupant for "unchanged" units in 1950 and 1956 (the figures are for 945,000 of the 1,020,000 unchanged units for which 1950 data are available):

| 1950 STATUS | 1956 STATUS | | |
|---|---|---|---|
| | White | Nonwhite | Vacant |
| White | 757,000 | 74,000 | 14,000 |
| Nonwhite | 1,000 | 83,000 | 3,000 |
| Vacant | 10,000 | 2,000 | 1,000 |

The foregoing observations are consistent with conclusions drawn from the analysis of small-area data which indicate that residential neighborhoods very infrequently revert from nonwhite to white occupancy, or that the white-to-nonwhite residential succession process is more or less irreversible (Duncan and Duncan, 1957).

*Growth of standard housing.* Standard dwellings increased and substandard dwellings decreased in each area between 1950 and 1956. Detailed statistics on the components of change in each area (similar to those presented in Chapter 2 for the city as a whole) are not available; however, with data available, one can

Table 6-24
**Components of Change in the Housing Inventory, by Occupancy Status and Color of Occupant: City of Chicago, 1950–56**

| COMPONENT OF CHANGE | ALL UNITS | OCCUPIED | | VACANT |
|---|---|---|---|---|
| | | White | Nonwhite | |
| | | in thousands | | |
| All dwelling units, 1950 | 1,106 | 956 | 131 | 19 |
| Demolished or lost by other means | —42 | —23 | —16 | —3 |
| Net change due to conversion and merger | —2 | —7 | 5 | —1 |
| Additions from new construction and other sources | 103 | 77 | 18 | 8 |
| Net occupancy-color shifts in unchanged units | ... | —85 | 76 | 9 |
| All dwelling units, 1956 | 1,165 | 919 | 214 | 32 |

Source: 1956 NHI, Vol. I, Tables 1 and 2.

see that the upgrading came about in different ways in the several areas.

At least half the increase in standard dwellings in the City as a whole can be accounted for by post-1950 residential construction. In the Deteriorated Central Nonwhite Area and in the Mixed Area about half the increase in standard housing resulted from new construction. However, in the Deteriorated Central White Area, the increase in standard units was wholly accounted for by factors other than new construction; whether the improvement came about through merger and/or conversion or through rehabilitation of unchanged units is not known. At least three-fourths of the increase in standard housing in the Outer Area can be attributed to new construction. The data on which these observations are based appear in Table 6–25. It seems clear that there is a variety of ways in which the supply of standard housing can be expanded although they cannot be detailed with the available data.

In the absence of information about the components of change, the processes by which substandard housing was reduced are unknown. Inasmuch as only 15,000 substandard dwellings were demolished in the City as a whole between 1950 and 1956 (1956 NHI, Vol. I, Table 2), not more than a fifth of the City-wide decrease in substandard housing can be attributed to demolition. Within some areas, however, demolition may have been the major factor leading to a reduction in substandard housing.

**Table 6–25**
**Change in the Housing Inventory, by Quality, 1950–56:**
**Five Areas of the City of Chicago**

| ITEM | CITY OF CHICAGO | DETERIORATED CENTRAL AREA | | MIXED AREA | OUTER AREA | |
| --- | --- | --- | --- | --- | --- | --- |
| | | Nonwhite | White | | North | South |
| | | *in thousands* | | | | |
| Number of dwelling | | | | | | |
| units, 1956 | 1,165 | 94 | 213 | 241 | 398 | 219 |
| Standard: newly built* | 78 | 5 | <1 | 8 | 32 | 34 |
| Standard: other | 911 | 39 | 154 | 185 | 349 | 183 |
| Substandard | 176 | 50 | 59 | 48 | 17 | 2 |
| Number of dwelling | | | | | | |
| units, 1950 | 1,106 | 97 | 216 | 237 | 367 | 189 |
| Standard | 849 | 32 | 125 | 176 | 340 | 176 |
| Substandard | 257 | 65 | 91 | 61 | 27 | 13 |
| Change, 1950 to 1956 | | | | | | |
| All dwelling units | 59 | —3 | —3 | 4 | 31 | 30 |
| Standard | | | | | | |
| New construction | 78 | 5 | <1 | 8 | 32 | 34 |
| Other | 62 | 7 | 29 | 9 | 9 | 7 |
| Substandard | —81 | —15 | —32 | —13 | —10 | —11 |

Note: Proportional allocation of not reported units within areas.
* Occupied units only.
Source: CSNHI, Tables 6–1 and 6–8.

VARIATION IN HOUSING CHARACTERISTICS BY TENURE

The statistics by area permit a series of comparisons. Households in the Deteriorated Central White Residential Area can be compared with households in the Deteriorated Central Nonwhite Residential Area. Within the Mixed Area, white and nonwhite households can be contrasted. Comparisons can be made among households in the Deteriorated Central White Area, white households in the Mixed Area, and households in the Outer Area which is occupied almost exclusively by whites. Finally, households in the Deteriorated Central Nonwhite Area can be compared with nonwhite households in the Mixed Area.

Comparison of columns (2) and (3) in Table 6–26 makes it clear that housing conditions in the Deteriorated Central White Area differ from those in the Deteriorated Central Nonwhite Area. Whereas 23 per cent of the units in the Central White Area were occupied by their owners, only 8 per cent of the units in the Central Nonwhite Area were owner-occupied. As was pointed out earlier, substandard housing was twice as prevalent in the nonwhite part of the Central Area as in the white part— 52 as compared with 27 per cent. On the other hand, units which lack central heating facilities occurred more frequently in the white part of the Area than in the nonwhite part; in the former portion of the Area, 44 per cent of the households were living in dwellings with no central heating facilities as compared with 17 per cent of the households in the nonwhite part of the Central Area. Although areal data on type of structure are not available in the CSNHI, it seems very likely that the higher proportion of units without central heating is associated with a higher proportion of single-family homes or duplexes as opposed to large, multi-unit structures. In both parts of the Central Area, some 88 per cent of the households were living in structures built before 1920. Differences between the White and Nonwhite Central Areas with respect to housing characteristics parallel those just described when home owners or tenants are considered separately.

Within the Mixed Area, the housing conditions of white and nonwhite households are somewhat similar. Twenty per cent of the whites and 22 per cent of the nonwhites are home owners;

## Table 6–26
## Selected Characteristics of Occupied Dwelling Units: Five Areas of the City of Chicago, 1956

| CHARACTERISTIC | CITY OF CHICAGO (1) | DETERIORATED CENTRAL AREA White (2) | DETERIORATED CENTRAL AREA Nonwhite (3) | MIXED AREA Nonwhite occupants (4) | MIXED AREA White occupants (5) | OUTER AREA North (6) | OUTER AREA South (7) |
|---|---|---|---|---|---|---|---|
| Number of occupied units (in thousands) | 1,133 | 206 | 89 | 123 | 110 | 390 | 214 |
| Home ownership (per cent owner-occupied) | 34 | 23 | 8 | 22 | 20 | 39 | 60 |
| Substandard housing (per cent substandard) | 15 | 27 | 52 | 21 | 17 | 4 | 1 |
| Owner | 3 | 4 | 13 | 12 | 3 | 2 | ... |
| Renter | 21 | 34 | 56 | 24 | 21 | 6 | 2 |
| No central heating (per cent with no central heating) | 19 | 44 | 17 | 11 | 19 | 9 | 16 |
| Owner | 16 | 38 | 15 | 14 | 21 | 7 | 16 |
| Renter | 20 | 45 | 17 | 11 | 18 | 11 | 16 |
| Older structures (per cent in structures built before 1920) | 60 | 87 | 89 | 71 | 68 | 47 | 36 |
| Owner | 46 | 87 | 92 | 58 | 62 | 39 | 31 |
| Renter | 68 | 87 | 88 | 75 | 70 | 52 | 44 |

... 0.5 per cent or less.
Source: CSNHI, Tables 6–1, 6–7, and 6–8.

17 per cent of the white households and 21 per cent of the non-white households are living in substandard dwellings; 19 per cent of the white households and 11 per cent of the nonwhite households occupy units with no central heating; 68 per cent of the whites and 71 per cent of the nonwhites live in structures built before 1920. Detailed examination of columns (4) and (5) in Table 6–26 gives the impression that white-occupied units are more or less like nonwhite-occupied units in the Mixed Area. The proportion of units with no central heating is clearly higher for white households than for nonwhite households. This suggests that the proportion of units in large, multi-unit structures is lower for white than for nonwhite households. It also should be noted that the proportion substandard is four times as high among nonwhite home owners as among white home owners in the Mixed Area. No doubt additional bases of differentiation would be evident if more data were available, but the difference between the housing conditions of white and nonwhite households in the Mixed Area seems to be less than the difference between housing conditions in the white and nonwhite parts of the Deteriorated Central Area.

Home ownership occurs with like frequency in the Deteriorated Central White Area and among white households in the Mixed Area. About 20 per cent of the households in each Area own their homes; by contrast, 39 per cent of the households in the northern part of the Outer Area and 60 per cent of the households in the southern part of the Outer Area are home owners. The proportion of substandard housing decreases as one moves outward from the Deteriorated Central White Area to the Outer Area; the proportion of units which lack central heating tends to decrease as one moves outward from the City center and the proportion of older structures decreases as distance from the City center increases. There are occasional exceptions to the patterns just described which can be observed by comparing the figures in columns (2), (5), (6), and (7). In general, however, it seems clear that the housing conditions of white households in areas which lie relatively close to the City center compare unfavorably with those of white households in the outer parts of the City.

Eight per cent of the households in the Deteriorated Central Nonwhite Area were home owners, whereas 22 per cent of the nonwhite households in the Mixed Area owned their dwellings. Some 52 per cent of the households in the Central Area were living in substandard units, as compared with 21 per cent of the nonwhite households in the Mixed Area; 17 per cent of the households in the Central Nonwhite Area were living in dwellings which lacked central heating, as compared with 11 per cent of the nonwhite households in the Mixed Area; 90 per cent of the households in the Central Nonwhite Area lived in structures built before 1920, as compared with 71 per cent of the nonwhite households in the Mixed Area. Comparison of columns (3) and (4) of Table 6–26 makes it clear that the housing conditions of nonwhites living near the City center were inferior to those of nonwhites living in the less centralized area.

Insofar as these selected aspects of housing conditions are concerned, it seems that (1) housing conditions in the white and nonwhite parts of the Deteriorated Central Area differ— the white part has higher home ownership, less substandard housing, more units without central heating; (2) housing conditions of white and nonwhite households in the Mixed Area are more or less equivalent; (3) housing conditions become more favorable as distance from the City center increases for both whites and nonwhites.

### VARIATION IN HOUSEHOLD CHARACTERISTICS

Households in the preponderantly white residential areas of the Deteriorated Central Area differ from those in the preponderantly nonwhite parts of the Area in a number of respects. Home ownership (shown in Table 6–26) is much more prevalent in the white parts of the Area than in the nonwhite parts— 23 as compared with 8 per cent. Table 6–27 shows that normal families account for 69 per cent of the households in the Deteriorated Central White Residential Area, but only 54 per cent of the households in the Deteriorated Central Nonwhite Area are normal families. In both areas, the proportion of normal families is higher among owner-occupants than among tenants; but for both owners and renters, households in the white parts of the Area are more likely to be normal families than are households in the nonwhite parts of the Area. The average household in the white parts of the Area consists of 2.8 persons, as compared with an average household of 2.7 persons in the nonwhite parts of the Area. In both areas, median household size is greater for owners than for renters. For owners, median household size is somewhat greater in the White than in the Nonwhite Area, whereas for renters, the average household in the White Area is slightly smaller than the average household in the Nonwhite Area. Were it possible to contrast households in these Areas with respect to other characteristics, it is almost certain that further differences would be found. The prevalence of home ownership in the White Area and the fact that normal families are more typical of the White Area than of the Nonwhite Area strongly suggest a whole complex of differences between the areas although both are deteriorated and centralized.

Within the Mixed Area, nonwhite households were as likely to be home owners as were white households; 22 per cent of the nonwhites and 20 per cent of the whites were owner-occupants. The nonwhite and white households were about equally likely to consist of normal families. For both owners and renters, the proportion of normal families was only three percentage points lower for nonwhites than for whites. The average nonwhite household in the Mixed Area was somewhat larger than the average white household—3.2 as compared with 2.8 persons. However, median household size for both nonwhite and white home owners was 3.4 persons; the difference in size of the average household reflects the fact that the average nonwhite renter household consisted of 3.1 persons by comparison with 2.6 persons for the average white renter household.

Certain comparisons of white and nonwhite households in the Mixed Area can be made with respect to patterns of residential mobility. The findings are somewhat ambiguous. Nonwhite households are only slightly more likely to be recent movers (moved into their present dwellings within the last two years) than are white households; 32 per cent of the nonwhites and 28 per cent of the whites reported that they were recent movers. Although one might expect the proportion of recent movers to be substantially higher for nonwhites than for whites in areas which are in transition from white to nonwhite occupancy, the statistics do not bear out this expectation. However, if attention is focused on the proportion of "long-time" residents, it is found that only 15 per cent of the nonwhite households as compared with 34 per cent of the white households have been living in their present dwellings since 1949 or earlier. The ambiguity may stem in part from the fact that moves within the Mixed Area cannot be distinguished from moves into the Mixed Area from other areas. It would appear that the proportion of recent migrants (moved into the Chicago SMA within the last two years) among nonwhites in the Mixed Area was slightly lower than the proportion of recent migrants among whites in the Mixed Area. In any case, households reported themselves as recent in-migrants rather infrequently (4 per cent of the nonwhite and 7 per cent of the white households). The statistics on mobility by tenure are generally consistent with the notion that home owners are less mobile residentially than are renters. In evaluating the foregoing results, the reader should recall that there was reason to suspect the completeness with which mobility was reported. Differential reporting by type of household and/or by area may well account for part of the difference observed between white and nonwhite households in the Mixed Area.

With respect to frequency of home ownership, proportion of normal families, and size of the average household, households in the Deteriorated Central White Residential Area and white households in the Mixed Area are similar. Twenty per cent are home owners, 70 per cent consist of normal families, and the average household includes 2.8 persons. By contrast, in the Outer Residential Area, home ownership is more prevalent, households are more likely to consist of normal families, and the average household is slightly larger. Forty per cent of the households in the North Outer Area and 60 per cent of the households in the South Outer Area owned their dwellings; normal families accounted for 76 per cent of the households in the North Outer Area, 80 per cent of the households in the South Outer Area; median household size was 2.8 persons in the North Outer Area and 3.2 persons in the South Outer Area. This partial picture of living arrangements of whites in the several areas fits in with the notion that "family living" becomes more prevalent as one goes outward from the City center.

Comparisons of households in the Deteriorated Central Nonwhite Area and nonwhite households in the Mixed Area show a similar pattern of differences. Eight per cent of the households in the Central Area are home owners, as compared with 22 per cent of the nonwhite households in the Mixed Area, which is less centrally located. Whereas normal families make up 54 per cent of the households in the Central Area, 68 per cent of the nonwhite households in the Mixed Area consist of normal families. The average household in the Central Area includes 2.7 persons,

## Table 6-27
## Selected Characteristics of Households: Five Areas of the City of Chicago, 1956

| CHARACTERISTIC | CITY OF CHICAGO (1) | DETERIORATED CENTRAL AREA | | MIXED AREA | | OUTER AREA | |
|---|---|---|---|---|---|---|---|
| | | White (2) | Nonwhite (3) | Nonwhite occupants (4) | White occupants (5) | North (6) | South (7) |
| Normal families (per cent husband-wife families, no nonrelatives) | 72 | 69 | 54 | 68 | 70 | 76 | 80 |
| Owners | 79 | 74 | 59 | 73 | 76 | 81 | 82 |
| Renters | 69 | 68 | 54 | 66 | 69 | 73 | 76 |
| Household size (median number of persons in household) | 2.9 | 2.8 | 2.7 | 3.2 | 2.8 | 2.8 | 3.2 |
| Owners | 3.3 | 3.3 | 2.9 | 3.4 | 3.4 | 3.2 | 3.4 |
| Renters | 2.7 | 2.6 | 2.7 | 3.1 | 2.6 | 2.5 | 2.8 |
| Recent movers (per cent moving to present unit in 1955 or 1956) | 26 | (n.a.) | 30 | 32 | 28 | (n.a.) | (n.a.) |
| Owners | 14 | (n.a.) | 5 | 20 | 8 | (n.a.) | (n.a.) |
| Renters | 32 | (n.a.) | 32 | 35 | 32 | (n.a.) | (n.a.) |
| Long-time residents (per cent moving to present unit before 1950) | 36 | (n.a.) | 35 | 15 | 34 | (n.a.) | (n.a.) |
| Owners | 54 | (n.a.) | 81 | 30 | 63 | (n.a.) | (n.a.) |
| Renters | 27 | (n.a.) | 31 | 11 | 26 | (n.a.) | (n.a.) |
| Recent-migrants (per cent moving to Chicago SMA in 1955 or 1956) | 4 | (n.a.) | 6 | 4 | 7 | (n.a.) | (n.a.) |
| Owners | 1 | (n.a.) | ... | 2 | ... | (n.a.) | (n.a.) |
| Renters | 6 | (n.a.) | 7 | 4 | 9 | (n.a.) | (n.a.) |

... 0.5 per cent or less.
(n.a.) Not available for area.
Source: CSNHI, Tables 6-3, 6-4, 6-9, and 6-10.

as compared with a median household size of 3.2 persons for nonwhites in the Mixed Area.

With respect to residential mobility, the proportion of recent movers is on the order of 30 per cent both for households in the Central Nonwhite Area and for nonwhite households in the less-centralized Mixed Area. However, 35 per cent of the households in the Central Nonwhite Area are "long-time" residents as compared with 15 per cent of the nonwhite households in the Mixed Area. Inasmuch as "ports of entry" for in-migrants generally lie close to the City center, one might expect the proportion of recent migrants to be substantially higher in the Central Area than in the less-centralized Mixed Area. However, only six per cent of the households in the Central Area as compared with four per cent of the nonwhite households in the Mixed Area identified themselves as recent migrants. As we pointed out earlier, nonreporting was high on the mobility questions and the number of recent in-migrants was probably under-reported. These findings, then, may reflect inter-area differences in the accuracy with which mobility status was reported.

In general, then, "family living" as indexed by frequency of home ownership, proportion of normal families, and size of average household is more prevalent: (1) in the Deteriorated Central White Area than in the Deteriorated Central Nonwhite Area; (2) in the Outer Area than in the more centralized white residential areas; and (3) among nonwhite households in the less centralized Mixed Area than in the Deteriorated Central Nonwhite Area. Within the Mixed Area, white and nonwhite households are equally likely to be home owners and to consist of normal families although the average nonwhite household is somewhat larger than the average white household.

The mobility statistics are available for only selected areas. Insofar as one can tell, the proportion of households identifying themselves as recent movers does not vary greatly among areas.

*232*

However, the proportion of "long-time" residents appears to be substantially lower among nonwhite households in the Mixed Area than among white households in the Mixed Area or among households in the Deteriorated Central Nonwhite Area. The proportion of households who identified themselves as recent in-migrants does not vary markedly by area although it appears to be slightly higher in the Deteriorated Central Nonwhite Area and for white households in the Mixed Area than for nonwhite households in the Mixed Area. Given the limited data available, it is difficult to generalize the pattern of areal variation in residential mobility and in-migration.

# Housing and the Family Cycle

An "average" family, formed by marriage and dissolved by the death of the husband or wife, passes through a series of stages; events such as the birth of the first child or the departure of the last child from the parental home signal that the family is entering a new stage. Glick (1957, p. 54) has detailed these stages for the "average" family in the United States as of 1950. The husband is 23 years old when the family is formed. During the next six years, the size of the family increases as the couple's two or three children are born. By the time the husband is 29 years of age, the last child has been born; and family size has reached its maximum. For the next 21 years, the couple will be sharing their home with their child(ren). Then, when the husband is about 50 years old, the last child will leave the parental home; and the family once again will consist of the husband and wife alone. Some 14 years later, or when the husband is 64, the family will be dissolved through the death of either spouse.

A sizeable number of married couples will defer establishing their own home for a year or more after marriage, and a few will never establish their own household. Glick (1957, p. 60) indicates that a fifth of the married couples defer setting up their own home for the first year of marriage, an eighth postponed establishing their own home for the first three years of marriage. However, over 90 per cent of the married couples with a husband 25 years of age or more had their own households.

The proportion of married couples with their own home is as high among couples with the husband 65 years of age or older as among couples with the husband, say, 25 to 44 years of age. However, as is suggested by the description of the "average" family, the family typically is dissolved by the death of either the husband or wife when the husband is about 64 years old.

In this chapter, a series of comparisons among normal primary families (families comprising the husband, wife, and relatives, if any, who maintain their own households) at different stages of the family cycle is presented first. Attention then shifts to older persons living in households, both household heads and other household members.

STAGE OF THE FAMILY CYCLE

*Age of husband.* Most of the generalizations about housing and household characteristics of families at different stages of the family cycle are based on statistics for families classified by age of husband. In the City of Chicago, the number of normal primary families increased by 11 per cent between 1950 and 1956, from 736,000 to 820,000. Families in the "expanding" phase of the family cycle, i.e., families with the husband under 45 years of age, increased from 385,000 to 413,000 or by 7 per cent; families in the "contracting" phase of the family cycle, those with the husband 45 to 64 years of age, increased from 289,000 to 323,000, or by 12 per cent; "older" families, those with the husband 65 years of age or over, increased from 62,000 to 85,000, or by 37 per cent. Thus, families in the later stages of the family cycle accounted for a larger proportion of the families living in Chicago in 1956 than of the families living in the City in 1950.

In both 1950 and 1956, home ownership was less prevalent among families in the early stages of the family cycle than among families in the later stages. Table 7–1 shows that 28 per cent of the families in the "expanding" phase and 50 per cent of the "older" families were home owners in 1956. In 1950, home ownership ranged from 22 per cent for families in the "expanding" phase to 48 per cent for "older" families. Thus, between 1950 and 1956, frequency of home ownership increased among families in each stage of the family cycle. Although in both years it was most prevalent among families in the later stages of the cycle, home ownership increased more rapidly for "younger" than for older families in the 1950's.

Substandard housing, on the other hand, was found more often among families in the "expanding" phase than among families in later stages of the family cycle. In 1956, some 13 per cent of the expanding families occupied substandard dwellings as compared with 7 per cent of the contracting families and 10 per cent of the older families; 22 per cent of the expanding families, 14 per cent of the contracting families, and 15 per cent

**Table 7–1**
**Selected Characteristics of Normal Families, by Age of
Husband: City of Chicago, 1956 and 1950**

| CHARACTERISTIC | ALL NORMAL FAMILIES | AGE OF HUSBAND | | |
|---|---|---|---|---|
| | | Under 45 | 45 to 64 | 65 or over |
| Number of families (in thousands) | | | | |
| 1956 | 820 | 413 | 323 | 85 |
| 1950 | 736 | 385 | 289 | 62 |
| Home ownership (per cent of occupied units owner-occupied) | | | | |
| 1956 | 37 | 28 | 46 | 50 |
| 1950 | 32 | 22 | 42 | 48 |
| Substandard housing (per cent of units substandard) | | | | |
| 1956 | 10 | 13 | 7 | 10 |
| 1950 | 18 | 22 | 14 | 15 |
| Family size | | | | |
| 1956 (per cent two or three persons) | 57 | 44 | 66 | 86 |
| 1950 (per cent two persons) | 32 | 25 | 37 | 55 |
| Median family income | | | | |
| 1956 (1956 income) | $5,732 | $5,572 | $5,965* | $4,528† |
| 1950 (1949 income) | $4,242 | $4,068 | $4,750 | $3,139 |

\* Husband 45 or more
† All primary families with head 65 or more
Source: CSNHI, Tables 8–3, 8–4, 8–6, 9–1, 9–4, 9–5, and unpublished tabulation; 1950
    *Census of Housing*, Vol. II, Chap. 36, Table B–8.

of the older families were living in substandard units in 1950. In the post-1950 period, the proportion of substandard housing was reduced for families in each stage of the family cycle. The reduction, however, was somewhat less for older families than for those with husband under 65 years of age.

On the basis of the hypothetical "average" family, one would expect family size to be relatively large when the husband was under 45 years of age. While only 44 per cent of the families with the husband under 45 years of age consisted of the couple living alone or with only one relative, 66 per cent of the families with the husband 45 to 64 years old and 86 per cent of the families with the husband 65 or more consisted of not more than three members in 1956. In 1950, married couples living alone accounted for 25 per cent of the expanding families, 37 per cent of the contracting families, and 55 per cent of the older families. Unfortunately, the size-of-family classification in 1956 is not comparable with that used in 1950, so one cannot determine whether family size at the several stages of the family cycle increased or decreased over the period.

The family's current income typically reaches a peak when the husband is in the late 40's. Median income in 1956 for families with the husband under 45 years of age was $5,600 in Chicago, as compared with a median income of at least $6,000 for families with the husband aged 45 to 64. On the average, the income of older families was well below that of families in earlier stages of the cycle; a median income of only $4,500 in 1956 is reported. In 1949, the incomes of families at each stage of the family cycle were substantially lower; but the pattern of income differences by stage is the same. Median income in 1949 was $4,100 for expanding families, $4,800 for contracting families, and $3,100 for older families. Because the income data are not fully comparable for the two years (Table 7–1), no firm conclusion about changes in the relative economic positions of families in the several stages of the family cycle can be drawn. There is some suggestion that the absolute increases in income were more or less constant over the stages of the family cycle and that the relative increase in income was greater for older families than for those in earlier stages of the cycle, at least in the average sense.

At the time when the family first attains its maximum size and has the maximum number of dependents—when the husband is around 30—the family has a relatively low income which restricts the quality and quantity of housing which can be secured. As the family's economic position improves, the family acquires more spacious housing quarters of higher quality. With the departure of children from the parental home, the family is likely to retain its living quarters; and, as Winnick (1957, p. 33) notes, "Older persons may continue to occupy more space than they 'need.'"

*Presence of children.* Table 7–2 makes it clear that it is not the presence or absence of child(ren) in the home *per se* that produces differences in housing characteristics. The proportion of home owners, the prevalence of substandard housing, median family income, and median gross monthly rent are virtually identical for normal families with no child and normal families with child(ren).

More detailed inspection of Table 7–2 suggests why no differences between families with no child and families with child(ren) are found. About 74 per cent of the families with no child are families in which the husband is 45 years old or over. In only 30 per cent of the families with at least one child is the husband 45 or over. The "childless" families are made up of about one-fourth "younger families with no child" and three-fourths "older families with no child." The families with child(ren) are made up of about seven-tenths "younger families with a child" and three-tenths "older families with a child." The "childless" families comprise families in the earliest and latest stages of the family life cycle, whereas the families "with child(ren)" include families in the intermediate stages of the family life cycle. The classification of families as "childless" and "with child(ren)" masks the differences by stage of the family life cycle.

*Classifications by stage of family life cycle.* As noted earlier,

239

most of the generalizations about variation in characteristics with stage of the family cycle have been drawn from statistics compiled by age of head or husband. For example, Glick (1947) examines differences among "husband-wife" families classified by age of husband. Lansing and Kish (1957, pp. 512–13), however, state:

> It is well known that changes occur in people's attitudes and behavior as they grow older, but many of these changes may be associated less with the biological process of aging than with the influence of age upon the individual's family memberships. Thus, the critical dates in the life of an individual may not be his birthdays so much as the days when change occurs in his family status, for example, when he marries, or when his first child is born . . . To understand an individual's social behavior it may be more relevant to consider what stage in the family cycle he has reached than how old he is.

The "Stage in the Life Cycle of the Family" scheme presented by Lansing and Kish covers all households. The major criteria of classification are family *vs.* single individual, older *vs.* younger head, and no child *vs.* child(ren). They demonstrate considerable variation by stage of the family cycle with respect to spending patterns, including home ownership, and income. Beyer (1958, pp. 171–73) proposes a scheme whose major criteria of classification are age of wife and presence and age of child(ren); the scheme apparently is restricted to families. He points to the relevance of such classifications for the area of housing design. Rossi (1955, p. 179), in a study of *Why Families Move*, states: "The changes in [housing] needs generated by the life cycle changes become translated into residential mobility when the family dwelling does not satisfy the new needs." He classifies households by stage according to type, e.g., normal families with child(ren), normal families with no child,

## Table 7-2
### Selected Characteristics of Normal Families by Presence of Children and by Stage of Family Cycle: City of Chicago, 1956

| CHARACTERISTIC | ALL NORMAL FAMILIES | CHILDREN | | HUSBAND UNDER 45 | | | HUSBAND 45 OR MORE | |
| --- | --- | --- | --- | --- | --- | --- | --- | --- |
| | | None | One or more | No child | Child under six | Child six to 17 | Child under 17 | No child |
| Number of families (in thousands) | 820 | 368 | 452 | 96 | 214 | 102 | 135 | 272 |
| Home ownership (per cent of occupied units owner-occupied) | 37 | 36 | 38 | 15 | 28 | 39 | 53 | 44 |
| Substandard housing (per cent of units substandard) | 10 | 11 | 10 | 18 | 13 | 8 | 7 | 8 |
| Median family income in 1956 | $5,732 | $5,788 | $5,705 | $5,801 | $5,346 | $5,989 | $6,308 | $5,783 |
| Median gross monthly rent | $81 | $81 | $81 | $78 | $79 | $79 | $85 | $82 |

Source: CSNHI, Tables 8-3, 8-4, 8-8, and 8-9.

broken families, single persons, and for other analyses by age of head and size of household.

Although increased attention is being directed to variation in housing characteristics by stage of the family life cycle, it seems premature to designate any single scheme as most appropriate for such analyses. In the CSNHI, the following classification of normal families by stage of the family life cycle was employed:

(1)  Younger couple—husband under 45, no child
(2)  Younger family, pre-school child—husband under 45, at least one child under six
(3)  Younger family, school-age child—husband under 45, no child under six, at least one child six to 17
(4)  Older family, minor child—husband 45 or more, at least one child under 18
(5)  Older couple—husband 45 or more, no child

The criteria of the classification are age of husband, presence of child, and age of child. The stages of the family cycle are listed above in sequential order.

*Characteristics by stage of family cycle.* A glance at Figure 7–1 suggests that the pattern of variation by stage of the family cycle frequently takes the form of a U or an inverted U. For example, substandard housing becomes less prevalent as the family passes through its "expanding" phase and then rises slightly among older couples. Home ownership becomes more frequent as the family passes through its "expanding" phase and then falls off somewhat among older couples.

The reader should be cautioned about inferring changes in the housing of particular groups of families through time from cross-sectional data such as these. For example, the proportion of home owners among older couples need not have been 53 per cent before their children left the parental home. It is by no means certain that the proportion of home owners among older families with minor children will fall to 44 per cent after their children depart from the parental home. In the absence of "life histories" for individual families, however, the sequence of changes in housing conditions which accompany the expansion and contraction of the family must be surmised from cross-sectional data of the type used here.

No "explanation" of the patterns of variation by stage of the family cycle is undertaken here. Home ownership clearly becomes more frequent as the family expands, rising from 15 per cent among younger couples to 53 per cent among older families with a minor child. The drop in home ownership observed among contracting families—older couples—perhaps reflects a tendency to relinquish the responsibilities of home ownership on the part of elderly persons. In part, it may reflect low rates of home ownership among older couples who have never had a child. The reduction in substandard housing which occurs as the family expands, from 18 per cent for younger couples to 7 per cent for older families with a minor child, presumably is accounted for in part by the improving economic circumstances of the family. It may also be that the "need" for housing of good quality increases as the family expands, with a consequent increase in the proportion of income allocated to housing and household maintenance.

Income shows a somewhat irregular pattern—it is relatively high among younger couples, falls among younger families with a pre-school child, rises as the family expands, and then falls among older couples. Probably the relatively high income for younger couples reflects the fact that sizeable numbers of younger wives without children work and thus supplement the income of the husband. The increase in income which occurs as the family expands seemingly is accounted for by the facts that income of the husband is likely to attain its maximum when

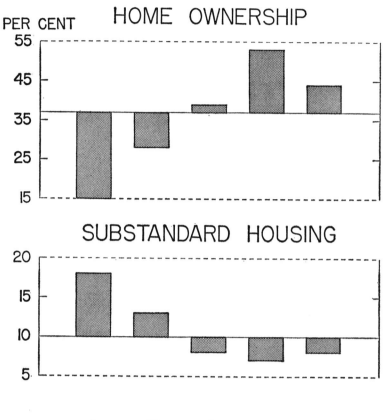

## STAGE OF FAMILY CYCLE

A—Younger couple
B—Younger family, pre-school child
C—Younger family, school-age child
D—Older family, minor child
E—Older couple

*Figure 7–1*
*Selected Characteristics of Normal Families by Stage of the*
*Family Cycle: City of Chicago, 1956. (Source: Table 7–2) [Base*
*line: per cent for all families.]*

he is "40-ish," that the wife may re-enter the labor force as her children reach maturity, and that older children living at home may contribute to the family's income. Among the older couples, substantial numbers of husbands will have retired from the labor force; and retirement typically means a sharp reduction in current income. The foregoing comments are intended only as illustrative of the complex of factors underlying the observed changes in characteristics.

Differences among families in different stages of the family cycle with respect to median gross rent are rather small although a slight tendency toward an inverted-U pattern is evident. The average younger couple or family was paying a gross monthly rental of $78–79, as compared with median rents of $85 for older families with a minor child and $82 for older couples. The statistics on value of one-unit, owner-occupied properties without business, which are not summarized in tabular form, suggest that the average family at each stage of the family cycle values their property more or less the same; median values were about $18,000 for each group (CSNHI, Table 8–16).

Selected structural characteristics are shown in Table 7–3. The proportion of families living in single-family homes increases from 12 per cent for younger couples to 33 per cent for older families with a minor child and then drops to 26 per cent for older couples. Conversely, the proportion of families living in large apartment buildings (structures which contain 20 units or more) falls from 24 per cent for younger couples to 7 per cent for younger families with a school-age child and then rises to 15 per cent for older couples. Variation among families in the several stages of the family cycle with respect to "age" of their dwelling is less marked than with respect to the type of structure in which they live. The proportion of families living in newly constructed units rises from 7 per cent for younger couples to 11 per cent for older families with a minor child and then falls to 6 per cent for older couples. The proportion of families living in old units, i.e., units built before 1920, decreases from 63 per cent for younger couples to 54 per cent for older couples.

Residential mobility appears to be substantially higher for younger couples and younger families with a pre-school child than for families in later stages of the family cycle. Forty per cent of the younger couples had moved to their dwelling in the last two years. Probably a sizeable number of these recent movers are recently married couples establishing their own household for the first time. About 43 per cent of the younger families with a preschool child had moved to their dwelling in the last two years. It seems likely that a substantial proportion of the mobile expanding families undertook a move to bring their housing into balance with their housing "needs." Among families in later stages of the family life cycle, 22 per cent of the younger families with a school-age child, 19 per cent of the older families with a minor child, and 16 per cent of the older couples were recent movers. On the other hand, the proportion of "long-time" residents (families who have lived in the same unit since 1944 or earlier) increased from about 5 per cent at the early stages of the family cycle to 42 per cent for older couples. It appears that families in the "expanding" phases of the family cycle are more mobile than families in the "contracting" phases of the cycle.

Table 7–3 also shows differences among families by stage of the family cycle in their distribution by residential area. The proportion of families living in the Deteriorated Central Area (described in Chapter 6) falls from 30 per cent for younger couples to 20 per cent for older couples. The proportion of families living in the Outer Area rises from 41 per cent for

## Table 7–3
### Selected Characteristics of Normal Families, by Stage of Family Cycle: City of Chicago, 1956

| CHARACTERISTIC | ALL NORMAL FAMILIES | HUSBAND UNDER 45 | | | HUSBAND 45 OR MORE | |
| --- | --- | --- | --- | --- | --- | --- |
| | | No child | Child under six | Child six to 17 | Child under 17 | No child |
| Single-family homes (per cent in one-unit structures) | 24 | 12 | 20 | 27 | 33 | 26 |
| Large apartment buildings (per cent in structures with 20 units or more) | 13 | 24 | 11 | 7 | 10 | 15 |
| New units (per cent built in 1950 or later) | 8 | 7 | 9 | 9 | 11 | 6 |
| Old units (per cent built before 1920) | 58 | 63 | 62 | 58 | 57 | 54 |
| Recent movers (per cent moved into unit in 1955 or later) | 27 | 42 | 43 | 22 | 19 | 16 |
| Long-time residents (per cent moved into unit before 1945) | 23 | 6 | 5 | 14 | 29 | 42 |
| Residential area (per cent distribution): | | | | | | |
| Deteriorated Central | 23 | 30 | 25 | 25 | 21 | 20 |
| Mixed | 20 | 29 | 22 | 17 | 20 | 16 |
| Outer | 57 | 41 | 53 | 58 | 59 | 64 |

Source: CSNHI, unpublished tabulations.

younger couples to 64 per cent for older couples. Some 29 per cent of the younger couples live in the Mixed Area as compared with about 20 per cent of the families in the intermediate stages of the family cycle and 16 per cent of the older couples. This suggests that typically families move to less centrally located and better quality residential areas as they progress through the family cycle.

*White and nonwhite families by stage of family cycle.* Selected characteristics of white and nonwhite families at each stage of the family cycle are shown in Table 7–4. Here, the concern is not so much with white-nonwhite differentials as with differences by stage of the family life cycle for white and nonwhite families respectively.

Sixteen per cent of the normal families living in Chicago were nonwhite in 1956. However, nonwhites made up 30 per cent of the younger couples and 18 per cent of the younger families with a preschool child, as compared with only 14 per cent of the younger families with a school-age child, 15 per cent of the older families with a minor child, and 11 per cent of the older couples. One might expect the proportion nonwhite to be higher among younger couples and families than among older couples and families given the relatively youthful nonwhite population in the City. However, we can offer no ready explanation of the high proportion nonwhite among younger couples.

Among both white and nonwhite families, the pattern of home ownership in relation to stage of the family cycle forms an inverted-U. For both groups, home ownership occurs least frequently among younger couples and most frequently among older families with a minor child. For both white and nonwhite families, the pattern of substandard housing in relation to stage of the family cycle tends to form a U. Among white families, the proportion substandard drops from 13 per cent among

## Table 7–4
## Selected Characteristics of White and Nonwhite Normal Families, by Stage of Family Cycle: City of Chicago, 1956

| CHARACTERISTIC | ALL NORMAL FAMILIES | HUSBAND UNDER 45 | | | HUSBAND 45 OR MORE | |
|---|---|---|---|---|---|---|
| | | No child | Child under six | Child six to 17 | Child under 17 | No child |
| Number of families (in thousands) | | | | | | |
| White | 688 | 68 | 175 | 88 | 115 | 242 |
| Nonwhite | 132 | 29 | 39 | 14 | 20 | 30 |
| Per cent nonwhite | 16 | 30 | 18 | 14 | 15 | 11 |
| Home ownership (per cent of occupied units owner-occupied) | | | | | | |
| White | 41 | 18 | 32 | 42 | 56 | 45 |
| Nonwhite | 19 | 8 | 12 | 19 | 35 | 28 |
| Substandard housing (per cent of units substandard) | | | | | | |
| White | 7 | 13 | 9 | 6 | 4 | 6 |
| Nonwhite | 28 | 29 | 31 | 23 | 24 | 31 |
| Median family income in 1956 | | | | | | |
| White | $5,985 | $6,478 | $5,576 | $6,259 | $6,686 | $5,968 |
| Nonwhite | $4,358 | $4,367 | $4,101 | $5,007 | $4,498 | $4,279 |
| Median gross monthly rent | | | | | | |
| White | $82 | $77 | $81 | $78 | $87 | $84 |
| Nonwhite | $77 | $80 | $75 | $83 | $79 | $74 |

Source: CSNHI, Tables 4–5, 5–5, 8–3, 8–4, 8–8, 8–9, and unpublished tabulations.

younger couples to 4 per cent among older families with a minor child, then rises to 6 per cent for older couples. Details of the pattern are quite different for nonwhite families; 29 per cent of the younger couples and 31 per cent of the younger families with a preschool child occupy substandard units, 23 per cent of the younger families with a school-age child and 24 per cent of the older families with a minor child have substandard housing, and 31 per cent of the older couples live in substandard units.

With respect to family income and rent, the pattern of variation by stage of the family cycle for white families differs from that for nonwhite families. Among white families, median income falls from $6,500 for younger couples to $5,600 for younger families with a preschool child, rises to $6,300 among younger families with a school-age child and $6,700 among older families with a minor child, then falls to $6,000 among older couples. For the nonwhite families, median income falls from $4,400 among younger couples to $4,100 among younger families with a preschool child—a less marked drop than that observed for whites—then rises to $5,000 among younger families with a school-age child; however, median income then drops to $4,500 among older families with a minor child and $4,300 among older couples. A complex of factors, including differences in labor force participation by age, differences in age at which peak earnings are attained, differences in number of workers per family, and the like, no doubt underlies the observed difference in pattern. Analyses of these factors fall outside the scope of this monograph. The patterns of relationship between rent and stage of the family cycle differ for white and nonwhite families. For neither whites nor nonwhites are the differences in median rent by stage of the family cycle very large; among whites, the range is from $77 for younger couples to $87 for older families with a minor child, and among nonwhites median rentals range from $74 among older couples to $83 among younger families with a school-age child. Finally, it may be noted that neither for whites nor for nonwhites does the pattern of variation in rent resemble closely the pattern of variation in family income or in proportion of substandard housing.

*Summary.* Analyses of housing by stage in the family cycle are not numerous. Therefore, it is not certain whether the patterns observed in Chicago obtain in most areas or whether they are somewhat unique. However, there is strong reason to suspect that a family's behavior in the housing market will depend in part upon its stage in the family life cycle, i.e., that newly married couples will behave differently from couples with children living at home and older couples whose children have left home.

Given the selected characteristics available, it appears that home ownership, occupancy of single-family homes, occupancy of newly built units, and occupancy of standard units become more frequent as the family expands and then become slightly less frequent as the family contracts. These characteristics are no doubt interrelated and may form part of a broader complex of housing characteristics whose prevalence increases as the family expands and decreases as the family contracts. On the economic side, either in terms of family income or financial characteristics of their dwelling, the pattern of variation by stage of the family cycle is more complicated. The statistics make it fairly clear that the average young family with a small child has an income well below that of the average young married couple and that the peak income occurs in the intermediate stages of the family cycle, i.e., among younger families with a school-age child or older families with a minor child. The same general pattern is evident in data cited by Lansing and Kish (1957, Table 1). The statistics on rent and value by stage of the family cycle do not seem to lend themselves to generalization in terms of pattern.

## OLDER PERSONS LIVING
## IN HOUSEHOLDS

Statistics from the CSNHI are restricted to households which include an elderly person, or less precisely to the older population which lives in households. Probably at least nine-tenths of the older residents of Chicago were living in households in 1956. In 1950, the most recent year for which relevant data are available, 93.2 per cent of the Chicago residents 65 years of age or more were living in households; 5.4 per cent were living in quasi-households and 1.4 per cent were classified as inmates of institutions (Chicago Community Inventory, 1954, Table B-4).

*Living arrangements of older persons.* Households which included at least one person 65 years of age or older numbered 218,000 in 1956. Of these households, 35,000 or 16 per cent consisted of an elderly person living alone. Normal families with an elderly husband numbered 85,000 and accounted for 39 per cent of all households with an older member. Broken families with an elderly head numbered 25,000 and made up 12 per cent of all households with an older member. An elderly relative was living with 40,000 normal families in which the husband was under 65; 18 per cent of all households with an older member were of this type. Some 14,000 broken families headed by a younger person included an elderly relative; they accounted for 6 per cent of all households with an older member. Finally, there were 19,000 households with an older member which included at least one nonrelative (not necessarily the older person himself); 9 per cent of the households with an older member were of this type. In summary, then, the statistics in Table 7–5 show that 16 per cent of the households with an elderly member consisted of an older person living alone, 75 per cent consisted of an older person (or persons) living with other relatives, and 9 per cent consisted of an older person (or

## Table 7–5
## Selected Characteristics of Households with an Older Person, by Type of Household: City of Chicago, 1956

| TYPE OF HOUSEHOLD | HOUSEHOLDS | | PER CENT OF HOUSEHOLDS | | |
|---|---|---|---|---|---|
| | Number | Per cent distribution | Nonwhite | Home owners | In sub-standard units |
| All households with an older person | 218 | 100 | 11 | 49 | 14 |
| Older person living alone | 35 | 16 | 8 | 34 | 32 |
| Older person living with relatives | 164 | 75 | 10 | 51 | 9 |
| Older husband of normal family | 85 | 39 | 9 | 50 | 10 |
| Only older person in family | 37 | 17 | 9 | 46 | 11 |
| Other older person(s) in family | 47 | 22 | 8 | 53 | 9 |
| Older head of broken family | 25 | 12 | 9 | 56 | 12 |
| Older relative in normal family | 40 | 18 | 9 | 59 | 4 |
| Older relative in broken family | 14 | 6 | 24 | 34 | 11 |
| Older person in household with a nonrelative | 19 | 9 | 25 | 50 | 26 |
| Primary-family household | 9 | 4 | 29* | 65* | 7* |
| Primary-individual household | 10 | 5 | 22 | 36 | 43 |

* Based on less than 50 sample cases.
Source: CSNHI, Table 9–1.

persons) living in a household in which he was not a relative of the household head or in which a nonrelative of the household head was living.

*Color, tenure, and quality of dwelling.* Nonwhites accounted for 11 per cent of all households with an older person, as compared with 19 per cent of all households in the City of Chicago. The relatively "young" age structure of the nonwhite population probably is a major factor accounting for the difference. The proportion nonwhite is shown in Table 7–5 for each of several types of households which include an older person. The proportion nonwhite was high (on the order of 25 per cent) in two type-of-household groups: broken families with no nonrelatives and at least one older relative; and households which included nonrelatives and at least one older person. In the other type-of-household groups, the proportion nonwhite ranged from 8 to 10 per cent.

Of the 218,000 households with an older person, 49 per cent were home owners. By comparison, 34 per cent of all households owned their homes. A tendency for home ownership to be relatively frequent among older families already has been noted. For most types of households which include an older person, the proportion of home owners was 50 per cent or more. However, only 34 per cent of the older persons living alone or as a relative in a broken family and 36 per cent of the older persons sharing a dwelling with one or more unrelated persons were owners.

Fourteen per cent of all households with an older member were living in substandard dwellings, as compared with 15 per cent of all households in the City of Chicago. Households which include an older person are about as likely as households with no older member to occupy a substandard dwelling. Substandard housing was prevalent among older persons living alone (32 per cent) and older persons sharing a dwelling with one or more

*254*

unrelated persons (43 per cent). For the other types of house-holds with an older person, not more than 12 per cent were occupying substandard housing. In evaluating the figures on proportion substandard for the several types of households which include an older person, some comparisons with similar households which include no older person may be useful. The proportion substandard is 32 per cent for older persons living alone and 34 per cent for younger persons living alone. About 43 per cent of the older persons sharing a dwelling with one or more unrelated persons and 25 per cent of the households consisting of a group of unrelated younger persons were living in substandard housing. Nine per cent of the primary families which included an older person as compared with 12 per cent of the primary families which included no older person had substandard housing. These data indicate that the probability of a household with an older member living in a substandard unit is about the same as the probability of a "younger" household living in a substandard unit. (For more detailed comparisons of "older" and "younger" households in terms of housing quality, see CSNHI, Table 9–1.) The possibility that other quality classifications might reveal a consistent difference in quality unfavorable for "older" households cannot be dismissed of course.

*Other characteristics for families.* Statistics on family size and income and financial characteristics of dwellings occupied by families are shown in Table 7–6. Note that the classification of households by presence of an older person is much less detailed than the one just described. All households with a primary family (including those with nonrelatives sharing the dwelling) are classified into three groups: the family head is under 65 and each household member is under 65; the family head is under 65 and at least one household member is 65 or over; the family head is 65 or over. For convenience in exposition, these groups are designated "younger families," "mixed families," and "older families."

A third of the younger families as compared with 53 per cent of the mixed families and 52 per cent of the older families were home owners. Twelve per cent of the younger families, but only 6 per cent of the mixed families and 10 per cent of the older families, were living in substandard housing. The average younger family comprised 3.3 persons; the average mixed family comprised 3.5 persons; and the average older family had only 2.3 members. Median family income varied from $5,700 among younger families to $6,100 among mixed families to $4,500 among older families. On the average, gross monthly rent was $80 for the younger families, $86 for the mixed families, and $78 for the older families; median value of one-unit, owner-occupied properties (without business) decreased from $18,200 for younger families, to $17,100 for mixed families, to $16,700 for older families.

Home ownership and quality of housing have been discussed earlier. Both family size and family income are lower for older families than for younger or mixed families; it is quite possible that income per family member was as great for older families as for the younger or mixed families although the evidence is not conclusive. Rent as a percentage of income probably was somewhat greater for older families than for mixed or younger families. Among renters with incomes of less than $10,000, the average older family had a rent/income ratio of 23 per cent as compared with a median rent/income ratio of 19 per cent for mixed or younger families (CSNHI, Table 9–9). The available data provide only a partial picture of the financial circumstances of older families, of course, and perhaps understate the gravity of their financial situation.

Table 7–7 indicates that older families are a little more likely to live in a single-family home than are younger families;

**Table 7-6**

**Selected Family and Financial Characteristics of Primary Families, by Presence of an Older Person: City of Chicago, 1956**

| CHARACTERISTIC | ALL PRIMARY FAMILIES | HEAD UNDER 65 | | | HEAD 65 OR OVER |
|---|---|---|---|---|---|
| | | All | No older person | Older person(s) | |
| Number of families (in thousands) | 964 | 849 | 791 | 58 | 115 |
| Home ownership (per cent of occupied units owner-occupied | 37 | 35 | 33 | 53 | 52 |
| Substandard housing (per cent of units substandard) | 11 | 12 | 12 | 6 | 10 |
| Family size (median number of persons in family) | 3.1 | 3.3 | 3.3 | 3.5 | 2.3 |
| Median family income in 1956 | $5,590 | $5,696 | $5,668 | $6,053 | $4,528 |
| Median gross monthly rent | $78 | $81 | $80 | $86 | $78 |
| Median value of one-unit property | $17,900 | $18,100 | $18,200 | $17,100 | $16,700 |

Source: CSNHI, Tables 9–3, 9–5, 9–8, and unpublished tabulation.

but they are less likely to have a single-family home than are mixed families. Twelve per cent of the older families as compared with 14 per cent of the younger families and 10 per cent of the mixed families were living in large apartment buildings. Differences among the groups of families with respect to age of dwelling are rather small. Four per cent of the older and mixed families and 8 per cent of the younger families occupied newly-built units; 61 per cent of the older families, 56 per cent of the mixed families, and 59 per cent of the younger families lived in older structures. The proportion of recent movers was only 8 per cent among older families as compared with 16 per cent among mixed families and 30 per cent among younger families; 58 per cent of the older families were long-time residents as compared with 37 per cent of the mixed families and 18 per cent of the younger families.

In viewing these differences among groups of families, it is well to keep in mind the stages of the family life cycle. The families headed by an older person are at a relatively late stage of the family cycle; probably most would fall in the stage identified as older couples. The mixed families, we suspect, typically are in the intermediate stages of the cycle. A majority of these families probably are headed by persons in the age range 40 to 64 and include an older parent or sibling of the family head. Disproportionate numbers of the younger families probably are recently married couples or young couples with a small child. It seems likely that the differences among younger, mixed, and older families reflect differences among them in stage of the family cycle rather than presence or absence of older persons *per se.*

*Other characteristics for primary individuals.* The available statistics on primary-individual households by presence of an older person are difficult to interpret. The statistics are for all primary-individual households, i.e., primary individuals living

## Table 7-7
### Selected Structural Characteristics of Dwelling Units and Mobility Characteristics of Primary Families, by Presence of an Older Person: City of Chicago, 1956

| CHARACTERISTIC | ALL PRIMARY FAMILIES | HEAD UNDER 65 | | | HEAD 65 OR OVER |
|---|---|---|---|---|---|
| | | All | No older person | Older person(s) | |
| Single-family homes (per cent in one-unit structures) | 23 | 23 | 22 | 36 | 25 |
| Large apartment buildings (per cent in structures with 20 units or more) | 13 | 14 | 14 | 10 | 12 |
| New units (per cent built in 1950 or later) | 8 | 8 | 8 | 4 | 4 |
| Old units (per cent built before 1920) | 59 | 59 | 59 | 56 | 61 |
| Recent movers (per cent moved into unit in 1955 or later) | 27 | 29 | 30 | 16 | 8 |
| Long-time residents (per cent moved into unit before 1945) | 24 | 20 | 18 | 37 | 58 |

Source: CSNHI, Tables 9–10, 9–11, 9–12, and unpublished tabulation.

alone and primary individuals living with one or more unrelated individuals. If no person in the primary-individual household had attained the age of 65, it is classified as a primary-individual household with no older person. If at least one member of the primary-individual household, the head or another member, had attained the age of 65, it is classified as a primary-individual household with an older person. Of the 168,000 primary-individual households, 123,000 included no older person and 45,000 included at least one older person.

Some 23 per cent of the primary individuals in households with no older person reported a 1956 personal income of less than $2,000; by comparison, 68 per cent of the primary individuals in households with an older person reported an income of less than $2,000 (CSNHI, Table 9–7). Note that if the primary-individual household consists of more than one person, one household member is designated as head or "primary individual"; the income figure for the household is the personal income of the primary individual. Some 85 per cent of the primary-individual households with no older person and 78 per cent of those with an older person comprised a person living alone (CSNHI, Table 9–1). This creates some problem about interpretation of the income statistics. In addition, no information is available about the financial "resources" and "prospects" (other than current income) of the older persons as compared with the younger persons. It seems possible that the older persons are more likely to have income from sources not covered by the definition used in the NHI, in particular, lump-sum inheritance or insurance payments, as well as greater accumulated wealth.

Among renters, the median gross monthly rental was $65 for primary-individual households with no older person and $54 for primary-individual households with an older person (CSNHI, Table 9–8). The ratio of rent to current personal income of the primary individual was substantially lower for the households with no older person than for the households with an older person (CSNHI, Table 9–9). Certain difficulties in interpreting rent/income ratios have been discussed in Chapter 5; furthermore, in the case of multi-person, primary-individual households, rent perhaps should be related to the aggregate income of the household members rather than to the income of the primary individual. The number of primary-individual households who are owner-occupants of one-unit properties without business is too small to provide reliable information about value of property.

It seems likely that many of the older persons in primary-individual households have lived in the same dwelling for a considerable length of time. Some 47 per cent of the primary-individual households with an older person had had at least one household member living in the dwelling since 1944 or earlier; in contrast, only 18 per cent of the primary-individual households with no older person had had a household member living in the dwelling so long (CSNHI, Table 9–12).

*Summary*. In the literature on housing conditions of the aged, descriptions of their household and housing characteristics tend to be interwoven with discussions of their housing "needs" or "desires." The following excerpts serve to illustrate this tendency.

Ashley (1957) indicates a number of characteristics of households with older heads.

> As a result either of retirement or of curtailed work opportunities, older people as a class have far lower incomes than those in the younger age groups (p. 3). . . . Going hand in hand with the smallness of the family groups among the aging is the noticeable lack of overcrowding in their homes (p. 4). . . . That older families do not give up their larger homes just because the children have gone off on their own is no

doubt due in part at least to the fact that . . . the proportion of home owners among this age group exceeds that for all others in the population (p. 5). . . . Undoubtedly it is the reluctance of many of our older citizens to relinquish their present quarters that contributes to the fact that a somewhat larger share of our older families (8.4 percent) live in substandard [dilapidated] housing than is true of younger families (6.9 percent) (pp. 5–6).

He concludes that "The weight of evidence from all the statistics from the 1950 Census of Housing pointed to the fact that there were tremendous unmet housing needs among our older citizens" (p. 6).

Dropkin (1956, p. 4) states:

Actually the percentage of homeownership among elderly persons is relatively high . . . and about 80 percent of elderly persons in the nonfarm population maintain independent households. It might then be said that the problem of housing for elderly persons has been magnified beyond proportion, a statement that superficially appears to be true. However, upon analysis we find that in most instances the housing is not suited to the needs of older people when household composition is examined.

Dropkin points out that one- and two-person households occur more frequently among households with heads 65 or more than among households with younger heads; that houses occupied by households with older heads frequently are "oversized"; that the average older owner-occupant places a lesser value on his property than the average younger owner-occupant; that the proportion substandard is "high" among older home owners and renters; and that older renters tend to pay relatively low rents although their rent/income ratios are higher.

Beyer (1958, p. 56) points out with reference to older persons:

It might be presumed . . . that persons or families owning their own homes have no problem. The large percentage of substandard dwellings, however, indicates that this is not necessarily the case. Many of the houses which these people occupy are too large for their physical capabilities, and others require more maintenance than can be afforded.

Comments such as the foregoing stress the somewhat special "needs" and "desires" of older persons. Perhaps somewhat contradictory to the foregoing notions is the observation of Ashley (1957, p. 15) that "public low-rent housing to be suitable for elderly families need not differ too substantially in design from the normal type of low-rent public housing since the housing needs of elderly families do not differ greatly from those of younger families."

The excerpts cited above may not sample adequately the general views held by the respective authors. However, they are not atypical of current writing on housing and the aged. Here we have undertaken only to describe the housing of older persons without attempting to evaluate it as "good or bad" or "desirable or unsatisfactory."

The difficulties in such evaluations are pointed out in the following statement by Sheldon (1958, p. 103): "To be sure, a small apartment with all modern conveniences may be attractive; however, the cold, impersonal efficiency—and occasional recalcitrance—of air conditioners, dishwashers, and garbage disposal units may not compensate for the satisfactions derived from the assured and habitual mastery of a crotchety door latch or a familiar oven in a state of genteel decay."

In the City of Chicago, households which include an older person are about as likely to live in substandard housing as are households of the same type which do not include an older person. Sheldon (1958, p. 109), after examining statistics on housing quality for the nonfarm United States, says: "In terms of sharp contrasts, the differences in quality of housing among the three types of households headed by persons 65 and over [male head, wife present; other male head; female head] are of more interest than are the differences by age of household head." The same observation might be made with respect to Chicago. The proportion substandard is about the same comparing primary-family households headed by an older person with primary-family households headed by a younger person and about the same comparing primary-individual households headed by an older person with primary-individual households headed by a younger person; but, more important, irrespective of the age of the head, the proportion substandard is roughly three times as great for primary-individual households as for primary-family households.

We have suggested that additional information on the economic resources and prospects of the various types of households are needed if the relative economic position of households with older heads is to be determined. The importance of such additional information is brought out by Sheldon (1958, p. 122): "The assessment of the economic position of older people is a complicated matter and does not lend itself to summary in a brief succinct statement . . . if assets are regarded as a supplement to income, income data *per se* overstate the financial stringency under which older people live. If, however, assets are viewed as insurance against emergencies requiring large financial outlays such as, for example, protracted and serious illness, then they appear to be less adequate; particularly when it is recognized that a major element in the value of total assets is the value of owned homes." The two major findings in our material are these: (1) The current income of households with older heads is, on the average, considerably lower than the current income of households with younger heads. (2) Within the rental sector, the ratio of rent to current income tends to be higher for households with older heads than for households with younger heads. But in view of the considerations summarized by Sheldon, these findings give only a partial basis, at best, for evaluating the financial status of households with older heads.

# References

Ashley, E. Everett, 3rd. 1957. *Older People and Their Housing Needs*. Paper presented at 12th Annual Short Course in Residential Construction, University of Illinois, Urbana, Illinois. (Mimeographed.)

Becker, Gary S. 1957. *The Economics of Discrimination*. Chicago: University of Chicago Press.

Beyer, Glenn H. 1958. *Housing: A Factual Analysis*. New York: Macmillan.

Chicago Community Inventory, University of Chicago. 1954. *Demographic and Socio-Economic Characteristics of the Population of the City of Chicago and of the Suburbs and Urban Fringe: 1950*. By Beverly Duncan. Chicago: Chicago Plan Commission and the Office of the Housing and Redevelopment Coordinator.

———. 1958a. *Population Growth in the Chicago Standard Metropolitan Area: 1950–57.* By Beverly Duncan. Chicago: Department of City Planning, City of Chicago.

———. 1958b. *Chicago Supplement to the National Housing Inventory*, Series of Bulletins submitted to the Chicago Housing Authority:

> No. 1. Change in Number of Dwelling Units by Quality and Condition, Tenure, Vacancy Status, and Color of Occupant: City of Chicago, 1950–1957.
>
> No. 2. 1956 National Housing Inventory Program of the United States Bureau of the Census.
>
> No. 3. Size and Type of Household and Number of Bedrooms in Dwelling Unit: City of Chicago, 1957.
>
> No. 4. 1956 Income of Primary Families and Primary Individuals: City of Chicago, 1957.
>
> No. 5. Gross Rent of Renter-Occupied Dwelling Units, Gross Rent as a Percentage of Income of Occupant, Value of Owner-Occupied, One-Dwelling-Unit Properties Without Business, and Value-Income Ratios for Occupants: City of Chicago, 1957.
>
> No. 6. Housing Characteristics of Delineated Areas: City of Chicago, 1957.
>
> No. 7. Characteristics of Households Which Moved into Their Dwelling Unit in 1956 or 1955: City of Chicago, 1957.
>
> No. 8. Characteristics of Primary Families by Age of Children Related to Head of the Household: City of Chicago, 1957.
>
> No. 9. Housing of Persons 65 Years of Age and Older: City of Chicago, 1957.

Chicago Housing Authority. 1957. *Tables Accompanying Annual Report—Year Ended June 30, 1957.* (Mimeographed.)

Commission on Race and Housing. 1958. *Where Shall We Live?* Berkeley and Los Angeles: University of California Press.

Department of City Planning, City of Chicago. 1958. *Status of Urban Renewal and Public Housing Projects as of September 30, 1958.* (Mimeographed.)

Dropkin, Allen H. 1956. *Housing for the Elderly.* Staff Report to the Subcommittee on Housing of the Committee on Banking and Currency, House of Representatives, Eighty-fourth Congress. Washington: Government Printing Office.

Duncan, Otis Dudley, and Cuzzort, Ray P. 1958. "Regional Differentiation and Socio-economic Change," *Papers and Proceedings of the Regional Science Association.* Vol. IV. Pp. 163–77.

———— and Duncan, Beverly. 1957. *The Negro Population of Chicago.* Chicago: University of Chicago Press.

Dunsing, Marilyn, and Reid, Margaret G. 1958. "Effect of Varying Degrees of Transitory Income on Income Elasticity of Expenditures," *Journal of the American Statistical Association,* 53: 348–59.

Frazier, E. Franklin. 1932. *The Negro Family in Chicago.* Chicago: University of Chicago Press.

Friedman, Milton. 1957. *A Theory of the Consumption Function.* Princeton, N.J.: Princeton University Press.

Glick, Paul C. 1947. "The Family Cycle," *American Sociological Review,* 12: 164–74.

————. 1957. *American Families.* New York: John Wiley and Sons.

Hauser, Philip M., and Kitagawa, Evelyn M. (Editors.) 1953. *Local Community Fact Book for Chicago: 1950.* Chicago: Chicago Community Inventory, University of Chicago.

Kitagawa, Evelyn M. 1955. "Components of a Difference Between Two Rates," *Journal of the American Statistical Association,* 50: 1168–94.

Lansing, John B., and Kish, Leslie. 1957. "Family Life Cycle as an Independent Variable," *American Sociological Review,* 22: 512–19.

Maccoby, Eleanor E. 1956. "Pitfalls in the Analysis of Panel Data," *American Journal of Sociology,* 61: 359–62.

Muth, Richard F. 1958. *The Demand for Nonfarm Housing.* Unpublished Ph.D. thesis, Department of Economics, University of Chicago.

Rapkin, Chester, Winnick, Louis, and Blank, David M. 1953. *Housing Market Analysis*. Washington: Housing and Home Finance Agency.

Rossi, Peter H. 1955. *Why Families Move*. Glencoe, Ill.: The Free Press.

Sheldon, Henry D. 1958. *The Older Population of the United States*. New York: John Wiley and Sons.

United States Bureau of the Census. 1943. *1940 Census of Population and Housing*, Families, General Characteristics. Washington: Government Printing Office.

―――. 1943. *1940 Census of Housing*, Vol. III, Part 2, Illinois. Washington: Government Printing Office.

―――. 1952. *1950 Census of Population*, Vol. II, Part 13. Washington: Government Printing Office.

―――. 1953. *1950 Census of Housing*, Vol. I, Part 1. Washington: Government Printing Office.

―――. 1953. *1950 Census of Housing*, Vol. II, Part 2, Chap. 36. Washington: Government Printing Office.

―――. 1953. *Statistics on Occupied Dwelling Units: Condition and Plumbing Facilities, Primary Tables*. Post-enumeration Survey, 1950. Results Memorandum No. 22. (Mimeographed.)

―――. 1955– . *Housing and Construction Reports*. Series H–111.

―――. 1958. "Income of Families and Persons in the United States: 1956," *Current Population Reports: Consumer Income*, Series P–60, No. 27.

―――. 1958–59. *1956 National Housing Inventory*. Vol. I: Components of Change, 1950 to 1956. Vol. III: Characteristics of the 1956 Inventory.

United States Bureau of Labor Statistics. 1956. *Study of Consumer Expenditures, Incomes and Savings*. Vol. IV. Summary of Family Expenditures for Housing and Household Operations. Philadelphia: University of Pennsylvania.

United States Department of Labor. 1939a. *Family Income in Chi-*

*cago: 1935–36*. Bulletin No. 642, Vol. I. Washington: Government Printing Office.

————. 1939b. *Family Expenditure in Chicago: 1935–36*. Bulletin No. 642, Vol. II. Washington: Government Printing Office.

Winnick, Louis. 1957. *American Housing and Its Use*. New York: John Wiley and Sons.

# Index